My two husbands

Kathy Golski is a painter and a writer. She has exhibited in Sydney, Melbourne, Canberra, Brisbane and Warsaw, and her work is well represented in public, corporate and private collections. Her first book, *Watched by Ancestors*, was published in 1998 to much acclaim, and chronicles an extraordinary two years spent with her young family in the highlands of Papua New Guinea. *My Two Husbands* is her second book. Kathy Golski lives in inner-city Sydney with her anthropologist husband Wojciech Dabrowski and various members of her family, including three of her six adored grandchildren.

Kathy Golski
My two husbands

VIKING
an imprint of
PENGUIN BOOKS

VIKING

Published by the Penguin Group
Penguin Group (Australia)
250 Camberwell Road, Camberwell, Victoria 3124, Australia
(a division of Pearson Australia Group Pty Ltd)
Penguin Group (USA) Inc.
375 Hudson Street, New York, New York 10014, USA
Penguin Group (Canada)
90 Eglinton Avenue East, Suite 700, Toronto, Canada ON M4P 2Y3
(a division of Pearson Penguin Canada Inc.)
Penguin Books Ltd
80 Strand, London WC2R 0RL England
Penguin Ireland
25 St Stephen's Green, Dublin 2, Ireland
(a division of Penguin Books Ltd)
Penguin Books India Pvt Ltd
11 Community Centre, Panchsheel Park, New Delhi – 110 017, India
Penguin Group (NZ)
67 Apollo Drive, Rosedale, North Shore 0632, New Zealand
(a division of Pearson New Zealand Ltd)
Penguin Books (South Africa) (Pty) Ltd
24 Sturdee Avenue, Rosebank, Johannesburg 2196, South Africa

Penguin Books Ltd, Registered Offices: 80 Strand, London, WC2R 0RL, England

First published by Penguin Group (Australia), 2008

1 3 5 7 9 10 8 6 4 2

Text copyright © Kathy Golski 2008

The moral right of the author has been asserted

Cover and text design by Debra Billson © Penguin Group (Australia)
Cover photograph by Olek Golski

Typeset in 12/15.8 pt Fairfield Light by Post Pre-press Group, Brisbane, Queensland
Printed and bound in Australia by McPherson's Printing Group, Maryborough, Victoria

National Library of Australia
Cataloguing-in-Publication data:

Golski, Kathy
My two husbands / Kathy Golski
9780670072217 (pbk.)
Golski, Kathy
Australians – Papua New Guinea – Biography.
Artists – Australia – 20th century – Biography
Painters – Australia – 20th century – Biography

995.605

penguin.com.au

For both of my husbands, those two great Poles apart,
Alexander Golski and Wojciech Dabrowski, separated
by life and death but linked by me.

And for my mother Phyllis Miller, who romantically thinks
of my book as a polonaise for three, as indeed it is – my dance
through life arm-in-arm with two gallant Poles, first one
and then the other…

Find me in every drop of rain,
find me in the colours of the rainbow,
find me in the smile of the sun,
find me there where the name for youth
is eternity,
because I am queen of the dreams,
wrapped with the veil of secrets,
hidden on the cross roads of memories,
on the cross of love and pain,
sadness and happiness,
somewhere there in the calm
where time has stopped.

Diana Jeleskovic

Introduction

Once, when Olek, our small children and I were living in London, a gypsy came to the front door and tried to sell me my fortune. To hasten her departure rather than for want of a destiny revealed, I allowed her to read my palm and the transaction was sealed. She left. I immediately rejected what she told me about my future as a generic fortune that had nothing to do with me.

'You will have two husbands,' she assured me. 'And you will be very rich!' Being completely happy with one husband, and seeing no need to get another, I thought little of the prediction. Certainly riches were unlikely to come my way, so why, I thought, should the more sombre part of the prediction carry any weight? I was excused from any serious consideration of the fortune the gypsy told to me. But then it seemed to come true. Years later, I realised there *were* two husbands, both of them from the same part of the world, Poland.

My first husband Olek, father of three of my children, died suddenly. He left stories half-told, which in their half-telling gathered power when he was no longer here to finish them. One of the stories was his own gypsy fortune, the reading which, when he was only six, foretold his destiny. And in the slipstream of his life I am left looking at receding images, remembering fading conversations that demand to be recorded, so that they and he can keep on living, and so that I can try to work out why it is that things in my life have run the way they have. Is it Olek's death that makes him stand so strong in the lives of me and my children?

My second husband Voy is, hopefully, my last husband.

But why choose – or be chosen by, however it happens – Poles both times? Two very different men from very different lives behind the same Iron Curtain.

After a very contented childhood I was an explorative young thing in my first life, perched precariously on the brink of abandoning my stable existence for the excitement of the unknown. So my second life began a journey into the unknown, when I ejected myself from my comfort zone and entered the territory of the other. I married my first Slav.

Clumsily – but with the good heart that I have – I attempted to negotiate the secrets of my new husband's past and his culture as he led me deep into his territory and away from mine. I tried to temper my strong reactions to these new demands on my sensibilities. Geographically I was on home ground, but that ground had shifted below me. And the strange past of my first husband became, by some process of osmosis, part of my new reality.

I grappled with the shift, trying to maintain balance – to withstand, for instance, the challenge of my first and only mother-in-law, who was intense, demanding, Jewish, and into whose orbit I was spun as she exercised furious, unbridled love for her only son. As I faced the horror of the death of my young husband when I was still too young and protected to understand any sort of loss, let alone death, my mother-in-law was still there with me, and wouldn't stop crying. Her tears became one of the companions of my life.

And then my third life began, as I plunged into marriage with another Pole, and my children had to turn their gaze from the void left by their father and adjust to living with another man who spoke the same language, the same sort of English. Voy took on the job of being their father. And he stayed with me and with them as they gradually left childhood for the more threatening phase of their lives. And he's still here.

With the help of my diary, and by way of much stony ground, I see that the rivers that make up my life have flowed, precariously at times, taking me with them as I have tried to navigate through calm, and through rapids.

When Olek died it felt right to address my diary to him, as a way of keeping him included in our lives. It didn't work as I hoped it might – he seemed to have retreated too far across that mysterious border of death as I continued relentlessly in the opposite direction, into life. But occasionally he would be there in dreams, approaching then retreating. So often my diary entries will appear as an address to Olek. It is with Olek's life that I begin this book, because it explains so much – his wartime childhood was the genesis of a crucial theme of my life and the lives of my children.

The first dream letter I had from him came from a cold place. I felt a tremor of sadness, even in my sleep. It was a letter from him to me and it asked me where I was, where were the children? Why had we become separated, leaving him lonely? There was an address on the back of the envelope, but I couldn't make it out. And when I woke, asleep next to me in place of Olek, the husband of my dream, was my living husband, Voy, oblivious to my nocturnal correspondence.

Looking at Voy that night, I felt enveloped by his warm living presence. But a feeling of desolation lingered, pulling at me gently. How had the passion and love I felt for him, my dream husband was trying to say, how had it found its way to another? Had it not been an exclusive love? Intended only for him? For answers I try to look within myself, but I find only stories. So it's these stories I can tell, and how they have woven themselves into the fabric of our lives.

Voy appeared in my life mysteriously and fatefully just days before Olek went to the place from which nobody returns. Voy's early presence was, I thought, angel-like. He had a solid stature and a quiet face. But then, staying, he became very human, as he was thrown into the turbulent and resistant scrum of a fast-growing family with all its challenges, a family that was increased joyfully by our son Rafal. Voy, with his ever-thoughtful approach, struggled valiantly to help guide us over the abyss of loss to our common land beyond, and as an anthropologist, to other lands as well.

This is my story, and the story of my two husbands. I have written it at my kitchen table, on the train to Newcastle, surrounded by canvases and paints, children, grandchildren and the chaos of my existence, warmly and sometimes painfully embedded as it was and still is between two cultures.

PART ONE

———

Looking back, I never realised the significance and impact of Olek's stories until after he had died, when I knew – but not in a flash, just over time, in half flashes – that his death had been written into his hand while he was still a child. And that he had lived knowing that.

I

Once upon a time

It was summer, 1975. We were camping at Lake Brou, on the far south coast of New South Wales. We had put the children to bed in the tent, and Olek was telling them bedtime stories. The sound of his voice with its strong accent recounting his particular version of 'The Magic Carpet' and 'Snow White' drifted out, mingling magically with the sounds of another evening encroaching on our bush camp. The wind in the stooped casuarinas had ceased its great sighing, and I could hear the friendly plop of jumping fish in the lake. Just over a rise of sand, beyond the mouth of the lake, the ocean continued its own sound – the crash, crash, crash of waves still lit by the dying sun, washing up the beach, impersonal, rhythmic, beyond time.

I was shoving kindling under the main log of our camp fire, kicking it to reignite the lazy embers.

Olek came creeping out of the tent, closing the flap slowly to avoid disturbing the little sleepers. Our evening was beginning; young parents wait for it. The children were finally asleep, and the parents had time for each other.

'I was enjoying that, the sound of your voice telling stories,' I said. 'Now you can tell me a story while we wait for our potatoes to cook!'

'What story you would like, Katush?'

'One about the war,' I answered. I had heard his war stories so many times, always as we were driving. I would be half asleep, lulled by movement and the soft rhythms of his pleasant voice, or looking out the window and listening in snatches. My concentration would sharpen during the scary parts, and then escape again into the present – to sort out a fight in the back seat, to stop the car and help a child recover from queasiness, to gaze at a sunset and follow its reds through the darkening sky, wishing I could trail it with my brushes and palette.

I often thought of writing Olek's stories. I tried, I began, I couldn't. There were too many gaps when I wrote, and his demanding adult presence filled the spaces in my mind. I was occupied with children – the days sped quickly into the evening's routines – and there was also my endless struggle to find time to paint. That night, by the campfire, I decided I wanted to hear this strange childhood tale properly. It was the appropriate idyll.

'About the war?' he repeated, already starting to mesmerise himself.

He looked into the fire, and at the black shadows beyond. He stood up and stretched, searching the sky full of sea mist and stars. We saw through the treetops, the Southern Cross – or what we deciphered as the Southern Cross – and he said how he loved it here under this bright galaxy, how he loved Australia for its bush, for its freedom, for the family it had given him. His soul had a poetic lining. He was a man with a practical profession. He was, he said, the carpenter of surgery, the orthopaedic surgeon, that member of the surgical brotherhood requiring the greatest physical strength. And he was full of poetry.

And so, once again, Olek began. He had his own grammar, usually omitting the definite article, but this didn't detract from the impact of his story. His voice, his presence, his feeling for the great power of language itself gave his tales special resonance.

'Once upon a time,' he said. He always liked that opening, reading it to children at the beginning of all their bedtime stories.

'Once upon a time. Which time? This time I tell you about, it doesn't seem so long ago, and yet it does. Now I am upon it, then I was in it! And it must have been autumn, because I remember trees, trees losing leaves, falling leaves, hazelnuts, and I was hiding in leaves, great carpets of fallen leaves.

'We were in small town in Belorus. Tatush was dentist. When I was small, about two years old, Germans invaded, and then, coming from east, Russians they also invaded. It had been Polish, Belorus, this region, that was before war started, then after invasion in '39 it was occupied by Russians and Germans, and Poland never got it back again, it remained part of Russia. We were Jewish, but not religious, never went to synagogue. My mother spoke Russian as her first language, because she came from the east, part of Poland that had been Russian occupied until this short period between two world wars. So, now Germans were coming in, they set up headquarters, barracks, they were organised. And then invading Russians just spread everywhere, some with their families, moving into houses and apartments of the town. People had to move over, make space for these families in their own apartments and cottages – imagine if you had to do that! Poles were never keen on Russians, but for us as Polish Jews it was OK, because Russians were not after Jews and Tatush had many Russian patients. It was sort of protection. Anyway, my father said it was too late for us to go anywhere abroad. He hoped he as dentist would survive with family, because there were never enough dentists, he knew he was well liked and with Mamushka and her fluent Russian we could live among Russians.

'Many relations of ours had gone already, left for overseas. Few years passed, I was five or six, and it was getting less and less safe, even as dentist, to be where we were. Germans were stepping up their anti-Jewish drive, they had invaded Russia, breaking German–Russian pact of '39, alienating Russians, and partisan groups had started fierce anti-German underground activities. We knew that there were many gangs hiding out in the great forests of Belorus where we lived. Some were Russian, Soviet, a few were Polish, even there were Jewish groups. They were the partisans, *partisanski*, and they had one common enemy, Germans.

'Mamushka was nervous. She wanted me baptised in local Russian Orthodox monastery. I had white hair, like flax, my parents said, my eyes were light, I spoke Russian, it was my language. I could pass as Russian boy, and Mamushka as my Russian mother. And my father, he was fair, his Russian was passable – he also could pass scrutiny.

'So I was sent to our local monastery. I learned to pray. I was baptised and I did pray, I liked to pray, for good outcomes we needed. My parents not being religious, never going to synagogue, they did not know to pray. Mama was suspicious at my praying, but never Tatush. He told Mamushka, "Don't worry, let him pray, prayers can never hurt." Anyway, I prayed.

'One night, I was not yet asleep and I heard whispering in Russian. I crept out, I peeped. I knew by his rough look it was partisan man, I heard the talk, he was needing urgently to see the dentist. Partisans lived deep in the middle of forests near us, their mission was blowing up German trains, interrupting German supply lines. Partisans were my heroes. I was fascinated with stories of their deeds. I imagined their bush hideouts, their secret, thrilling missions.

'Germans were nervous of partisans. They were being made look fools by these gangs that they could not even find. So they were publicly executing anybody who was reported to them for helping partisans. There were hangings in the town square, there were shootings.

'My father of course was trained in old way, if person needs medical treatment, then you treat. Hippocratic oath. All doctors must live and die by this oath. So he did treat this partisan, and then my parents became extremely nervous. Fear put its cold hand into our household. My parents shivered any time the Germans carried out a public hanging, imagining it to be themselves. There could have been eyes peeping at our comings and goings, to report that partisan man. We could not stay as we were, we could not stay there any longer.

I was student of a Russian prior, and he offered to hide us in his monastery. So we decided to leave our house and went to his monastery, creeping there at night. And there we lived in a room off a cellar, a room down below dark staircase, where the monks stored potatoes, apples and their big barrels of sauerkraut, food for those long cold winters where snow lies on the ground and nothing grows. I was small like Mishka here, but I remember that cellar. It smelt of sauerkraut.'

'And yet you still love sauerkraut,' I interjected. 'Doesn't the smell make you feel fear? Every time you smell it, doesn't it remind you of hiding from Germans?'

'Ah, Katush! I liked that monastery. Sauerkraut is what I know, what I knew, what my body knows, my food through so many winters. It is valuable source of vitamin C when there is no fresh fruit, no fresh vegetables available! Not like here, not at all, you have fruit and vegetables all year. In Poland, even after war, and now as well. One can have only apples, potatoes and sauerkraut in winter.'

Olek kept on talking. I heard him through the smell of smoke and its sting in my eyes, through sounds of the night in the bush behind us, the occasional crash of wallabies, and the slow wash of the ocean. Suddenly, I wanted a rest from the story, to dwell on my growing image of this wiry boy with hair like flax, curled up near the barrels of sauerkraut by night, and by day careering along stone cloisters, ducking between monks with arms folded and their sandalled feet slapping along stone floors, their swinging cassocks catching beams of autumn light slanting through vaulted archways.

'Slow down, boy!' the monks would have said, laughing a bit, glad to have this lively kid disturbing their orderly routines, reminding them of rowdy childhood.

Now I know, I thought, I know why he likes Orthodox music, why he talks about going to the monks retreat monastery in Berrima. Perhaps the time he spent at the monastery is also why he likes sandals, and why he would like to have a samovar in our house.

'Do you think that's why you love sandals so much?' I interrupted.

'Ah, Katush, here you are with this love again! Sandals are comfortable! Allowing feet to be free! To exercise small muscles in foot one can wear sandals rather than tight shoes!'

'You've always deliberately flouted convention by wearing sandals to the hospital, to all the hospitals you've worked in, even in London as a trainee specialist . . . I mean, Dad is a conservative doctor, always pin-striped and elegant, so no doubt your sandal habit does raise a few eyebrows! Now I guess that's why sandals appeal to you so much, it was from that time with the monks,' I suggested.

'You may be right. It did not occur to me. I liked those monks, they were safe. Life in the monastery was separate from war, in monastery we were with them. But then it got bad, very bad, because one day our time there came to an end. My father had some maps, he wanted to explore – maybe to find a partisans' camp?

'We were out in forest behind the monastery, I remember it very well. We heard voices and commotion, shouting in German. We tried to run, to hide. I buried myself under fallen leaves, I whispered to my parents, "Come," I said, "here under leaves!" But they could not bury themselves. I was good at it, children are good at hiding. Instead, we hid behind trees. I was sure they could hear my heart, it beat so loud. They caught us.

'We were taken in back of a big truck to a camp, a transit camp. We stayed there for a while, behind barbed wire, sleeping on bunks. And we were living in apprehension, fear of what next day would bring. Winter started, days got shorter, in that camp. It was always dark. We were shivering because of cold, because of trying to control fear. Our fates were random – everybody's fates were random. When we lined up in morning, they checked us, they were choosing some people. Those people did not come back. We never saw those people again. That camp, it was scary place.'

'Did you have enough to eat?' I asked, thinking guiltily of my own growing appetite for the potatoes under the hot coals. We had already eaten a good dinner. Steak, chops, a salad. But I was becoming aware that whatever desire we had to gobble up those hot potatoes could not be called real hunger. The expectation of hot potatoes, ready to be smothered with butter, teases the appetite and compels gratification. How different must that be from the gnawing pit of a shrinking stomach sending alarm pangs through a body, protesting against its depletion? That, Olek told me, that is war hunger.

'There was one guard, a German guard – somehow I remember even his face, Katush. He gave me eggs, secretly. Nobody saw him, only me. Now I know he was treasure. In that hierarchy of evil, eggs were precious, courage was very precious, and he took risks for me, and I think perhaps for other children in that camp. We were hungry, I remember that, although pains of hunger go from memory. We had bits of bread, some bad soup. Mamushka saved hers for me, she saved those bits of bread, hiding them, to give me a bit extra. There were other much bigger dangers, that they could separate us, split our family. They were doing that, taking a child or a father, or the mother, wrenching them away, leaving the rest of the family like wreckage, never to recover. It might be one of us today – that's what I thought in the mornings. I feared separation, I feared it much more than anything else. "All of us or nothing," I said to my parents.

'Then it was our turn. And my prayers came true. We were all selected. We were lined up, faces to wall, there were others, three men. We were to be shot. But then I felt brave, I was with my parents. Where we were going, we were going together. "Don't be afraid," I said to them, "we are all going together."'

This was getting too hard for me to listen to, but I had made it my mission. I stared into the campfire as images flooded my resisting mind. I could see the roughly shorn flaxen hair, the lively child who had been romping down monastery cloisters, now facing the brick wall, his little face puckered and silent as he bravely met his fate, eyes tightly shut. Where did he put his hands? Up on the wall? Together in prayer to the new god? In his pockets? His thin body – was it crouched in fear, shivering out of his control as he awaited the deadly shot that would crumple him and his family to the ground forever, but together?

'How old were you then?' I asked, contracting with revulsion, thinking of our children asleep in the tent, warm, protected, soothed against their nightmares, having the right to their childhood, to their dignity, to dream and to play, to ask for their breakfast upon waking, pester us to take them out in the dinghy, or to take them fishing, or swimming. 'Shhh, Katush, let me tell you the rest. I was five, or six. First let us eat potatoes.'

We ate our potatoes and took a break as we worked our way through the hot bits, cramming them with butter and chucking the burnt charcoal jackets back into the fire.

'Your face looks too serious – the shadows of the fire make you look tragic!' I murmured, in awe of what was to come.

'So here are we,' he continued, 'lined up, waiting for the shot. Suddenly there was shouting in German, "Halt! Halt!"

'Firing squad stopped. We heard conversation in German, very urgent, and were then pulled roughly away from the wall and pushed into an office. From there I heard shots I knew were for those three men we had known, and I said my prayers for their souls to go somewhere safe, and prayed to my new god that we would be together, whatever was going to happen.

'"You are going to another camp," said commandant. "We need the doctor there."'

The potato stuck fast in my throat. I needed another respite from the story. It was too close to our lives. It was making my teeth chatter out of control. He was describing himself at the same age as Mishka, or Jan, and it was only their faces I saw, the mercurial intensity, the look of the boy child.

'Perhaps I can tell my story? How I met you?' I asked invitingly, needing an escape from the relentless unfolding of Olek's childhood terror trip.

2

Olek meets Katush

We – that is, our story, his story and mine – we began with a careless meeting.

'Do you remember that first meeting? At the bus stop outside St Vincent's? You were walking past. You wore a white clinical jacket and a stethoscope protruded from a top pocket, signifying the profession I knew best because my Dad was a doctor. It was Christmas time and I had a lot of bags. You helped me get them on the bus, handing me my parcels and glancing at my eyes with a little smile. It was an act of gallantry, it lasted only a second, and it caught me in its fleeting, flirtatious magic. But I had to continue my mission, climb up the steps into the bus, fumble for change, find my seat. It was a stolid response to such magic, but it seemed to be out of my power to reverse it.

'Well, you stared after the bus, not seeing me, where I was sitting. And I looked back. And then you disappeared, no doubt, I thought, back to your patients, as the 389 bus roared out of vision. But I knew where you worked. I knew St Vincent's – its wards, its corridors, its polished linoleum floors. I knew it from going there with the trolley from the Little Shop, a kiosk in the hospital's foyer started by my mother and her friends to raise money for a scholarship. And now I saw you there, in your white coat. And I kept that inside myself like a warm secret which had not been there before.

Then ten days later, I met you anyway. It was New Year's Eve. The Bajkowskis' house, Strathfield. I was there with Irene Bajkowski, a good friend from uni. You arrived late. This time there was no clinical jacket, no stethoscope. Just a white short-sleeved shirt, long, over-sized old man's trousers, hitched up well past the navel, leather sandals on very large feet. And those eyes, recognising me across the room. I turned away, feeling the heat rise up my neck. I fumbled with my cigarette in its long holder, concentrating with unnecessary intensity on adjusting it, thankful for the diversion, as the action in the room continued around me and I felt your eyes, interested, watching me.

'When I arrived, early and full of anticipation, wearing my red muu-muu with its white hibiscus pattern, my mother's hoop earrings and carrying my long cigarette holder, the mother and various aunties were still busy taking the great, crusty cabbage pies out of the oven and cutting them into slices. They were the first things my hungry eyes noticed, and I learned later they were a Russian speciality. Cabbage cooked as a delicacy? I'd never heard of that before. I had always been bored by cabbage, almost repulsed, but cooked this way, seeing its crust, smelling its fragrance, I could not wait to taste it.

Out the back, there were a couple of men and a large woman dancing to gypsy music that started on a slow uneven beat, and got faster and more frenetic, building up to a wild chorus of violins. I knew this kind of music. I had been collecting it, playing it loudly when I was alone at home, dancing to it through the living room and up the hall to my room.

'"Turn that noise down, will you?" someone would shout when I wasn't alone, one of my brothers, my sister, or my father. My choice in music was not appreciated at home, and was referred to as "Kathy's wailing Spaniards".

'Well now, I was here, I was in the music, my music, living it, breathing it. I was at the origin of it. There was clapping to the music. And stamping. There were men, jumping from squatting positions, kicking out one leg and then the other, their arms out. A woman gyrated her hips and whirled, faster and faster until her skirt became a hoop around her torso.

'The hostess, her brother and the other guests were drinking vodka from tumblers, throwing it right back in one gulp. A man with thick lips and very thick glasses, and a woman in black were perched on the edge of an old couch, linking arms, drinking, kissing and singing.

'*Brüderschaft* is what that's called. They showed me. Linking arms, drinking and kissing. "It's the beginning of intimacy!" I was told.

'The beginning of intimacy. Here in Strathfield my life seemed at last to be making sense. I was born to come here, to find this music, these people. To be intimate. One group was singing, skolling vodka, occasionally smashing an empty glass into the fireplace. I was welcomed, they called me Katya and fed me slices of the cabbage pie and some small *pierogi*. I was handed a small, cold tumbler of straight vodka. I had only ever drunk vodka mixed with tomato juice, in pubs. Bloody Mary, we called it when we ordered it. It tasted innocent but made us so tipsy.

'"Drink, Katya, all of it, now!" my new mentors instructed me.

Obediently, I gulped it down, and felt the fire in my throat. This did not taste innocent. Everybody seemed to be smoking, the room was thick with it. So I got out a black Sobranie from its black and gold packet and placed it in my cigarette holder, and I felt that at last this sophisticated equipment was being used in the right setting.

'And then you arrived. You knew, as you walked deliberately towards me that I was the girl at the bus stop. I knew that you were the serious young man in the white clinical jacket whose flirtatious glance had hijacked my attention. We had both been thinking about that day, I suspect. I wonder if I knew then that we would . . . well, anyway, I pretended not to notice as you walked over to where I was

18

sitting, but I watched you from the corner of my eye. You stopped to borrow matches from someone, and then suddenly you were stooping over me to light my Sobranie.

'"Why you smoke?" you said, as you ignited the end of my cigarette, cupping it in your hands. I watched your hands, I remember I wanted to touch them. But I didn't, and my own hands trembled as they supported my cigarette holder. You sat down beside me. I remember being glad to feel my mother's hoop earrings flashing and twinkling in place of conversation as I downed my second straight vodka and almost choked on the smoke as I attempted to puff elegantly on my lit Sobranie.

'Before you came in, I had been starting to become this girl Katya. So I was able to throw back the drink as I had been taught to do by the host, and I stole another look at you. Your profile was dashing and proud. My heart leaped and words abandoned me. And then, a little drunk, I made a spontaneous decision to throw my glass into the fire, too, to be part of the spirit of the evening. But of course the glass failed me, do you remember? It dribbled from my hand and bounced across the floor, betraying me as the impostor that I was in your company.

'"What you do? Why you do that?" you asked, quite gently, through the smoke, as you picked up the rejected glass, looking reproachful, as though there had been no wild throwing and smashing going on at the party, as though I alone had distinguished myself with my clumsy attempt to waste the glassware.

'And then you threw the glass yourself, so deftly, with such daring and style that it smashed obediently. At that moment I was conquered. Your sober recognition of my failed attempt at Slavic panache undid me. You were exerting authority so softly that my heart just unravelled, and the desire to succeed in everything that glass throwing represented was becoming a roar in my head.'

'So a few days later, back at work, I sat with a cigarette in hand as a stream of sunshine came over my desk. I allowed you to consume my thoughts, and surrendered to the delicious feelings thoughts of you provoked.

'Who were you, anyway, I wondered, ignoring work awaiting me on my desk. You had taken my number, but experience had taught me that that didn't have to mean anything. So to avoid getting hurt I tried to think of you as a funny little bloke, just to keep my feelings in check. And you were really foreign, I told myself, and perhaps too keen as well. Or perhaps you were always like that, charming, to everyone, one of those types – a true Continental, to be regarded with extreme caution and suspicion. But would you call me?

'Feeling more and more uncertain of the answer, I discussed the matter with the girls in the office. Office mates are the keepers of all knowledge, and I knew that they were bound to empathise, if I presented evidence in the right way. "Will he ring? Do you think he will ring?" I asked them, at least four times.

'After interrogating me closely on the few words we had exchanged at the party, along with the detailed description I gave them of the looks, gestures and the method of parting, Maria and Elle finally diagnosed that you would call. I had to relate to them our conversation, word for word.

'"Where you work?" he asked me.

'"At the Atomic Energy Commission," I answered.

'"Ah, so, you must be radioactive woman!" he said.

'"Did you laugh, Kath?" they asked, scrutinising my face for any lapse in honesty.

'"Perhaps – but why should I? Everyone says that. It's stupid! But he's not stupid, if you know what I mean. And I was a bit drunk."

'"So that could have been where you went wrong, Kath," they assured me. "You have to laugh at their jokes even though they might sound dumb. Oh, Kath. Perhaps you'll get another chance. If he really looked at you like that, then he'll ring," they said.

'And we all waited for that call, ignoring requests from Mr Thomas for action to be taken on matters to do with atomic energy. The only item of discussion was what I should wear on the outing they had decided you were going to take me on.

'"Definitely that little blue number with the white taffeta collar that you wore to the office Christmas party," said Maria. "You know, Kath, it looks, well, innocent, and a bit sexy at the same time – and it makes you look a little taller than you really are, and slimmer too. And you remember, Kath, at the Christmas party, how the men were lurching at you?"

'I did recall the lurching, through not with much pleasure because those lurching were all old and married. But maybe it was the right dress. A dress with impact.

'And then the telephone rang. An outside line. Maria answered and we knew it was you, we knew by the look on her face, by the roll of her eyes.'

3

Olek and the gypsy

'Let's build up fire a bit, Katush,' said Olek, 'and boil the billy . . . I'd like to return to my story.'

He always liked to boil the billy and put the gumleaves in with the tea and swing it three times around his head. This, he claimed, was the Australian bushman style. I stood far from the wildly swinging billy of hot tea in his cultivated surgeon's hands, and waited for the tea to have a safe landing. I was getting shivery from the cold night (or from the story?), so we dragged some more big logs onto the fire.

'So here we are, we are in this camp. We were about to be shot, and then we were not! We had returned from being the dead. My father was being told that our lives were spared because he had to work. His dentistry and medical skills were badly needed at another camp.

'"What use am I without instruments or medicine?" he asked them, after being too shocked even to reply.

'"You will have instruments," they told him, "and medicine."

'The second camp was different, less scary because Tatush was needed. The camp was run by Ukrainians. There were five huts. We were in one. It was snowing when we arrived, it was still before Christmas. We stayed there, I remember Christmas in that camp,

I wanted to be part of it, the tree with its lights, the secret passing of the bread, whispering wishes and longings. I felt a bit of a Christian, but not so familiar with its public rituals.

'I don't know how long we were there, was it weeks? Months? A long time, it seemed. There were some gypsies in our hut. They were making fires when we arrived.

'Prisoners were suspicious of gypsies – the prisoners were miserable enough – and their food, warm clothing, bits and pieces. People hid their things, they thought that gypsies would steal. They had this reputation of stealing everything they could. I liked those gypsies, they showed me how to make their fires – you see, I still use their method.'

'So that's the story of you and fire,' I said. 'It was the gypsies you first watched – they lit the first fires in your life. Now you teach our sons to make fires, first the very small twigs, crisscross, then when the fire has a bit of strength, the next size, crisscross, and so on, crisscross, further layers, until the fire can devour the big logs, like this one here!'

'Yes, the gypsies knew about fires. They had music too. They played with everything – spoons, dishes, they had a violin, they sang. Mamushka warned me against them, but sometimes she sang with them – she knew their words. Gypsies had played at her wedding, she said. Anyway, my mother loved to sing.

'And then one night a prisoner came over to the fire and spoke to the gypsy woman. "*Tsyganka!*" she said, "Tell my fortune!" The gypsy took the prisoner's hand and sat her like this, right next to fire.'

'Did the woman have to pay?' I asked, aware of the fiscal nature of fortune telling.

'A cigarette she gave to the gypsy. Cigarettes were a sort of currency in camps.

'I watched intently, and it seemed that she was hearing terrible things from the gypsy, because she protested, and then she looked ill. She even put her head in her hands and cried loudly. Other prisoners followed. Their lives were so uncertain – to hear their futures being told from a gypsy looking at their hands was all they had to go on. The prisoners gave cigarettes, bits of precious bread, and this gypsy, in return, told them their lives. Nobody wanted to believe what they were being told. Hope, Katush, was a glimpse of a world outside prison – people needed to catch those glimpses, to know there was a future. And this gypsy had given them no hope and no future.'

'How do you remember that, when you were so small at the time?' I asked. 'I don't remember too much from when I was that age, just bits and pieces. My grandfather dressed as Father Christmas, me and Christina playing in the roots of the old fig tree in the playground at our primary school, my mother crying on my windowsill when her grandmother died – I suppose it's a lot but it's bits and pieces, not continuous or in any sequence —'

'I think, Katush, that children must remember the dramatic, the dangerous things from their early lives, because this I will never lose. Don't forget, there was no normal life for me any more. My arrest, life in the camps, nearly being shot – all of that is, you know, images imprinted forever. From our previously happy lives, I do not remember so much, but when we started to be ruled by bad forces I remember many incidents. I too was on alert. Children are aware for themselves, for their parents, that is their survival instinct, to be always acutely aware.

'And these prisoners from our hut number five, they did have their chance, because when we arrived there, they had some hope, because the construction of our escape tunnel was nearly finished and they were all going to crawl through it and come out on the side of freedom. The secret was kept so tight. All inmates of hut number five had to agree to escape, because any who remained could be a security risk.

'Mamushka gave three cigarettes to the gypsy, she wanted a good fortune, one for each of us, her family. I was the only child. I went first. Others were looking at me. The woman took my hand, turning my palm to the fire, and she traced it with her finger. And then she smiled.

'"Acch!" she said. "This is good. You will survive. You, you will grow to be a man, you may travel far, to a land across oceans where sun shines so hot, like this fire burns."

'She slapped my hand, from the bottom, like this, Katush,' he said, demonstrating on my hand, doing a light pushing gesture against my knuckles.

'And then she went on to the next prisoner.

'The others, they were all going to die by fire. That is all the gypsy revealed. She said they would die while hanging over fire in prison camp . . . They, the prisoners, they knew about this punishment for escape, and they were afraid. They complained against gypsy woman.

'"She must be mistaken, that stupid gypsy!"

'That's what they were saying to each other, because was not their escape so carefully planned? How could they get caught? That's what they thought. What could go wrong? Gypsies can be wrong, they said, escape was our new life. Everybody wanted so desperately to believe this. But it was still like a rip of fear which shook everybody, and their excitement over that tunnel of hope was turning now to panic. Should they just keep on and try to escape? Or should they just close the tunnel, forget it?

'And then she read Mamushka's hand. Her hand told the gypsy that Mamushka would live to be an old lady, so Mamushka was happy that she would live that long. Tatush refused to give his hand, and Mamushka could not persuade him. He just didn't like it. The prisoners were starting to talk.

'"We must be more cautious," one man said. "This might be a warning."

'"Yes, perhaps a warning," said another. "Sent by God to help us."

'"It's a premonition," said one old man. "Nothing can be done about it. Our fates are set."

'"Oh, surely a premonition can be altered by exercising greater care, by better planning, and we must be aware that gypsies are only sometimes right!"

'This was what my father said. Tatush was not superstitious – he was the doctor, trained to be a pragmatist, to follow scientific approaches rather than run after superstitions. I think he was trying to lift the mood of the group, which was so frightened. "A warning," that's what he was suggesting.

'"But is it not the same as a premonition, doctor?" said one of the men.

'"No, it is not," said Tatush. "A premonition is the event itself, seen by chosen people in advance of its occurrence. A warning, however, can reverse a planned situation because some things in the plan can be altered to avert an impending disaster. This could be a warning. Let us not panic! Let us not be the victims of superstitions, dear friends and fellow prisoners!"

'Everyone wanted to look at my hand. What looked so different? Of course I was only five or six years old. I would not let them see my hand, anyway.

'"It's my hand!" I said. I remember I did not want them to steal that life she had read in my hand.'

'And your future? Did she say anything else to you?' I asked, as I huddled closer to the burning log of our safe little south-coast campfire. I heard the waves pounding on the dark beach, heaving and sighing, washing away footprints and leaving mysteriously virginal sand for us to trample again in the morning. The Easter moon was getting high in the sky. And I was far from sleep.

'Yes she did, she said I would have children, these children,' said Olek, gesturing at the tent. 'She knew about them —'

'And did she tell you that you would live to be an old man?' I prompted. I wanted our happiness to be guaranteed by the gypsy's words. She promised Mamushka old age. Had she withheld that promise from the small boy?

'Shhh, Katush, shhh! No, she did not say that. Nobody can really know what will happen in life. But we must protect ourselves anyway, be wise, for the sake of our children.'

His story was making me nervous again. Was he trying to

hide something from me? 'So, what if we take a little break from your drama, and I tell you a bit more of my story, about meeting you?'

'Oh yes, please, I like it, your story . . .'

4

At the Balalaika

'So, what was I up to? Yes, the office. My heart had stopped for a second, when Maria said, her hand over the mouthpiece, "It's for you, Kath! Psst! Sounds like him!"

'"Whoops!" I said, "I'll take it from my phone!"

'So I returned to my desk, motioning the two gossips out of my room. I knew that they would be listening outside my door anyway. Part of me was glad of that. They could tell me if I sounded all right.'

'"You like to go to restaurant with me tomorrow?" That's what you said, just like that. No preamble. All confidence. Perhaps you knew my answer.

'Feeling as though my burning face was going to melt, I agreed. Radioactive woman indeed – I could hardly stammer out an address!

'"We go to Balalaika. I pick you seven. Perhaps ten past." You sounded very precise! I really didn't have a clue about you, did I?

'Anyway, the next day at the office, I was thrown into planning my outfit. I ignored all the work in my in-tray. The girls placed a little eye mask and some cold tea-bags over my eyes to get rid of the puffiness, and I lay in repose on the couch in the tearoom. Maria kept a lookout for me. Our entire department had become devoted to preparing for my date.

'Well, at 5.06 p.m., along with the rest of the Atomic Energy office, I bundied off and rushed home. And I did, after trying a few other combinations, settle on the blue taffeta dress with the white organza collar, which, I observed in the mirror, showed up my deep January suntan. I played with make-up – not too much for this man, I told myself – but just enough.'

'What? Such preparation? For me?' he laughed, looking at the fire. Pleased with the impact of my story, I continued.

'And I waited for the doorbell to ring. I looked at my watch. I listened for the door, for a knock that I may have missed. Mum and her sister Mary, my aunt, sat with me in the sunroom, aware that I had prepared myself with more care than usual. I was annoyed that they seemed conscious of my anxiety. The female guardians, protective of the young one in this world of capricious males.

'"Hasn't he come yet?" asked my mother, and, glancing at her watch, "or rung, to say he's late?"

'"Mum, please, he's the reliable type, he wouldn't stand me up. He *is* a doctor, after all!"

'"A doctor? Ah, well, he'll be with a patient then. Patients always come first," reasoned Mum, the doctor's wife. The MD, in my parents' eyes, was the pinnacle of reliable male achievement, signifying the right mixture of noble self-sacrifice coupled with the promise of financial security. And Dad was one. So it must be right. But, I was starting to wonder, where was this pinnacle? Because you never came, nor did you ring to explain why. No news of medical emergencies, no excuses, I was just left, a stranded hopeful in her best clothes, witnessed pityingly by mother and feminist auntie. You, the doctor, essence of reliability and security, you failed me and you made an idiot out of me. Now you can explain!'

'Yes, I remember, I changed my mind when boys at hospital told me who your father was! I lost all my nerves!'

'Well the next morning there I was, still waiting, asleep on the sunroom couch in my navy-blue taffeta frock with its white organza collar. I changed only to go to the office where the girls had put aside all the files related to atomic energy to wait for my news. They saw my face, and that it brought bad news. But they were resourceful. Girls, they always want continuing action! More gossip to while away those long hours in the service of the government.

'"Well, Kath," said Elle, the tough one. "I wouldn't just sit down and take that sort of behaviour if I was you. You ring him up and giv'im What For!"

'And they forced me to ring you. They encircled me, there was no escape. I called St Vincent's Hospital and they paged you – you took a long time to come to the phone. I would normally have hung up. But the girls were watching me. When you finally answered, your voice was loud and confident compared to my feeling of being, well, let's say, hopelessly on the back foot!

'"Hello," you finally said, "ahem, here is Doctor Golski . . ."

'All my lines, carefully rehearsed with Maria and Elle, distilled themselves into a squeak.

'"Hullo!"

'"Oh! Katya! How you are? I would take you to restaurant tonight! I pick you at seven, same place." No apologies, nothing.

'And I agreed, thinking, same place as what? You had never even turned up or rung the night before, you had left me to suffer humiliation in front of my mother and my auntie. "Poor old Kathy," they would have been saying behind my back. "Such a nice girl, and nice looking too. What is it about her?" How demeaning to have them talk about me like that.

'Anyway, that night, I abandoned the slept-in taffeta dress with the organza collar, and instead chose my red satin Chinese-style cheongsam, skin-tight with a high collar. I liked it for its vampish, I-don't-give-a-damn look. It showed exactly how big my bum was, and my chubby legs were peeping from the slits down the sides. Mum said I looked like a tart – but it didn't matter, did it? Because you wouldn't come! So that's what I told her, and that I didn't care any more how I looked. She looked disappointed too, you know . . . she also wanted you for me, because you were a doctor!

'And then you knocked on the door. Action!

'"Mum!" I whispered. "Keep him there, make him a cup of tea – give me five minutes in the bathroom . . ."

'I did a quick, desperate tidy of my make-up, but had to keep the cheongsam on in case you had already spotted me in it through the window. And then I whipped you away swiftly before Mum could get a chance to interrogate you about your movements the night before, or something else fatally embarrassing. I had decided to say nothing. That was my strategy for the time being, arrived at after deep consultation with the girls at work – to pretend I had not even noticed any behavioural transgression.

'At the Balalaika, at the Cross, a blind gypsy played the wailing violin just for us, do you remember? We were the only ones there, and we danced to "Black Eyes" and you quietly translated the words, so outrageously passionate, desperate and romantic. I was in another dimension! And you looked directly into my eyes and I felt them becoming velvety and black, velvety like the music, black like the embers of the love that was glowing in my awakened soul. I was Black Eyes and the song was for me.'

I waxed lyrical with my revelations, me, whose feelings usually lurk far behind speech. Olek was enjoying my story. His version of our getting together would have been a lot different to mine – all the background talk that must have gone on with Mamushka and Tatush stating their demands and lodging complaints about me – but I never really got to hear it, or to know how difficult it would have been for him. I leant back and saw the moon again through the lacy treetops.

'Have a little vodka!' he offered. 'And please, tell me more!'

'OK, so we're at the Balalaika. The *pierogi* and *borscht* were pushing uncomfortably against the tight seams of the cheongsam, restricting my breathing and movement. I was wishing then that I had worn a dress that could have swished around me a bit on the dance floor. Or was my breathing restricted anyway? Did I feel breathless because it was you I was dancing with? And because I already knew I had put my future into those arms that moved me expertly around the room, goaded by the slow and fast rhythms of that tragic violin?

'I was confused, I think, by your unusual behaviour and that's partly what made me fall for you. You made me curious, because you were so sure, but you had done this unexpected thing to me, standing me up, and then you had immediately questioned my right to smoke, asking "Why you smoke?" within seconds of meeting me. Oh but there were many things, so many things about you, I had never met anybody like you. I guess you made me curious.'

He thought for a while, smiling sheepishly, and reached for my hand. Squeezing it, he then launched into his explanation.

'I was rather impressed, you know, that you never mentioned me not coming, or ringing – it was rude, no? But when I found out from boys at hospital who your father was I felt cool about you – you were suddenly for me in different context, you know? It's good you rang me with girls' pressures, I may never have got back to you! So I'm grateful to them! But I like your story about us, keep telling it!'

'OK,' I said. 'So the next day at the office I said nothing to the girls. There was nothing to say any more. It was all becoming rather heated up, filling me with thrills and confusion. But still I knew nothing about you. My in-tray remained untouched as I gazed at my scarlet-painted fingernails, my mind swimming in the beam of morning sun that was always slanting across my desk. The girls knew already. Girlfriends always know, for they are the holders of knowledge that one keeps hidden even from oneself.

'"Ah, Kath," they said, "this is It!"'

5

Escape

'You know, you realise that the same night the gypsy read your palm – my own fate hidden in its creases – I would have been a toddler, playing with my brother Johnny in some safe garden in Bowral, where we had moved to escape the new threats to Sydney from the Japanese. Anyway, I was small and remember nothing.

'We were far from the real grip of war. Dad was in the Middle East, also a medical officer, but not an imprisoned one like your father, who was forced to work rather than be shot. What a horrible childhood you had!'

'No, Katush, I don't remember it being horrible,' said Olek. 'I don't remember exactly my fear. I remember my Mamushka's face, her conversations with Tatush, always so agitated. I remember how everything looked, but fear, that feeling always there with us, it went eventually. Things got better, because we did escape to live in forests with partisans . . . and then we were no longer just victims, in prison. We felt in control, to some degree, of our destiny. Look at our children, how they would be –"Snow White" and "The Magic Carpet" still are the limit of their adventures into the unknown – but they love it, Snow White in forest, all those dangers. Our children snuggle together, they are so sweet, I smell campfire in their hair, I sense their imagination inviting dreams, they listen to my stories.

We must tape them, these stories, in case we want to sit outside our tent and they can sleep listening to tape.'

'I already taped you telling "Snow White" and "The Magic Carpet",' I told him, 'but I forgot to bring it.'

The shadows from the fire danced against the black trees, the distant surf repeated its mantra, and we continued his story, my story. We broke the stories from time to time with bushman's tea, and the moon moved further across the treetops.

'We did escape through that underground tunnel, which had been in preparation for several months. The other prisoners, apart from one man, an engineer, refused to go with us because of me. They thought I would cry and alert the guards. They suggested killing me by strangulation, rather than run the risk!'

'I know that story,' I said. 'I've heard it from your mother. She told me you were so brave, but I just can't imagine a child being able to withstand those tests!'

'Oich!' Mamushka had told me, 'they wanted to, you know, Katya, do like this to Olek!' and she made strangling actions, clutching gruesomely at her own neck, until Tatush winced and told her 'Czekaj, Tanya, czekaj! Wystarce,' which means 'stop, Tanya, this is enough . . . please, no more!'

I continued. 'There was no stopping Mamushka when she told me that story. Doing the actions, she continued to describe your bravery when the other prisoners hurled objects and you, her stoical son, took your injuries in silence.

'"Acch!" Mamushka relived the moment when she defied your would-be killers.

'"First kill me!" she threatened the other prisoners. "You will never touch him!"'

I continued impersonating my mother-in-law. 'No tear did give Olek, not a cry! Nussing!'

Mamushka's pride in her son's dogged resistance to provocation lasted decades. It was recited regularly along with Olek's other noble deeds, such as the brave reassurance to his parents as the family was about be executed: 'Don't worry! We all go, we are all going together!'

'So when you were five, and six, and seven, and eight,' I thought out loud, 'while I was playing supervised by my mother, war had forced you away from your childhood, into a terrifying adult reality . . .'

'That is true; I became a sort of man-child. And after war I was always different.

'I did not feel like child any more, after war was over. I felt like soldier. But I see now, through my children and what they are like, that I was also child. Adults calculate their decisions in different ways. My priorities were those of the child. Anyway, we escaped.

'The tunnel was narrow, dark, we had candle, I went behind Tatush and Mamushka went behind me, then Igor, that engineer who had volunteered to accompany us. Dirt was dropping on me, it got in my eyes, I did not cry. It was wet, and narrow, the space. I hung on to Tatush. But then we came up the other side, and crept one at a time past the beam of light into the trees of a very dark forest.

'Igor the engineer, he had decided to go on his own when we were out the other side. The other prisoners, who did not want to go with us, they were all caught. They were strung over fires by their hair, and they died.'

'What?' I asked, incredulous. 'Those gypsies too? Everyone? How could they hang people by their hair? Didn't men have short hair then? And what about bald men?'

He looked into my eyes. 'Hush, Katush, I am telling you, this is what we heard later. I hope too that it wasn't true, but so many cruel things were done during that war. Some things too bad to say, to speak about. War brings out good in some – there were many small heroes – and it brings out bad in very many. Cruelty.

'So once out on the other side, we wandered in cold night, in forest, then followed a frozen river, then farmland, and snow and ice. We were slipping, stopping, we were cold, hungry, staying huddled for warmth, then looking for some haystacks, for shed to sleep at night. We left early, very early, before being discovered by a peasant who could report us. Tatush wanted to sit down and die, Mamushka made him keep going.

'And me too, I urged him not to rest. And then we were found by a man in a horse and sleigh, who spoke in Russian to Mamushka. She seemed to know he would be there, at this certain place, waiting for us. This was the spot we had been trying to get to, following landmarks. We climbed onto his sleigh, it was so good to be not walking, we were sitting in seats being pulled by a horse, smelling the horse's warm breath.'

'But how did he know you would be there?' I interrupted. 'Who told him?'

'You know Katush, I don't know – I must ask Mamushka one day.

'Anyway, doctors, you know, they were needed desperately. Everywhere. More than salt, perhaps. Or sugar. My father had his instruments that the Germans had allotted him, he had brought them through the tunnel. Most of all, he had his knowledge. My father was known, even outside the prison, for his expertise. More than once we were saved by Tatush's reputation.'

Once again, I interjected. 'But Tatush is a dentist!'

'Ah yes, but you know, before dentistry, you must in these times first study medicine. Dentistry was a specialty. Anyway, to be a dentist was good in war. People can put up with pain, but no one can stand toothache. No drugs, no painkillers, no antibiotics, not even aspirin were available, remember. So to be a dentist guaranteed survival.'

He stared off into the distance. 'Now you tell your story, I like

this, our story. So what happened next? With us? This is very pleasant, hearing your version.'

'Yes, well, yours is a bit more of a story. But I will return to mine
anyway, since you seem to like it and it's your story as it is mine.'

6

Until death do us part

'Do you realise that you never ever proposed marriage to me? When I was the bridesmaid at my brother Johnny's wedding, you suddenly swept into the side chapel where the bride and groom were signing the registry, and we were all there with them, my family, her family.

'Straight to Dad you went, I could not believe my eyes. What was going on? I hadn't been told a thing by you, nothing! You were on duty at the hospital that night, I was at my brother's wedding, you had never met my family apart from Mum, and here you were. Taking over . . .

'Everybody watched as you became the centre of attention. No one noticed the bride and groom any more . . . Dad is always the master of every occasion. I remember he turned in his elegant manner, adjusting his monocle in order to peer at you in his theatrical, specialist-doing-his-rounds way. He always loved theatre! And you, a doctor, charging into the group, you gave him the golden chance to exercise his famous wit.

' "Excuse me, sir!" you said. "Could I have hand of your daughter?"

'All eyes turned on me. The monocle swivelled, from you to me. Nobody said a word. The silence shouted at me, and I really blushed.

I must have been scarlet. I was embarrassed, confused, half furious and wondering why did you do that? I hardly knew you and we
had become this instant spectacle . . . they must have thought that
perhaps Kathy the show-off was desperate to upstage the bride, but
I never asked any of them what they made of it all. My quiet life
was about to change.

'Of course Dad noticed the stethoscope dangling from the pocket
of your white clinical jacket. It was the honourable stethoscope that
saved you. His monocle, I noticed, magnified a bit of a twinkle. Dad
was having fun.

'He prepared his answer, remember? Do you recall what he
said?'

'I don't remember. I think he asked me to come and see him.'

'Well, I remember. "I have two daughters, young man!' he said.
'Which one do you have in mind?" That's what he asked you, I heard
him . . . I remember his eye magnifying horribly through the monocle
and that you stood your ground. Amazing. Then you pointed at me
and said, "That one!"

'The inspection by monocle must have obliterated my name
from your mind. Anyway, to my father I was Katharine. To you I was
Katushka. Had you remembered, Dad may not have understood
whose hand was being sought, he would have definitely denied having a Katushka in his brood. But he said something like, "Come and
see me tomorrow. I am presuming that you know where we live?"'

'Yes, he told me to come to your house! He wanted to warn me
about you and your habits!' said Olek, remembering.

'Well, he may have wanted to warn you, but I tell you now, there
was no way Dad was going to say no to a doctor, even if your behaviour had proven to be seriously unorthodox. Besides, he was always
anxious to offload his children into other households – he was sick
of living with us and wanted Mum to himself. So, what did he tell
you about me?' I was curious.

'He told me you were silly with money, loyal, strong, that you
would follow me anywhere, you had a nice nature, an artistic

temperament, that sort of thing, all designed to appeal to me. I was caught, anyway —'

'Oh! Well, why the hell did you do that? Coming to the wedding, barging in like that? It was outrageous . . . did the boys put you up to it?'

'Boys at hospital, yes – they told me that's what I must do. They told me step by step, and I did it like that!'

'Well, they probably just wanted a laugh and they definitely got it. It was a bit embarrassing for me at the time, yes, very embarrassing. But I guess the standard ways of doing things are instantly forgettable, while your way will go down in history. What did you tell the boys? That you wanted to take out the daughter of the iconic Sir Douglas Miller? And did they insist that before you date her you have to first ask her father's permission to marry her? They must have had the time of their lives, goading the funny foreigner into making such a display. Aussies can be so rude to foreigners, and you would have been the only doctor with even an accent. But you carried it off with my father, and not many do – everybody's scared of being the victim of Dad's sharp tongue!'

'Six weeks later I faced you at the altar. You had announced yourself as Russian Orthodox and had produced an Orthodox baptism certificate, so we had a Catholic wedding. It never occurred to me at the time that you and your family may have wanted a Jewish wedding. You didn't say a word, you didn't even push the Jewish thing at all. Did you have to argue behind the scenes about that with Mamushka?'

'I did not listen to all her objections,' said Olek. 'Besides, she was never religious, she never went to synagogue. They were left-wing sympathisers, her family. They had a Jewish wedding, she and Tatush, gypsies playing, wild fiddles keeping everyone dancing till dawn, but they didn't do the other religious stuff.'

'How magical, a wedding with gypsy fiddles. I would love to

TOP Katush and Olek, toasting the future, 1966.
BOTTOM Katush and Olek, dancing for life, 1974.

Photo: Olek Golski

Photo: J. Laguna

TOP Babies can be fun! Kathy and naked Nadya in Malabar, 1968.
BOTTOM Nadya, Katush, Olek and Jan – a day at the beach, UK-style, 1971.

Photo: J. Szczepanski

Photo: J. Szczepanski

TOP Nadya and Jan climb too high to catch, 1974.
BOTTOM Mishka, Canberra, 1977.

ABOVE Jan, Nadya and Olek carrying Mishka, running
through the wind, United Kingdom, 1972.

Photo: J. Szczepanski

TOP Nadya has lost her voice; Olek reassures her it will return, 1974.
BOTTOM Mother and son: Mamushka and Olek, 1978.

ABOVE Nadya, Jan, Mishka and Kot with Voy – a happy family again, 1980.

Photo: Mishka Golski

ABOVE Kathy paints Nadya's portrait, 1986.

Photo: W. Dabrowski

Photo: Abigail Howells

TOP Kathy among tribesmen, Rulna, Papua New Guinea, 1982.
BOTTOM Jan and Mishka reach the banks of the Niger River, 1989.

have had such a wedding! But I remember it, our wedding. Going into St Joseph's with Dad, music playing, a small choir, me nervous, dressed in white.

'There we were, making eternal vows, you and me. Unfortunately we were a long way from gypsy fiddles, but we made the same desperate promises made in all marriages – the vows your parents made, my parents made. Then suddenly I realised how new you were in my life, and my legs wobbled. You appeared before me on the steps of the altar, strangely dressed for you, your bushy, ruffly hair harshly trimmed and formal, wetted back from your poor scrubbed temples!

'Without warning my new life flashed before me, its darker mysteries thrilling but also filling me with a trepidation for which I had not prepared myself, I was so preoccupied with preparing for the wedding.

'There was no sign of hesitation about me on your face. You didn't seem to be put off by my dramatic appearance. I had that lofty headdress constructed from a coiled sock, whipped in at the last moment, to support the antique mantilla which was "something borrowed".

My homemade attempts at an eyelash tint had made a dark smudge on my left cheek, and that fashionable beauty spot beneath my lip covered a zit. You probably didn't even notice. During the vows my cheeks were burning and you just looked me straight in the eye and your responses never even wavered. Your accent and your eyes were familiar but the rest of you looked strange. And your grip on my soul was tight. I guess I was swept along by your sureness, the sureness that is your mark.

'That same night, after the reception at Eastbourne Avenue, I stood there with you and tipsily threw my champagne glass against the stucco wall of my father's house. I made you throw yours, too, remember? The surroundings were not very Slavic, but I was on home ground, they were my family's glasses. The pieces of crystal disappeared into the hydrangea bushes, and I suppose they're still there . . .'

Olek smiled, remembering that. He had hesitated to break Mum's crystal, but I had recklessly insisted.

I see the broken crystal now as a symbol of the pieces of our marriage that prevail, inextricably embedded into our children, and now into their children, and in the intense slivers of Slavic Jewish culture that have blended with mine, changing my eating habits, my dreams, my memories, my choices, my way of seeing things, and infusing my life with a curiously rich and vital flavour.

7

Entry to partisans

Olek kept taking me further back into his memory, stirred by the embers of the campfire.

'I am sitting on the horse-drawn sleigh, next to the driver. Mamushka is sleeping, exhausted by the escape, the fear, the cold. Tired from protecting us, me and Tatush. The forest, it's getting dark. Snow makes it quiet, so quiet. Horse is snorting, sleigh goes gently. Mamushka sleeps, her head on Tatush's lap. I am scared, a bit excited too, going into the unknown. It's a forest. Tatush sleeps too. I wish that they would wake. I am sitting next to the driver. I feel so alone, so responsible for our destiny.

'"Where you drive us to, *tovarisch*," I say. That means comrade, communists used this. But he looks straight in front, ignores my question, laughs, gives me reins to drive his horse.

'"You say the way," he says. "You go, boy! Hey Ho! *Poshli!*"

'I don't want to drive,' continues Olek, 'but horse doesn't care who drives. He knows where to go. I smell his breath. It smells warm, it makes me sleepy too, but I should not sleep – I must watch this man. I am on watch.

'Mamushka had negotiated that we would be taken to the same group of partisans in this forest, we must be together. He wanted to take us to different groups.

'"Only together," she said. "If not, my husband will not work as the doctor."

'Tatush agreed. He was tired. She always spoke for Tatush, and he stayed silent, because he spoke Polish better than Russian, he came from Warsaw. She spoke Russian, it was her first language. Yiddish and Russian. Me too, I spoke mainly Russian. Anyway, he doesn't speak too much, my father. He is not the main talker.

'And now both my parents are sleeping. I am left to keep alert. So I must watch him, this driver, that he keeps his word. Trees become taller, more dense. Sky is dark, I can't see much. Trees are so high, Katush, more high than these trees here. Here you see stars. There not. An old forest. Some huge trees. And ground, white, even at night. Horse treads softly. Sleigh creaks a bit. You would like it, Katush, this sled, going through the snow. Usually they have bells, but not this one, because it is wartime.

'"Hey, Max!" The driver flicks reins over horse's rump. I ask no more questions. I start to get sleepy again, the cart it sways, it creaks. But I must fight sleep. It is up to me to make sure this man does not cheat us, take us to another prison.

'And then I smell fire. Max picks up his pace. Clob clob clob, soft clob clob on snow. Then stop. Clearing in forest, sky again. It is evening, snow falling, so quiet, so light. A big fire, in a shallow pit. People sitting around. A boy, standing on the edge of the clearing, singing a Russian song, like this, "Na ni na, ni na." He is older than me, he has balalaika. He is wearing soldier's jacket. I want one too, like his. His name, Pavlik.

'Mama is awake now, and Tatush. Two men come, they speak to my father. Mama answers, she speaks Russian. We have been brought to partisans. The men stand to greet us formally, Russian-style, kissing my father on both cheeks. They are surprised about me, so young, it is not the law of partisans, they say, to keep children. My parents explain that I will be as a man, that I have proved myself. The fellow he slaps my shoulder then, and shakes my hand. He calls me *tovarisch*. I was impressed, Katush.

44

It looked like a place for men, and I felt like a man.'

'And how did it look, the partisans' camp?' I asked.

'It was a camp. Like here. Not quite. But forest, sky, fire, people, there is much that is same. This is why I like to camp. Thirty-two people were in our camp, living in dugouts in forest. Only a few women, the teenage boy, Pavlik, and now me too. I was the youngest. I was given soldier's jacket too, like Pavlik.

'Now I too was a small soldier, that's what our leader told me. Our leader was disciplinarian. He had to be. You could be shot for going against orders. I was happy with that, their rules were fair, prison rules were unfair, it was good to be away from prison in that forest that protected us from enemies. We had dug-out rooms. We could hide, become invisible from above, from planes.

'So I stopped feeling my fear – fear of prison guards, fear of the fear in the eyes of fellow prisoners, always on the watch. Partisans' camp was our new home. We had food, mainly potatoes, and made bread in fire, dampers, like we make potatoes, they buried dough under ashes. We slept in dugouts. When we slept I heard snow, it was the only sound to be heard in forest. When I woke snow was on ground and on trees, it was quiet again. After noises of prison, shouts of guards, crying prisoners, coughing, those sounds of fear were gone.

'Our room was also a surgery. A pit with wooden ceiling. It had rough examination table, dug-out shelves, place to sleep, army blankets. It was safe. Tatush took his instruments out of his coat lining and laid them out, Mamushka helped him. He was ready to work. He had a patient as soon as we arrived. I had to attend, I watched him extract a tooth. It was quite horrible, there was no anaesthetic, they had to hold him still, that guy. I did not want to be dentist, I thought then, once again. I wanted to be doctor.

'Tatush explained to me, "You must know this, how to do this. I will teach you about teeth," he said, "in case Mamushka and I get taken and only you are left."

'So my father taught me to extract teeth, in case I would be left

45

without parents, so I would have skills to survive the war.'

'Can you still do that? Extract teeth?' I winced.

'If I had to, yes, I could. But I would prefer not, only in emergency I would do it.

'My parents still used the phrase "get taken" a lot. Even in the partisans' camp they thought about that. People could still get taken, and their children left behind. So aged six I got to know all instruments, their use, I had skills at age seven to pull teeth. I did not have height, or strength, but I knew what to do, not to break the tooth. Mamushka went to peel potatoes with other women. We ate potatoes, women cooked together, there were only few women, they cooked and joked and sang while they prepared potatoes.

'Russians love to sing. They sing harmonies. All join in, singing their own parts, men's parts, some different voices. Their harmonies at night by the fire I will never forget. That's what I like to sing with Nadya, now by our fire, those same harmonies I teach her, she understands these songs, she has the feeling in her soul.'

'And you were never discovered? By the Germans?' I asked.

'No no, never, they never found us. We were not near any forest tracks. Sometimes it was close, there were search missions in the distance, and we could quickly disappear underground. In summer forest is dense, there is no visibility, but many times we heard planes, and all fires had to be put out quickly. Everyone scuttling to dugouts, like rabbits. Then planes would go away. Other groups of partisans sometimes got bombed, not us. Only one horse was hit, a sort of a wild horse – they live in this forest. It was outside our camp, not too far. We had to cut him up for meat. We were lucky to have the meat, we were lucky it was not us who was killed. The forest was our friend, it protected us. In autumn we found mushrooms, different sorts, we dried them and hung them on strings, we cooked them over fire. And the trees even gave us our milk – the *berioski*, we call them. They were the birch trees. We tapped their trunks for their juice – it was our drink. One day when I was getting the milk I found an injured bird, he could not fly, he could hop a little, so I

46

took him back to the camp and after discussion they said I could keep him. He became my pet, Skoczek, Little Hopper.'

I continued to press him for information. 'What sort of partisans were they?'

'They were communist partisans, our group. Mainly Russian, a few Polish, we called each other *tovarisch*. There were quite a few groups in that same forest. It was big forest, Białowieza. Such a beautiful forest, Katushka. To live in forest and watch the seasons as they change – it's something you could never really know here, where trees are forever grey-green, where there is no snow, where there is no such great difference between winter and summer.'

8

Child of war

You were such a mystery, Olek. I have to carefully put together the bits and pieces you told me that night to fill in the gaps in my knowledge. When your family got caught, were the Germans looking for you or was it accidental? And if they were looking for you, who told the Germans that you were there? When you left the monastery that day to go exploring in the forest, was it part of a considered plan? And was that why you were in the forest with your things, including Tatush's dental gold? Or had you heard rumours from the monks of an impending raid and were hiding there out the back until the raid was over? Or was it just the fear in your parents' minds that kept you moving?

If your story was right, then you may not have been that long at the monastery. Yet you knew the prayers, the chants. And you said it was autumn when your childhood stopped. Children don't have a great sense of time, measuring their lives by imagination rather than calendars. These are my only real clues.

Once you were in that transit camp where the kind German guard brought you eggs, and where you were nearly shot, were you there for some time? Weeks? Months? Seasons? And had your father struck a deal with the partisan whom he treated that if you ever needed to hide, you would have a place there with them in the forest? Is that how you knew where the group was? Did your father have a map through the more invisible paths of the forest, whispered by the grateful patient and secretly committed to memory?

And how did the man with the horse and sled, how did he know where to find you after you escaped through the tunnel? How would he have known the timing of the escape? He had been sent to bring you to the Russian partisans – our friend Bajkowski remembers it was the Parhomenko brigade . . . or one of its forest cells. Had your father sent word from prison, notifying the group of your planned escape? It all seems impossible. There were no phones, no field phones, no telegrams. Communication would have only been via some resistance operation, perhaps a runner, sent into the forest with a drawn map. We may never know.

I should have asked you these questions and taken notes. Instead, I listened to your stories in a half daze, and they seemed unreal against the quiet landscapes of our small camping holidays in the bush.

I thought you would always be there, a living archive of your own life. There seemed to be no need to put together the bits and pieces, it was already a whole because your physical presence, your warm voice telling the stories, seemed to fill in the gaps and make it all seamless.

You called life with the partisans an ideal childhood – the best part of your boyhood. It was better than prison. It was hidden away, concealed from the malevolent eyes of the occupying army. It represented empowerment in a world where so many were simply victims, waiting for the worst. The partisan groups in the forest were constantly undermining the German occupation. Their war movements and transport contingents were all potential targets of partisan-led sabotage strategies. You were living the life of a boy in the forest helping the guerilla group defeat the dreaded enemy. It was a far better life than prison camp, and even after the war, when post-war communist Poland was grey with restrictions.

Your relatives – those who were not killed in the camps, or in the uprisings – fled to America. They went to New York and there they thrived. And you were left behind the Iron Curtain, where optimism and basic resources had been routed by the war, replaced by the ever-watchful, sombre eye of communism. There, a war-weary population was prevented from post-war recovery by its new oppressors.

Life in the forest for you, a boy unconcerned about the future state of the world, was bliss. You woke, climbed out of your dugout and yawned into the dawn filtering through the treetops, through the flakes of snow falling weightlessly, the black and white of winter, or when spring broke the eastern winter's long stronghold, the sudden calls of forest birds. You witnessed the joyful birth of palest green foliage creeping onto the graceful black limbs and branches of the old forest. The first daisies covering the ground, announcing spring. Your pet bird, Skoczek, that small orphan, would have chimed in with the twittering, tempted to join his kind in the canopy but choosing to stay with you, his keeper.

And then in summer, as the long northern twilight kept the night at bay, you, Skoczek and Pavlik tramped around searching for wild berries to liven up a diet of potatoes and the occasional horse or doe that had been bombed or strayed, and then used to nourish your group in the forest.

You had your parents with you, Olek, you felt safe. A child feels safe with its parents. You lived there, with them, through many sea-sons. The forests hiding your group were the mysterious landscape that became one of the strong layers in your soul. The white bark of the birches – the givers of milk – the massive trunks of the oaks, occasional kings of the forest, white winters, blossoming hazelnuts in spring, the long white nights of summer. It resonated with you all your life, even transferring happily to the Australian bush with its different secrets, its stronger light, more raucous bird sounds, longer summers and the pounding surf always crashing, crashing, crashing.

The partisans took you on their sabotage missions. They gave you a soldier's jacket the same as Pavlik's to make you a real soldier – you were not there for play. And you had *valenki*, rough, thick boots made of grey felt. You must have liked those *valenki* because you were always looking for a *valenki* substitute in shoe shops. As an orthopaedic surgeon you even wanted to design them for the children, saying that the boots were good for the little muscles in the foot. You never found *valenki*, never got to design them, but you wore sandals to work. Monks' sandals?

Your job as mascot for the partisans – accompanying them on their sabotage missions, pressing the bomb detonators – thrilled you to your core. The head partisan guided your hand. Did your small hand tremble with the responsibility, under the stern guidance of the partisans? Or were you quite calm, a war child, seasoned by your experiences, and watching the train crumple into the river, crashing through the broken bridge as our boys would watch a video game?

Did Mamushka cry, 'Oich, oich! No, not my son!' as the men led you away on their deadly missions? Or, disciplined by partisan lore, did she manage to control her anxieties and keep them to herself?

You told me your father put his hand over your eyes one day, when, walking through the warm summer forest on a reconnoitre, the head partisan spotted and then shot dead a coupling Russian woman and a German soldier taking a few seconds of blissful time out from the grim rules of war.

'I was angry with my father,' you said. 'I wanted to see them being shot. In partisan law, you were forbidden social or romantic contact with the German oppressors, so they had done wrong. I did not want to be protected by Tatush's genteel pre-war sensibilities, I did not want his hand blindfolding my eyes!'

What sort of child were you then? What other harsh experiences shaped your strange childhood, making it so different from mine?

How do I find the answers to your childhood? Tatush was a gentle man – the rough customs of the partisans must have constantly repulsed and horrified him. He said that he remembered the experience with extreme distaste, but as a child you became a devotee – you understood partisan lore.

When you came to Australia you had one ambition – to work as a barefoot doctor in Papua New Guinea. You had completed a few months in Papua New Guinea as a student, but you failed the entry requirements to practise there once you'd qualified – you could not spontaneously name the last five Australian prime ministers – so you stayed in Australia and met me.

I try looking at your children. I find some answers, just from the way they are – which is like you and, I imagine, not particularly like me. When a young person dies, they leave a powerful wake. The things you believed in, the things you said, the things you did all acquired legendary status with your children. Your maxims became beacons of light to be followed, often mentioned, often quoted, incorporated into their ways of being, and setting their life plans adrift in a sea of legends and dreams.

9

The death of Pavlik

Months later, we were back at our campsite and I was asking more questions.

'So, apart from potatoes and damper and the odd horse,' I asked, 'what about food?'

'There was food, we had food. We sent scavenging parties, ambushed German supply lines, sometimes partisans forced villagers to hand over rations like flour to survive the rest of the war. Villagers had trouble. They were the poorest. Cleaned out by Germans, and then by partisans, some were starving. We had food. Not too much. Potatoes, we planted them, harvested them. Sometimes there was meat, we were hungry for meat. There were no fat people there but I don't remember hunger in forest, not so much. It would have been subsistence amounts of food. In spring there were berries, there was the milk from the birches, the *berioska*. It was sort of thin milk, bit like breast milk, no special taste.'

I had heard about the birch trees and their miraculous yield. 'How? How did you get it out of the trees? Was it the sap you got?'

'We tapped trees with tin, to catch it, yes it was sap. I had to collect tins. Me and Pavlik. It was our job. Some *berioski* were quite far from camp, not in dense parts in middle of the forest. We knew where they were, on edges, near clearings, near the river.

'And Pavlik, that boy in the soldier's jacket, he was my friend. We had our duties because we were partisans and we had to be like men, so we gathered wood for fire, we cleaned camp, we collected sap, we pulled potatoes from the ground and washed them in the river. And I was taken on expeditions with the men. But when jobs were done we made a secret treehouse where we could hide. Sometimes when men were off somewhere, we could still play like children do. Not the cowboy and Indian, our heroes were always partisan men, our baddies were German soldiers.'

'And what became of Pavlik?'

'When war was finishing in our area, in '44, when Russians, the Red Army, had pushed Germans further west, Germans were running, escaping, and partisans disbanded. We quit our camp and went to find the town. We were standing at the edge of forest watching them. They rolled past – Russian tanks, soldiers and defeated Germans in front.

'Pavlik was next to me. He was trying to run over to the column of soldiers, he was angry and full of fire. I tried to pull him back but he struggled away from me. He ran in front of a tank and sang the anthem, he was shouting "The Internationale", he was so proud to be communist. The tank kept moving, it rolled over him. Perhaps the driver didn't see that small boy, didn't hear his anthem. I did not want to watch, I tried to hide from this myself, behind my father's hand, but it happened too quickly – I saw. I still see small crumpled soldier's jacket in tracks of tank. We waited until they had passed, then we dug a hole, men carried him, we buried him. We made a cross, Russian cross, and with my knife I scratched his name: Pavlik Who Died in Battle. I struggled, I tried not to cry. I was soldier, I told myself. But now I know soldiers do cry.

He lapsed into silence, staring at the last of the campfire, then dowsed the fire with water from the lake and we crawled into our tent and snuggled down next to the children, smelling the smoke in their hair, hearing their little snuffles. I thought about them for a sleepy moment, imagining one of them living in a forest, driven there by war, wintering in a cold, clammy dugout, knowing no other life.

I fell asleep, and in my dreams the face of the boy had the features of my own children. It was they who were there, small against the big trees, lost and away from familiarity. I was endeavouring to get to them, but my legs would not move, my calls to them made no sound.

10

Fighting for food

Mamushka, Olek's mother, thought her son had a shocking child-hood. When Olek and I had dinner at her home in Marrickville one night, I decided to be proactive rather than sit there warding off second and third helpings. I interrogated Mamushka on her partisan experience.

'We don't like talk about this,' said Tatush.

But Mamushka had no problems about recounting horrific experiences – she seemed to need to relive the drama, and endlessly recalled bits and pieces of the war as it affected her.

'Oich, oich! Terrible. You can't imagine! Underground, Katya, we lived!' Mamushka called me by the Russian version of my name.

'No salt,' she said. 'No soap. No sugar. No milk.'

'What did you miss most?' I asked her, always interested in the partisan tales. I liked to think of Mamushka, petite and daring, also dressed in an army jacket, singing and joking with the women while cooking. Would it have been like that? Would there have been the time and spirit to joke? Mamushka had a wonderful ear, and she knew many songs. She had a bawdy sense of fun. She was extroverted and sociable. I'm sure she would have found opportunities to be herself, even in the shadow of war.

But she remembered it differently. She did not recall the partisan experience with any sort of pleasure.

'Salt. Sugar. We had no sugar! You can't imagine! Acch, Olek, he was so poor! Such shoes he wore you can't imagine.'

'But Mamushka!' Olek protested, 'We were alive! We were together! I liked my *valenki*. We didn't have sugar but we imagined sugar in our tea that we didn't have. We sat round with our tea, with string hanging from a branch. Tied to the end of this string we imagined that lump of sugar. And when we watched it swing on the string, our tea tasted sweet. *Napre glasko*, we called it. And when we didn't have string, we imagined string, and we imagined a single sugar lump hanging from string. *Napre dunko* we called that. I tell you, it also made tea taste sweet. Even *napre dunko*!'

'Well, of course!' I said, trying my hardest to conjure up a situation where imagined sugar could taste sweet just because it is so longed for. And wondering if there would be a difference between the relative taste of tea when imagined with a string and then with no string. Olek thought there was a difference, he remembered it, and he was very persuasive. And the imagined taste of that non-existent sugar represented by the invisible lump still fired in his imagination, leaving our more easily acquired packets of supermarket sugar way behind, as far as desirable consumables were concerned.

Mamushka thought otherwise. 'Acch!' she declared, completely dismissive and scornful of the pleasures afforded by *napre glasko*. She saw it as sheer deprivation.

'Oich! Terrible! *Strachne*! You can't imagine, Katya, not having sugar! Nussing – we had nussing!'

'*Czekaj czekaj*, Tanya, Olek, *nie mow*. It's finish,' protests Tatush, trying to shut them both up. 'Now is beautiful here, Australia,' he said, pointing out the window at the Cooks River, snaking its way cheerfully between suburbs and beneath the cliff in front of the sunny block of flats in Hilltop Avenue, Marrickville.

Tatush, so quietly spoken, often seemed to get ignored. He could not bear to mention the war, to stimulate the residual horrors lurking in his mind. He failed completely in his attempt to silence Olek and Mamushka. But compared to the other bits of the war there seemed to me to be no ghastly horrors in the partisan story. Especially not for Olek as a child, living in the present and unaware of the future.

For his parents, the rough life in the forest must have verged on unbearable. Living in muddy holes, they would have been crushed with very real fears for the future – even if they did manage to survive the war. This, added to the physical hardship, must have been overwhelming.

Mamushka told me about her dramatic and dangerous sortie to the village to get real milk and soap to wash her filthy child-soldier.

'Acch! Soap, Katya, to wash the child. We with Olek, we went with gun, you know. One peasant woman she give me soap and milk!'

'Yes, Mama, we had sawn-off shotgun!'

'Oich, Olek! What is "sawn-off"? To wash you I go with gun, for milk I go with gun, I ask one peasant, "For my son," I said . . .'

Did Mamushka, plucky little thing that she was, really drag the protesting boy-soldier Olek from the depths of the forest and appear in some primitive, war-ravished village with a sawn-off shotgun in order to get soap to wash her filthy child? And why take that risk for a bit of soap and milk?

Would it not have been better to stay within the safety of the forest and let him remain grubby? And allow him to continue in perfect safety to tap the birch trees for his milk? Perhaps desperation makes mothers irrational, but how, on the other hand, did she get away with breaking camp, ignoring partisan rules and making her own journey to the village to get soap? So many things I can only guess at.

Perhaps Olek, on the other hand, took it for granted that this was the standard way to get soap. Like going to the chemist or supermarket for us. Perhaps it was he who suggested the expedition. Perhaps he it was who carried the weapon.

'I gave shirt off my back for you, Olek,' she continued, and he nodded in tacit agreement. 'Everything for you, my son!'

'And what about meat, Mamushka?' I asked, angling in stealthily, astride an issue close to her heart – food.

'The meat sometimes from horse, Katya, in partisan. Was very good – sweet, you know, *smakue nawet*. Sometimes the men they shot one. Sometimes deer too, they get. We were hungry for meat. Potato potato, all time, you know, potato?'

A horse-lover myself, I winced at the thought of eating those beautiful beasts, but did not vocalise my distaste for fear it would reveal a complete lack of sensitivity to a situation so desperate it was way beyond my ability to even imagine it.

'How did you find horses?' I asked her, wondering if horses wandered round the forest over there, in the company of wolves and bison.

'One time horse was killed by bombing, you know? Not far from camp, you know, one wild horse. And one time the men they steal from *tsigani* the horse. *Tsigani* they keep horses. But to steal from *tsigan*! You can imagine such situation to steal from *tsigani*? *Tsigani* they steal, but to steal from them? *Strachnie!*'

'What is *tsigan*, Mamushka?'

'It is gypsies!'

11

My in-laws

His mother Tanya. I haven't talked about her too much, have I? My Mamushka – my little mother, it means in Russian. She was small – in fact, she even made me look tall. She had dark eyes, blond hair and a perennial suntan, induced by strolling at Bondi Beach or by lying under her sunlamp. And Tatush, her husband, my father-in-law. A dignified person who usually kept his counsel and was also sun-tanned, making his eyes look lighter, more blue, behind his steel-rimmed glasses.

Far from the partisans, far from grey communism and long winters my parents-in-law enjoyed Sydney – they loved the freedom of movement, and they loved the weather. They like their mod cons in the kitchen, and they like to buy fruit at all times of the year.

We used to stroll, the four of us, when Olek and I first met. In the sun, along the promenade at Bondi, Mamushka and Tatush, me and Olek would walk four abreast.

I had never promenaded. Used to arriving at the beach in swimming costume, towel and bare feet, and smearing my body in oil, I had only ever gone to the beach to gain a deep tan or loll around in the waves. The concrete strip at the top of the sand at Bondi and the grass behind was for Europeans with different beach habits. New Australians. They brought proper food, they set up tables and ball games, they came in all their generations, often remaining clothed, and if they wore swimming costumes they were different sorts of costumes. It was them up there, I thought, and us, the locals, lying below the concrete on the hot sand. We called those others the grasshoppers.

Then, without ever wishing it to happen, I had switched. I had become one of the others, a grasshopper, inhabiting the promenade with other grasshoppers.

Dressed in a flowered frock I strolled with my new family at an even pace along the promenade. I gazed strangely at the oiled and sun-drenched bodies lying motionless and carefree on the hot sand. Had I not been one of them, just a few weeks ago? Would I ever be one of them again? I didn't know. Part of me seemed to have been dissolved. Was it serious?

And what about hot chips? Chiko rolls? Around me I could still smell their tantalising scent. But for me now it was back to Marrickville for a proper lunch, a lunch partly prepared by my new parents-in-law before they had left for the beach, the remaining courses waiting to arrive on the table after the return from the beach. We sat and waited as the food came in waves, brought eagerly by the ever-bustling Mamushka. She never sat down herself but observed us with a burning gaze as we ate, to see whether we were eating fast enough or sufficient quantities or whether we really appreciated her cooking.

And how about that Sunday, three weeks after we had met, when Olek took his new Olympus Pen camera along. He had bought it with his first pay as a fully fledged doctor, and wanted to photograph me. I was posing self-consciously next to him, possibly blushing shyly in front of my in-laws, when Mamushka banished my shyness forever. She who was supposed to be taking the photograph of us together, made a spontaneous leap onto her son's shoulders, having first handed the camera to me, motioning me to take the photograph of her astride Olek's shoulders! My finger hesitated before clicking as I struggled with an upsurge of feeling totally upstaged and being pushed out of my own picture. I looked at Tatush for help. He just smiled indulgently, looking admiringly at his wife, still so coy after their many years of marriage. I did not take the photo. And when it was my turn to pose, I refused. I could not persuade myself to cooperate with the terms that had been set. Something inside me rebelled furiously against the sweet and obliging acquiescence which was expected of me as an incoming daughter-in-law. Trouble loomed.

How life for me has changed, I thought. I had married a man with a mother, the likes of whom I had never encountered. It seemed to me that I was completely lacking in strategies with which to counter her outrageous demands.

Who was I becoming? I was no longer Kathy, Katy or Katharine. I was Katush or Katushka for Olek; for Mamushka I was Katya; and for Tatush, Kasia. I sat at the table in Marrickville, eating obediently, rapidly putting on the weight that I had lost for just long enough to catch Olek's eye. I looked down at my body and gazed with horror at all the new bulges. Olek didn't mind – I was his cute dumpling Katushka. They didn't mind – I was their Katya, and the fatter the better.

I did mind, and I remained silent. But my compliance was masking simmering resistance to this takeover of my old persona. I was not sure what it was about. Was it really about food? Or about where we were going to eat? I sat in my office, the same office where I fantasised about Olek before our failed first date. I ignored all matters connected with atomic energy and instead became obsessed with the energy of Mamushka, which could beam straight into me even when she wasn't in the room. I was constantly aware of her thoughts, as they sought to subvert any of my potential escape plans.

'Where are they going to eat dinner tonight?' I imagined her saying to Tatush. 'At my table? Or is she planning to waste money and eat bad food at a restaurant? Will she ring up to me, my daughter-in-law?'

I was aware of Mamushka's desire to place a curfew on any activities that precluded eating at her kitchen table. And I counterplotted. I did not ring her. I felt rebellious. Instead I dialled the hospital number and paged Olek, forcing his attention away from a patient in crisis. I didn't care.

'Are we going to eat at home?'

'I think it would be quite pleasant to eat at Mamushka's.'

Pleasant was the wrong word, but he liked to use it in many inappropriate situations, insist on his right to use it, and cite the dictionary as proof of continuing correct usage.

Unpleasant would have been a more accurate description, but I withheld my opinion and concurred. 'Right. Okay. See you at eight.'

Far from satisfied with my lame acceptance of this answer, my face burned with frustration. I thought of all the things I could and should have said.

'And why do we need to eat at Mamushka's again?'

Thinking of the answers Olek could give.

'Because she's prepared dinner for us.'

'Because you need a rest, Katushka. You go to work – why should you get tired in kitchen? Why should you bother to shop and then study recipe books in order to produce what Mamushka can just prepare with her eyes shut?'

And anyway, what could I really say? I imagined Olek with his bushy hair and appealing frown of concentration at a hospital bedside, someone's pulse under his sensitive fingertips, and then being interrupted by me on the phone, loaded up with a furious but trivial desire to deflect the dedicated doctor from going to his mother's house.

I was also becoming increasingly aware that Olek himself was under pressure to attend dinner there every night he was off-duty. It was so much easier to go along with her rather than oppose her, possessed as she was of this furious need to feed her only son and fatten his wife, observing us as we ate. But compliance was not on my mind.

Disguising the concern that was starting to dominate my waking hours, I strained my ears to interpret what he was arranging with Mamushka. Could it be that now Olek was actually trying to defend us from another dinner at Marrickville? Had he detected some rebellion in me? But surely this was wishful thinking on my part. My hopes that he would state our case successfully were rarely rewarded. My resistance made him upset, and somehow, whatever the outcome of our discussions, whatever alternative plans we made, we still found ourselves going to Marrickville. Mamushka always won. The dinner would be laid out in advance. The gold–edged white china, the shallow soup-bowls, the large oval-shaped soup spoons, rye bread, chopped herrings, beetroot soup, paprika chicken. For starters.

And then I would be full. Before even beginning on the *bigos*. Eating more and more, the family would argue excitedly in Polish. And what about me? Stupefied by food, I caught the occasional mention of my name disguised by linguistic inflections. But by this time my curiosity was dulled, along with my appetite. It didn't matter what they all said. Tatush always butted in, on my behalf, suggesting that they break into English for my sake.

'*Mow po angielsku dla kasi*! Kasia you are like rose, young rose,' he said in English.

Olek seemed to be listening to me as I chatted to him, telling him my part of the story. He had a half-smile with a slightly stubborn twist to it, and he kept on stirring the fire, avoiding my eyes. He said nothing, occasionally glancing at me in mock protest. And I kept going, in my mind.

English, as Mamushka and Tatush knew it, did not afford them ground to discuss, or gossip, or complain, or tell jokes. It simply provided them with the threadbare basics of practical communication, minus tense, minus all nuance, learned through a dictionary. Tatush liked to reassure me of their combined love for me – when he smiled at me his blue eyes were warm. He appeared to trust me, as long as I continued to eat Mamushka's food, and it was only he who suggested speaking in English.

'*Mow po angielsku dla kasi!*' he said again. Tatush called me a rose, even a young rose, but I was starting to feel more like a slug, an old slug, stupefied by food as I struggled between sleep and small talk. A rose did not describe the way I perceived myself during these dinners, not at all.

As the Polish conversation gathered its usual momentum the couch always caught my eye, offering its sweet self until its pull became too strong. And then I would flop there, relief coursing through my over-fed body, my eyes closing despite the strong fluorescent light. Then I would be woken.

'Ah, Katushka!'

Olek would squeeze my hand, bend to kiss me, his face alive and flushed after the conversation with his parents. And then, half-asleep, full of herring and *bigos*, dazed from being woken and driven off into the cold night, I knew I was not going to win any arguments. But I still tried.

'Why does your family always argue?' I asked, provocatively. Born a chatterbox, I now felt like a mute. And I could feel chasms opening up between Olek and me, as our different cultures moved like armies into their own trenches – his with its in-built drama, mine with its drama dispersed by passionless Anglo logic. We reached out for each other from the trenches, we searched for common ground, but the ground was already mined.

'Argue? What argue? We don't argue, Katushka!'

'Then why do you have so much to say to each other, anyway? And what about me?' I was close to tears.

'The English are different. You are very quiet people. Pleasant. Quiet, and English.'

Right. I was still half-asleep, and feeling grumpily negative. Actually, I thought, I had had just about enough. But had enough of what? I felt neither quiet nor English. Anyway, I wasn't English. And why did I resent this cultural description of me and my people? Should I not have been happy that I was quiet and pleasant and didn't get into fiery arguments with my parents over dinner?

I felt as though I was being categorised as coming from a race so orderly, so controlled, and so passionless, that for him and for his parents it appeared as exotic. The other. The inscrutable English. That's what they thought. I had been forced into an enemy camp where I didn't even feel I properly belonged. But my blood was up and I was going to defend that camp anyway, no matter how unattractive it appeared to me.

'How can you say that? It's so unfair!'

'What is unfair? I said good things, I like this about English! I will never marry a Polish girl. Or Jewish. It is pleasant to rest from all that!'

Oh, I thought then, is that what I am? A rest from all that. A pleasant rest from passion, from fiery altercations, from life, from colour. From excitement. From chucking vodka glasses into the fire. From *brüderschaft*. Chosen because of my equanimity and the equanimity of my kind. Chosen by default. Perhaps even seen as a placid pushover. No, not even placid, just pleasant. Well, I decided, I'll show them. But how? And how could I defend my common ground from this shameful description when Olek meant the description as a respite, a haven from anxiety, over-reaction and hysteria?

So I was stuck. Well and truly stuck. I had to face it. What could I say? Yes, we did get worked up, us Anglos, but mainly in parliament, or at the Domain on Sundays. Or at the football. But anyway, if we did get excited in a particular domestic situation, I thought protectively, then at least we would be aware that we had been arguing. We would feel uneasy and furious after such an excitable dinner. We would mutter and pace and dream up angry rejoinders and plot revenge all the way home in the car.

Not so with my new in-laws. Olek and his mother would argue and shout, waving their hands about. Tatush would join in to quieten Mamushka, and then just as I would begin suspecting that there was really a serious issue, they would leap up and kiss and hug warm and passionate goodnights. Olek and I would just drive off to our little flat in Darlinghurst, his mind full of the stimulating conversation he had just had with his parents, me quietly plotting how to avoid dinner at 20 Hilltop Avenue on his next night off.

How could I hope to compete with the closeness of a little family that, being Jewish, had survived the war, been through two camps, escaped from one through a tunnel, lived with the partisans in a forest so deep and vast that no land and air searches could even get close to spotting them, and suffered through Stalinist communism? My childhood was spent riding my pony through a bush gully near my house. I was free to dream and to swim in the waterhole in the heat of summer. I went to school at the Loreto convent and was protected and nurtured. I was oblivious of deprivation, political oppression, and politics.

12

Fighting off food

I dream about you now that you're gone, Olek. Did I dream about you then, when we were both children? Did I dream my future, as you trudged your way to school in communist Poland, your head already heavy with serious issues? Did I have little flashes of my future as I sat on the train on the way to school, looking out the window, my mind free to wander in other realms

Where did I live? Deep in the North Shore of Sydney, surrounded by orchards and the nearby bush. No whiff of insecurity ever disturbed my family life with my parents. There was my senior neurosurgeon dad and his orange orchard where we picked oranges for pocket money at weekends, and my mum, the strong and cheerful mother looking after the smooth running of the large family – my three brothers and one sister. There was my pony, our two dogs, Sally the cat, the white Leghorn chickens that laid eggs for our breakfast, and two geese named Hansel and Gretel. I had an adventure life woven from an unfettered imagination as I rode my pony and let my daydreams feed on the bush and gullies around our place.

What could I say to be as fascinating, as familiar to you as your lively mother? How could I ever compete with your past, which had fused you more fiercely than I could ever imagine? And should I even try and compete? Was it a competition? You loved the bush, your own partisan camp; I too loved the bush, but preferred riding in it, galloping home again at the end of the day. My family was not forcibly deprived of its home and forced to hide out in our neighbourhood bush from the enemy – such an idea would have been unthinkable. Ridiculous. Crawling through the undergrowth, detonating explosives, living all of us together in an underground bunker? In peacetime the disruption of war is an unthinkable, repulsive concept.

It occurred to me that your family had every right to be close, to exclude me and all that I stood for from the inner circle of your thoughts and preoccupations. The fates had dealt a much fairer hand to me, so far at least. Nevertheless, I wanted to muscle in and occupy first place in the mind of you, my new husband. I wanted to dislodge my mother-in-law.

So at the end of the next dinner at Marrickville, after I was woken gently from my deep sleep on the couch, I said to Mamushka as sweetly as I could, 'Next time, don't cook for us, we will go to a restaurant.'

I was, of course, thinking that the change in location could give me the advantage I needed. But I did not offer this as my reason. I said we could give her a little rest from the kitchen. She must have been tired, I added, trying to explain this to her.

I was fantasising that perhaps we could try the Balalaika again, this time without my cheongsam, which no longer zipped up anyway – too many *pirozhkis* tucked into my new profile.

But my ostensible reason was quickly countered – obliterated, in fact.

'What for to go to restaurant, Katya darlink? What for to waste money? And you know, to eat food at restaurant?'

For yes, food eaten at a restaurant could only cause harm. It had been made clear to me.

I looked to Tatush for help. I imagined that this taciturn, pleasant man was somehow on my side, and recognised that I did have a point of view. Silent people sometimes seem to harbour understanding for other people. Other people like me, for instance, who had recently become another silent person.

'Acch! Katya! Best eating, in home! And no problem. You are tired – come here, Mama cooks for you. No problem!'

Tatush was in total agreement with Mamushka – that I was the tired one, and needed to replenish my strength with Mamushka's cooking – no one was on my side. Because how could there even be another side in the face of such absolute truth – that her cooking was unsurpassed?

You kissed them goodnight. Then you told me in the car on our way home that my suggestion to eat elsewhere had been construed as offensive. You were displeased. I felt tears stubbornly blocking my throat, burning, because I didn't want to start blubbering. At last I was alone with you. That's what I had wanted. You were my new husband. But so what? I had offended your parents, and being alone with you in this state of disapproval was not what I had planned. I had wanted to be the centre of your world, not just a young wife whose smiling compliance with your family ways would bring me favour, whose complaints about them would bring me disgrace.

As I looked out the car window at the Greek shop signs on Marrickville Road, I felt trapped between two worlds. I was further from my own world than I had ever been, yet I resisted being absorbed into the strange one-way street of your culture to which I was fatally attracted. The culture of *matsoh* ball soup, cabbage, *pierogi,* sour cream, and devoted sons. I had to work out a survival strategy.

So I increased my appetite. It was increased anyway, with force-feeding from your family.

And I learned to cook. With a huge effort of my will, and disobeying my most basic urge which was to sulk and fret, I asked for lessons from Mamushka. She was the delighted teacher, instructing me how to feed her son, how to care for such a treasure. I was the compliant student. She was happy.

So why did I resist? I tried not to. I put lids on stubborn, stewing resentments and learned instead how to put lids on pots of *golomki.*

I learned to scald cabbage leaves and bash their little spines to make them limp so that they could be wrapped around parcels of mince-meat and rice. Then I was shown how to lay them neatly, side by side in the baking dish, layer upon layer, and put a skin of cabbage leaves along the top to keep the juice in, and an inch or so of sour cream just before the end of the cooking.

'You must do *barszch!*' instructed Mamushka. 'And boil chicken foot. Very economic, Katya, and no fat! You see he will be happy.'

And a new world opened for me and for my former family, on whom I tested the new cuisine. I wanted to show them that beetroot no longer needed to be sliced and leak purple puddles onto large lettuce leaves – rather it could be chopped and made into a pretty blood-red soup and served in Mamushka's large shallow china bowls, daringly garnished with blobs of sour cream and some chopped dill. Hard-boiled eggs, quartered, could be added to the soup by hungry guests.

My younger brothers liked the soup, but not the floating eggs in the soup. *Bigos*, the meat, sausage and cabbage dish supposedly prepared by huntsmen in the morning and left on the fire all day as they galloped off across the steppes, was loved by my whole family. As was the chicken paprika. Salted herrings, prepared by soaking the pieces of fish in chopped onions were appreciated only by Dad, the adventurous one. As far as Mum was concerned, they were 'those terrible herrings of Mamushka's' and after the first attempt she would not eat them for fear of the raging thirsts which followed consumption of 'ze herring'. As for the chicken soup, it was gobbled up by the whole family until one day my younger brother spotted the talons of the chicken clawing gruesomely through the surface of the simmering broth, and it was thereafter known as 'Dracula stew.' Mamushka told us that Dracula stew should be given to sick and ailing family members. But not, my brother Adrian said, to him, in either sickness or in health.

Piroshki, the dainty pancake parcels filled with sweet creamed cheese and lemon rind were Yum! My family begged me to make them for every occasion.

In Mamushka's eyes I was making progress. This was what she wanted, to instruct me in the art of caring for her son. In my mind, however, I was in competition with her, competing for the appetite of her son who had recently become my husband.

And then I got pregnant, and the thought of cooking anything made me ill. Cooking lessons stopped. I felt either sleepy or queasy. Turned off the preparation of food myself, I started going to Mum's to eat what I considered to be normal meals, when you were on duty.

At Hilltop Avenue the force-feeding doubled upon your proud announcement.

'For two now darling you eat! Not one!'

But I became more sluggish, and less interested in food.

'Eat, Katya! Is more, don't worry! Acch! You have child!'

'Zostaw, Mama! Ona jest chora, to jej wystacy!' (Stop, Mama! She is sick, it's enough!) You intervened on my behalf, having learned in your studies that my symptoms could be genuine. I was allowed to snooze on the couch even earlier in the evening. And I was at last almost exempt from being force-fed. Tanya continued to bustle energetically from the kitchen to the dining room and back, never really sitting down herself, just in case she might be needed to get more salt, or a little sour cream, or *herbata,* or another *ciastka* to perhaps try on Katya and add to the health of the unborn. In her mind, our survival depended on us eating her food.

Mamushka had survived the war, the camp, the aftermath of the war. We were her household. She had to make sure that we would not perish.

I had, I thought, learned to cook. Now I resolved to learn Polish, to find out what was going on in your combined minds.

And on one of our rare nights at home I ignored my nausea and tried cooking. I was exercising my new skills, still competing.

Pierogi. Bigos. Barszcz . . . You came home. And I led you straight to the table, laid for two.

'What you have cooked, Katushka?' Tasting, dabbing your lips with the napkin.

72

'Is quite pleasant,' that's what you said. 'But fortunately I have eaten at hospital. I am not so hungry.'

Fortunately. For whom? For you? So that you did not have to try my food? Fortunately for me? To know that I had been disqualified from the competition before it had even started? And had I ever heard you excuse yourself from Mamushka's spread? Telling her, that fortunately you had eaten?

My huge effort went unsung. You failed to recognise that I had prepared your national dishes. And for the first time, I broke down, and all my resentment came boiling out. In a dramatic demonstration of self-pity I threw the whole dinner into the bin and stomped off to the couch, tears pouring down my face. Tears of fury. Tears of everything.

And you just looked amazed. You had no idea what had been brewing, apart from your meal.

13

The failed bribe

'And what was your mother like,' I asked you, 'as a young woman, before the war chased you ignominiously into the forests?' Asking you about Mamushka in a positive way was part of my real attempt to come to terms with her and accept her with grace. I wanted to be curious about this small powerful woman who had mysteriously turned my world around, making me permanently conscious of her presence in my life, insisting that I ring her every single day, manoeuvring me into sullen capitulation. And forcing me into a cooking competition that I was programmed to lose. It was all so petty. But she had been such a hero!

'My mother was a flirt,' you told me disapprovingly. 'She was always very full of life, never did her studies, was boasting all the time how many men had loved her before she married. I was angry for Tatush – he wanted to be her only love. But after war finished she became very jealous of him, so possessive. She told me all her suspicions, she tried to confide in me that he was having an affair with his dental nurse, and I got so angry with her. I knew my father was always very steady. In the end she became his dental nurse, his only nurse, then they never left each other's side. They are always together.'

I asked you how they met, and you told me as much as you knew.

'Mamushka sometimes says to me it was not really love marriage; Tatush says for him it was a great love. Mamushka's family thought he was a bit unknown. He was from Warsaw, from a family nobody had heard of, and he had not finished his studies. They were not sure, they said, that he was from "a good family".

'But, argued Grandfather, he was a medical student with prospects, so the family finally approved him. They had a wedding in Lida. Gypsies played at their wedding – they must have danced and feasted on a summer's night.

'Tatush continued his studies and when I was born we remained living at my grandparents' house in Lida. We moved away when he had finished studying, and he worked in a surgery in a small town – I remember only bits of it. I was five or six then.'

'And can you tell me more about Tatush?' I asked you.

'Tatush, I never knew his family. His brothers in Warsaw did not survive the war. They were all killed in Warsaw Uprising. He never ever mentioned them after that.'

From my point of view, as his daughter-in-law, Tatush represented no threat. He was quiet and shy. Perhaps it wasn't only because he never trusted his English, he just liked to sit back. You told me, and Mamushka also boasted, that after the war he ran a very busy dental surgery in Chorzów, the coal-mining town where you settled after disembarking the exodus train from the east.

But after coming here, Tatush only had an illegal practice in their flat in Marrickville. His nerves always failed him in the exams set by the Dental Board of New South Wales. Poor Tatush, with all his long experience of dental practice in the partisans' camp, and all those neglected teeth that he restored after the war in Poland, he could not get out one word of English that any of his examiners recognised.

Fail. Fail. Fail. After the last exam he came out to the car where you and Mamushka were waiting faithfully. You sat in the driver's seat of the old grey Humber Hawk that you had bought as an incentive for them to go for their Australian licences and become less dependent on you. And home you drove, in the Humber, Tatush silent, Mamushka making plans for when he passed the exam – you and he quietly knowing that he had probably failed and would never pass.

And then he refused to sit the exams anymore and settled apprehensively for practising illegally on his own community, who preferred him to others anyway. His dental chair was cunningly concealed behind a curtain dividing off the back of the living room, ever since the day a new patient came for treatment. An Australian patient.

Just as Tatush was about to drill the patient's teeth with the old-fashioned drill he had brought with him from Poland, the patient leapt from his reclining position and produced from his pocket an identification card, saying that he was not a patient but an agent from the Dental Board. Tatush had been caught in the act of practising without registration, and would be issued with a large fine. He was lucky not to go to jail, he was told, and should cease treating patients from that minute.

Mamushka disappeared in her white coat, and then came back with a special envelope that she presented smilingly to the agent. He opened it, and with a stern expression, handed it back to Mamushka complete with its wad of cash.

Her ploy had failed. You returned from university to your parents waiting for you, the link to this new, strange culture, to discuss the attempted bribery incident. Tatush was distressed about Mamushka's lack of sensitivity, and Mamushka was railing against 'the English' and their incomprehensible ways.

Bribes had worked for her in so many situations in her life. Here, the bribe was refused. You, already caught between two cultures and aware of the danger of such a transaction, had tried unsuccessfully to divert Mamushka from her plot to pervert the course of Australian justice. Tatush, no doubt also sensing failure in such manoeuvres, sided with you. But Mamushka's stubborn nature prevailed. After all, how many times during the war had her hidden coins or dental gold saved the situation?

So that is the story of how the curtain was constructed and drawn tightly across the surgery area, like a false wall, in case the spy spawned another spy to snoop around. And from then on, the ethnic identity of each patient was carefully scrutinized. Patients, if they were to see Tatush, could not have an Anglo-Saxon name.

Meanwhile, the illegal practice thrived and I became one of his non-paying patients. Alas, my teeth, compromised by my affluent childhood, struggled to prosper even with a devoted dentist in the family. While yours, toughened by a childhood of imaginary sugar, never needed any treatment whatsoever.

14

Children/blood ties

For the second year of your internship you were offered a job in Tasmania, and that seemed a more exciting option than remaining in Sydney, where I would have to furiously defend myself against extra food portions from Mamushka as I carried her firstborn grandchild. We accepted, and left Sydney to cross Bass Strait on the *Princess of Tasmania*.

When that first baby was born in Hobart and she was a girl, Mamushka was overjoyed. She came immediately to stay with us, and the bond between baby and grandmother was instantaneous.

And then I was seized by possessive feelings for the new tiny creature.

'You hold her like this, Mamushka! Not like that . . . put her down now, let her sleep, she must sleep now!'

Knowing nothing whatsoever about babies myself I was nevertheless editing her fierce, unbridled love for our little daughter – as far as she was concerned, her first grandchild.

If I trusted my own mother's calm, sure baby-minding skills, why then did I not trust your mother? Had she not gotten you through the war and survived? Did she not have the maternal talent to do that? I could, I reasoned with myself, have trusted her anywhere with our baby, for to her Nadya was her child – whom she would have defended with her own life. And here was I fussing about when Nadya should sleep, how much breastmilk she may or may not have consumed, and when she should be put down. Looking after a baby in peacetime. Keeping my mother-in-law at bay, surely another peacetime activity.

When Jan, our second child, was born – and a son at that – Mamushka scarcely seemed to notice him. Jan was born in Crookwell, New South Wales, in 1968, when you were acting as a locum for the over-worked country doctor and saving the good money to go to the United Kingdom for further studies. Crookwell was hot and sleepy. There were plenty of flies, and apart from sifting gravel in the local creeks for sapphires, there was not a lot to do. I was heavy and hot, and Nadya was lively and demanding.

And then Jan was born on the eleventh hour of the eleventh day of the eleventh month of the year, and the place stopped being sleepy and I no longer noticed the flies. How immaculate could the timing of his birth be? I was amazed, but relieved, that Mamushka and Tatush did not get into their Humber Hawk and motor straight to Crookwell to inspect their first grandson, born, of all days, on Armistice Day. My parents came. So did my brother David, the medical student who, while reading me an engrossing poem he had written for his latest love interest, nearly sat on little Jan as he lay snuggled sleepily into our couch. It was funny that David ended up an obstetrician and champion of home births, and then writing about it, inspired as he was by the true poetry of delivering new life, and perhaps instigated by relief at not having squashed his very recent nephew.

Mishka astonished me with his blond and blue-eyed look. He was born two years later when we were living in the United Kingdom. He arrived three weeks early, while you were at work, so you had to come home in your theatre robes and jumpstart the car parked uphill from the house, and I aimed at the open door and leapt in, clutching my bag and holding my contractions as the old Renault hurtled down the hill in third gear, unable to stop until it reached the hospital. Perhaps recalling his hair-raising pre-birth dash, Mishka developed a taste for fixing old cars in his later life.

Mamushka never came to the United Kingdom while we were there. She and Tatush waved us sorrow-laden goodbyes at Darling Harbour as we left, guiltily, with their precious Nadya and the tiny Jan. My parents came to England to visit the new baby, along with David, reading poems for yet another love interest. But Mamushka just waited in Australia for Nadya to return.

Later, when Nadya was a little schoolgirl in Australia she went to stay with Mamushka and the bonding proceeded untrammelled. At Mamushka's Nadya was allowed to commit any excess that entered her child's mind. Jan – the second born, and a son at that – was scarcely noticed by my mother-in-law. I was amazed. And as for Mishka, well, cute as he was, and blond as well, Mamushka's gaze just never left Nadya.

Why did we call her Nadya, our first-born? Why did we call any of them those names? Mamushka wanted us to call her Lisa, after her sister who had perished in the camp, but you didn't want to think about camps – rather the opposite – so you called her Nadya, which comes from the Russian *nadezhda*, meaning 'hope'. I agreed with the choice. I liked the sound of Nadya – it seemed soft, exotic and full of mystery. Actually, full of hope. It suits her.

Jan was named for his godfather, another Jan, another Pole, another doctor. No family connections, no problems with that name, except that people want to spell it Y-A-R-N, as in a ball of wool, or pronounce it Jan, as in the girls' name.

In naming our children I did take a few moments to study the old photo Mamushka produced of her family members, with Lisa in it, and the other siblings. I felt myself, strangely, looking in on this family group I had married into – a group who were unaware that their serenity and composure were about to be hopelessly and permanently shattered by the war looming on their west. Just as they look unaware of me, the *goy* whose face would appear in future family photos in such a faraway country.

Lisa's face looked friendlier than the others. Lively, coy, standing there in her times, the 1930s, in her place – Lida? Was it Lida? Lida was where they came from. They are lined up in a setting still mysterious to me. There is Paula, the youngest – always, they say, the most elegant one. She left in time, went to Switzerland, then Australia, then to Los Angeles, and later New York. She had married a Zionist doctor who in America became a cardiologist and famously, lived next door to Kirk Douglas in Beverly Hills.

Then there was Ella. She also went to the States, with her sister Fanya who became a dentist. Fanya's husband Sam, while being the despised house-husband, collected old European paintings and irritated the more educated, house-proud Fanya by stashing them behind furniture, in the kitchen, under their bed, more and more of them, until they had taken up all of the available space in their small apartment. So he started to sell them to make space. And then he bought her a bigger apartment, in a better part of Manhattan. The paintings rose in value. Fanya ceased practising dentistry and she became the childminder. When we went to visit them years later Sam had died, the children he had looked after were both dentists, and the vivacious Fanya was living through her grief in a large Fifth Avenue apartment with the pick of Sam's collection still gracing their walls and corridors.

Mishka, the eldest one in the photo, corpulent and almost busting out of his Russian shirt – and a bit on the plain side, in my secret opinion – died. How did he die? You said he had a heart attack. Your New York Uncle Zalmon said he perished as a war victim of the Gestapo. There seems to be a rather major discrepancy. Who was right?

But anyway, back to the naming problem. Being motivated only by shallow considerations, I remembered this old family photo when our third baby was born in England. I argued a bit against calling him Mishka because I suspected that he might grow as fat as his great-uncle if shape was dictated by such a name, and then he would have a heart attack from being overweight. But it seemed tactless for me to say this about the dead uncle, who you remembered as being kind and funny. He could make people laugh with his sly wit, you recalled, or were reminded of this by Mamushka. So our new baby was anointed as Mishka, and he is also blond, like his great-uncle, handsome, not at all fat, and has selected some wonderful qualities, presumably some of them from his uncle.

'We had fun with him, with our Uncle Mishka, he was always eating *piroshkis*, making us children eat too,' you told me. '"Eat!" he said, "Eat like the Russian!"

'He wore the Russian coat, white one, with high collar and belt round the middle. We liked to tease him, make him chase us. He could not catch us! We were fast and he was lazy and there were so many places to hide in that house – that's what I remember about the house, the hiding places . . .'

And would they have been playing in the main family house, on visits? Or did the relatives come to visit the town from which the little family fled? Another unanswered question, lost in the veils of time.

Leon, whose story always fascinated you, went overland with General Anders' Army to Israel, carrying with him Ruth, his baby daughter, by then motherless. Why? Why was she motherless, Olek? How did he carry her? Was he on a horse, with the baby Ruth in a satchel? I think that's what you told me. And how many months did their journey last, trudging in their thousands from Kazakhstan to Palestine? They, Leon and Ruth, settled in Israel.

And then there were your grandparents, they died in the camp as well. Or did they? Uncle Zalmon in New York said that they did. You never told me that.

My eyes wander over the group in the photograph again, locking first on to Tanya my mother-in-law, pert and confident, head held proudly. And her new husband, dignified, refined. Then I look at the coy one in the flowered dress, whose daughter was your playmate until she was stolen from you. I shudder, imagining being snatched from my family, or my family being snatched from me. I remember looking at my daughter, Nadya, for hope, cosily asleep in the cot beside my hospital bed. How could that happen? How could a parent survive the horror of losing such a precious creature? I asked you about her, your little cousin.

'We played, me with my cousin Etka, she was older, bossy like girls are. There was a big staircase. We were having pillow fights, and sliding down the banisters on pillows. She fell off, they thought I pushed her. She must have lost consciousness, because she lay still, not crying. They thought she was dead. The doctor came, he measured her pulse. I watched his face to see what his expression could tell me. It told me nothing. So then it was my will, I willed her to wake up and speak to me, she came to, she asked for me, and they called me from under the table where I was and I was allowed to whisper to her. That's when I wanted to be a doctor. In case I needed to save her again, in case my will would not be enough.'

But if I ever asked you the location of the house with the banisters, then time must have erased your answer. So where, I wonder, was that great house, with its shady trees, its wide oak staircase, its many places for children to hide, its green summer lawns? Was it Uncle Mishka's house? Was it the grandparents' boarding house in Lida? Was this boarding house the same house in the town where Mamushka grew up with her big family, where Lenin's wife's family owned the hairdressing salon?

'Krupskaya,' Mamushka told me. 'They had beautiful salon.'

'That was Lenin's wife, Krupskaya,' you explained.

'What? Lenin's wife?' I had studied enough Russian history to receive some impact from this bit of gossip.

Mamushka told me they had a big salon there in the town, (was it Lida?) for *fryzier* (hairdresser), and in my imagination I filled in the rest. I could see Vladimir Ilyich, returning by train and exhausted from his revolutionary fervor, sitting brooding in the back of the salon, waiting for his wife to stop coiffing the local heads.

'I'm here now, woman! Forget those useless hairdos, luxuries of the bourgeoisie!'

No that couldn't be. Or could it?

My imagination runs too fast. But I'm sure Vladimir Ilyich was that type, demanding, impatient. One can see it in his face – not too much softness in that face, the determined pointy beard, close together blackcurrant eyes, tight mouth, the face of the man with the great mission, his wife merely there to serve him and his purpose before he left again for months. But the salon? History must swallow so much precious human trivia as it concentrates on the great movements. Why didn't I quiz Mamushka a bit more on the womens' gossip around the great Lenin, known by his neighbours as Vladimir Ilyich?

15

When the war was over

Olek was the only one I knew among my generation who remembered the end of the war. How many times did he tell me about it in different ways? He would have been a little boy – skinny, earnest, with roughly shorn blond hair. A too-big army jacket. His beloved *valenki*, also too big. Eyes grey-blue and alive with purpose. Like his children. That's how I see his face as a boy. Mishka's hair, Jan's mouth, Nadya's eyes – a purposeful combination.

'So tell me', I asked him as we sat by the campfire, 'about when the war finally ended.'

'Well, Katush, the partisans disbanded. For me they were sad, those goodbyes – there were strong feelings. Tatush was very happy to say goodbye – he was sick of living with rough partisans in dank hideouts. We must have been very different sorts of people, but so dependent on each other, we had lived like big family. I felt like a true comrade, a *tovarisch*. And yet I was told by my father that we may never see these forest comrades ever again in our lives.

'So after we left, even when it no longer existed I was convinced it was all still there. In my mind now it is still there, as it was. The clearing, the secret tracks through the forest, a fire, our dugouts, the early mornings, feeding my leftover crumbs to Skoczek, cleaning up, the songs we sang – Russian songs, always about war, about leaving, about love, about the countryside, plus our simple survival routines. Now the war was over, no reason anymore for our home to be in the forest. Pavlik was dead but I thought if I went back he would be there, waiting for me, with Skoczek. It was, for me, home.

'My parents wanted to go to west of Poland. Tatush said he had enough of living with Russians after that camp. He wanted to go as far to west as possible, away from Russian border. Germans were being pushed back by Russian army, advancing west. They were on the run, we had lived in the shadow of their terror for so long, and it seemed as though now life could begin again. We could get on with Russians, many Poles chose to stay there. But Tatush was determined to leave the east. Soviets were there, new masters, different from Germans, but erratic, and not really trusted either. Only I liked them. I was brainwashed a bit, from my love for partisans.

'About Pavlik, that he was dead, about Skoczek, that he was left, my parents were not thinking – their minds were of course on our future, getting out, getting back to whatever was still there, to create a life for us. I would like to see Skoczek, I knew he could be attacked by other birds without me to protect him, he could not fly, because of his damaged wing. Together with Pavlik we had tried to make a splint for his wing, to repair it. He liked his splint. When I had to leave him in that forest, when we quit partisans, he did not want to escape any more to other birds, but continue with me. He tried, then I put him on a branch with my last crumbs of bread for his breakfast and we crossed over the river, the little Narewka River, stepping across stones and wading, and Skoczek could not follow any further. I looked straight ahead, holding my bundle, and walked out of the forest, with my parents, with some other partisans. We left our forest life forever.'

Squinting through the smoke of our campfire I imagined myself in another forest thirty years before, standing near the little river next to the tree on which a confused bird sat ignoring his crumbs, sadly watching his keeper stride away to another life, distress visible in the boy's determined gait.

'My parents, they were busy trying to get papers. They had no Polish papers to return to Poland because they were Jewish and had been living in a place that was now going to become part of Soviet Union. There were places to forge every sort of document – even in these small towns, you could get those papers. Many people needed identity, to move, after years of war. My parents still had coins and a bit of dental gold concealed in bits of clothing. Tatush had started to treat patients again in the town where we first stayed. They were waiting until it would be safe to leave this place near the forests which had been both their prison and their refuge for the last few years. They were attending to responsibilities of having to create life, home, livelihood, after the long war that had made such a huge mess, and they longed for stability.

'Children do not concern themselves with future, they live in the present. So I missed that forest. Not my parents – they were trying to sort out something through the rubble that had become both the past and the present of their lives, and of everybody's lives. Any order that existed before, it had disappeared. What to do? Where to go and live?'

'So where did you stay when you left the forest?' I asked.

'We stayed in this small town. Everybody was friendly, jubilant in beginning when Russians came through and Germans were gone. I remember the house, a Polish family, the food being brought up from cellars, vodka, adults drinking, on the news of the Germans' retreat – perhaps they were drunk. I remember lying next to the *piec* –that is a big wood oven where children and families sleep, some behind *piec*, or some on top of *piec* on cushions. I remember listening to people talking. I was trying to work out what could be happening. Nobody knew anything, but they knew they were at last safe from Germans. This is how I remember it.

'When were we leaving, where we were going, who could say? We must have stayed there for months, I suppose, or a year, with that Polish village family, me sleeping beside *piec,* waiting for news of what was happening further west. Waiting till war was officially declared over.

'That was May nine, forty-five. I was eight or nine, same as Nadya. I will never forget that day, when they said End of War. Victory. Throwing, waving, running, cheering! In the streets!

'But Warsaw had been destroyed, bombed, burnt, wrecked. News came, and most of it bad news. People came in trucks with news, men in uniforms, soldiers with red stars on their caps. They were Soviets, soldiers of the Red Army. I just wanted to be one. I wanted a cap just like they had. With the red star.

'Our train did come, I remember it pulling into the station. It was a few months later, winter had begun, everyone was cheering the train. It was going to the west. The engine came and passed, it hissed and roared, people cheered, ran along beside carriages and then it slowly stopped. What had happened? Where had they come from? Travellers always have news, but these ones especially.

'For days and nights we were on this train. Passengers came down onto the platform, looking around, trying to buy food. They were not carriages like we know them now, but converted cattle trucks, no proper seating. Train kept stopping, to collect passengers, let some off, buy food from people on platforms, clear snow from tracks, gather round fires on platforms. I remember how it was snowing, I remember fires on platforms, fires in drums. We went to those fires, we got hot food, potatoes, *kvsa,* sort of yoghurt, to eat with the potatoes. It smells like now, our campfire.

'The smell of potatoes, it reminds me!'

'So stop a second, these potatoes are ready!' I interjected.

We dug our potatoes from the white embers in their blackened silver-foil jackets and ate them silently, flicking the burnt jackets back into the fire. I reflected on how late it seemed, how high the moon was in the sky and if we should turn in. But I wanted just a bit more story.

Olek continued. 'So for me then the train became home, because I remember it, how it looked. Our spot in the crowded train, me always trying to look out a window. We were going to some big city, not like before when we had lived in a small town, knowing people, neighbours, baker, butcher, you know, perhaps like here in Bodalla. Now some of my uncles had gone to America before the war, my auntie and my cousin had been taken. Killed in camps. Father's brothers gone, killed in Warsaw Uprising. But we did not know that yet. We did not know where anyone was. So my parents decided to go as far west as they could, to Chorzów.'

16

Red star

'Can you tell me again,' I asked Olek, 'about the hat with the red star?' This was the next night. Our conversations around the little campfire had meandered on, waiting until the evening in order to continue, waiting until the children were asleep once again in their tent. 'Tell me how your things got stolen?'

'Well that train, how well I remember it, the roar of the steam engine, the chugging of the wheels on tracks, the sound of the whistle when it was going to leave, everyone running back to their spot, we to ours, me racing for a window, to see platform get left behind. Well, like I said, we got out at stations, it stopped for ages, there did not seem to be any hurry. Everybody was doing some sort of business on platforms – peasants selling eggs and cooking potatoes on fires. Soldiers were everywhere, Russian soldiers. I still had on my *valenki*, you know, felt boots, and my soldier jacket, it was Russian soldier jacket. And I still felt like soldier, even more so now. I had to carry on what I had learned. So I needed full uniform.

'And then I had my chance to get a hat with star on it, the red star. I was standing, like always, minding our things, Tatush's instruments, they were our things, and my parents had gone off to do some business, or buy food or something.

'Two soldiers came over to me, started to talk, and one noticed me staring at his hat with the red star.

'"You want to try my hat, boy?" he asked.

'He put it on my head, laughing at me, telling me how I looked like Red Army soldier, calling me *tovarish*. And then I saw what the other soldier was doing. He took my bundle, which I had dropped to try on the hat, and he heaved it over the fence and then they both jumped the fence and ran. I shouted, I tried to jump too, to climb, but I couldn't get up, and when someone helped me up they were gone. Gone with Tatush's instruments, our livelihood. It was like we had lost our Aladdin lamp, you know?

'My parents noticed all the commotion on my end of platform, and came running towards me. When I said what had happened Mamushka started to scream and cry. She was hysterical, shaking me, her face was like, it was despair. My father just stood there at first, shaking his head.

'"*Czekaj*, Tanya, *czekaj!*" he begged her, "Leave the boy!" He sat on the ground. He put his head in his hands and he wept. My father crying, sobbing, and me to blame for that. Never during whole war had he cried, he was always quiet, dignified, even when soldiers were going to shoot us. And now this small thing, and after war was over. It seems small, does it, after everything? But it must have been all our future in those instruments. They had saved our lives, they were going to make us survive again. I had allowed a brute soldier to take our livelihood, for a hat with a red star. And now my real punishment was not my parents' anger at me, but the shock of seeing my father's grief.

'You know, they are still angry about that, they never really forgave me. I took that hat, with its red star, I threw it into a fire drum and watched it burn. And I don't think I really trusted people in uniform, ever again. And my parents became silent as their worry went deeper, their hopes of having a household, livelihood, further away.'

'And you continued on to Poland? With no instruments?' I asked.

'Yes, the train kept taking us, without the instruments, and we went slowly towards the west,' he said.

'Mamushka and I had always lived in the east in Belorus. We had never been to west. Tatush came from Warsaw. They realised what had really happened to their country, to Warsaw, well, and to them, to their lives. Their hopes had been in war ending of course, and Germans being defeated. We had been away from news, in forest with our partisans.

'I still dreamed of the partisans. In my dreams, I appeared there, in our camp. And they would open their arms to me, "*Tovarisch*, Sacha! Sacha!" They would call, in my dream. That's what they called me there, in partisans. And I would run to them, and then in my dream they turned into people without faces, and the camp it became a silent graveyard. Then I woke and I knew I was getting further from it, but I was determined not to lose any details as we went further away from the partisans, into this world of uncertainty. My parents looked frightened, anxious.

I kept thinking about the instruments, how I could get more, where could I find some, how? In my boy's mind there was every possibility of recovering them. Whenever the train stopped there was confusion, but I searched the platform for the thieves in uniform. Warsaw had been burnt, bombed, destroyed. And it was raining. Snow stopped, it just rained and rained, out the window of the train I saw how sad was the countryside that I had always heard from my father was so beautiful. Polish country-side. *Krajobras*.'

'We settled in the south-west, a town called Chorzów, a mining town. Tatush started working again, and Mamushka found out about her sister and Boubou, about all her losses, and she collapsed. She lost her will. Tatush struggled with her, he needed help. A woman came and helped her, and helped Tatush with patients, until she recovered after two years, then she got up and she became his dental nurse again.'

'So Tatush got more instruments, after all?'

'Yes there was plenty of work. I never found those soldiers, but he got instruments. It was an industrial city, mines, coal mines – the town where everything turned black, buildings, your clothes, your skin, and there were lots of patients. Tatush after a few years, he had a big clinic.

'I had to go to school, the local Polish school. I didn't like it. I did not want to wear clothes like the other children. I didn't like being one of those children and they didn't want to be like me. I felt more like a partisan than a child. I still wore my *valenki*, I insisted that I kept my head shaved, as we did in partisans, I was a young partisan, loyal to their code, very different from normal children.

'I fought with my teacher. We were singing in class. I loved to sing, after the partisans. She, the teacher, she was playing the violin. I felt happy. And then she told me my voice was too loud, and that I sang out of tune. She said that I should be quiet and not sing at all. I had always sung so loud in partisans and I was feeling so, you know, happy at last to be singing at school. When the teacher told me that I must not sing I was suddenly furious. I went up to her, I took her violin stick, I broke it in half. I really wanted to kill her.

'Teacher got in hysterics. I was sent home. It was winter. Ponds were frozen, kids came to school on skates, but I didn't have any skates, just my *valenki*. Some kids chased me – they fought me, a gang of boys, cutting me with their skates. I fought back as I could, but they were armed, I was not, I looked like a bit of a mess when I finally got home, covered with blood.

'Mamushka wanted to know why. I told her I had left early after being told not to sing, and I left out the bit about breaking the violin stick.

'"It's because you are Jewish she wouldn't let you sing, and why you get beaten up!" she said to me. "I will buy you skates, and you fight back. Always you must fight back!"

93

'That was my mum. She thought they beat me up because of being Jewish, that I was told not to sing because I was Jewish but it was not that, it was really that I was just different. My shaven head, my *valenki,* my soldier's jacket, I still insisted on wearing it to school. And, of course, all my experiences, they made me a misfit. Partisans had spoiled me for school. I was like a painted bird. My parents could not persuade me to be a normal schoolboy, wearing normal clothes. Poles disliked and distrusted Russians, and I was wearing Russian army jacket. They begged me, Mamushka even tried to bribe me. But it was my code of loyalty to partisans to wear those clothes and I continued to go to school looking like that.'

Olek's story continued. They lived in Chorzów, and Olek became a serious young communist. He cried, he said, when Stalin died, and only gradually did he come to fully realise the oppressive and sinister side of the harsh regime in which he had put his trust; even to the point where he was questioning his parents and trying to 'save' them from their pre-war bourgeois sensibilities. He was almost ready, as he admitted to me, to report them for hiding gold. But then he did not report them. There must have been a huge margin between the feeling and the deed itself.

When he became suffocated by communism he wanted to leave. He said he felt strangled. In 1957, as a fourth-year medical student, he left Poland with forged documents, with money hidden in the bottom of a honey jar. As an assimilated twenty-year-old medical student, Olek was not free to leave. His parents, classed as Jewish, were given exit visas. The family went to Italy together and caught the Italian liner *Fairsea* to Australia from Italy, arriving as migrants. Tatush had sent some money before the war to a friend in the United States, who transferred the money immediately when Tatush contacted him upon their arrival in Australia. They bought the place in Hilltop Avenue, Marrickville, and Tatush set up his dental practice there. Olek worked in the GMH factory in Sydney, then enrolled in medicine, receiving his degree in 1966, just after I met him.

I accompanied the family to Olek's graduation ceremony. In the august atmosphere of the Great Hall, two people alone stood up in the discreetly clapping audience when it was Olek's turn to receive his degree from the chancellor. They were Mamushka and Tatush. 'Bravo! Bravo!' they shouted. Tears were streaming down their faces. Tentatively, I stood up too, the third to break ranks from my polite peers, and join those upstanding. 'Bravo, bravo,' I whispered, as the tears leaked onto my cheeks and down past my nose.

PART TWO

———

The gypsy's prediction stalked our happy life, remaining humbly in the shadows, biding its time to strike. Then Olek died. And suddenly, I was left with the children, his mother, whiffs of his past, and without his warm and powerful presence guiding us into the future. The fates, however, had decreed that we were not to remain alone. I was to have another love.

17

Is that what the gypsy said?

Until 6 May 1978 Olek and I were married. Twelve years. Three children. We had lived in seventeen different rented houses, and finally we were in the house we had helped to design, on the rural outskirts of Canberra. We were happy.

And then on that night you froze in time. You had played your last game of chess, had your last walk with the children, and also, towards the evening, your last walk with me. The normal small unfoldings of a Saturday – it was the last Saturday – have since become light-houses in the fog of memory.

Your mother was staying, being her usual difficult self – and I was being my usual difficult self around her. Poor you, I think now. Poor me, I thought then. You had hospitalised her for a few days – she had heart problems – but she had returned without notice in a taxi, before her official discharge date. I reacted predictably. I complained to you.

And then you dropped the bombshell. A good bombshell. You told me when we were walking along the track through the waving kangaroo grass that you realised she was 'a very difficult woman', and that I must be a genius to cope! Your few words, loosening me from the greatest and perhaps only significant struggle of our married life, took me aback.

Why have you only realised this now? I thought. I was staring at the kangaroo grass. The late-afternoon sun was making it shimmer pink and golden.

What can she have done to have unblinkered your view of her, I wondered. Mamushka was the hero of your childhood. She held up a peasant to get soap and cow's milk for you. She gave you the 'shirt off her back'. She was the gutsy partisan heroine, surely the main reason for your survival.

I stopped in the middle of the track. You stopped too and looked at me, and your face, framed by its unruly grey hair, backlit by the autumn sun as it slanted below the hill, was dark with poetic sentiment. It was the last time I looked into your face, and your expression remains with me.

The nurses, you had said, had not been able to cope with her. 'You are a wonderful man, and sorry Doctor, but your mother is the most impossible patient!'

An impossible patient is something most doctors are sensitive to, including you. So finally, via the nurses, you had seen my situation. I was moved. I held back my avalanche of relief, holding the tears in my throat.

Your look deepened, your voice became serious. 'And Katush, I love you very much – more than ever!'

Your rush of eloquence caught me out. Expressions of love came so easily from your heart to your lips because you were a poet, raised in a culture where emotions can be expressed. In me they just got stuck somewhere inside, and now they were tangling up with joy about you finally seeing Mamushka as the difficult and capricious person that she was.

Of course I love you, I thought, cursing once again my reserved Anglo ways.

Then you laughed and peered at me a bit. I was trying to hold back my tears but you saw them anyway, leaking down my cheeks. We started to walk again, arm in arm, through the kangaroo grass, and kept going, me in snuffly silence until we hit the path.

We came to the road and then to the local Greek grocery. We bought a bottle of Greek brandy. I guess it was to celebrate our new united stance – the new Mamushka management team. And we had our first secret sip on the walk home, so as not to be subject to Mamushka's critical scrutiny.

That was late in the afternoon on the fateful Saturday. We had guests in the evening for dinner. They were driving from Sydney. And Voy was with them. Mamushka was muttering about these guests whom she did not know, devouring food which she considered should be used to make her grandchildren grow – especially Nadya, whose healthy proportions did not beg extra rations, unlike her skinny brothers. We laughed at that, and you did not even bother to engage in your usual combative way with her argument. We laughed with each other.

And then we were going to Carole's to watch the soccer on TV, leaving Mamushka to babysit. Our dinner guests were staying overnight, including Voy. He was a visiting Pole. He had arrived a few weeks before with two male friends, all from Warsaw. You liked him, and I liked the three of them – the way they all kissed you on both cheeks and you kissed them back, on both cheeks, Russian style. But it was also Polish style – and, I knew, partisan style. I watched, fascinated, as you transformed yourself, becoming one of them. They stayed for a few days and in the evenings they helped me make dinner. They were very cosy – chopping things, frying, cleaning up. While I put the children to bed you all talked into the night about news from Poland, then you told me bits of it and what had been said. Then they put on their rucksacks and left to continue their travels.

Voy was interesting – a bit charismatic, I thought, but more serious than his friends. When he rang from Sydney to thank us we invited him back with a few others for this weekend. You wanted to ride your bike to go to Carole's. I considered going by bike, but it was too dark, too cold and my bike had small wheels. So one of the guests, another doctor, borrowed the neighbour's bike, which had bigger wheels, and she rode with you. I went in the car with the others, including Voy. But I was not to know during that short trip how significant he was going to be in my life.

Those of us in the car arrived in time for the opening ceremony of the soccer match, which was theatrical because it was being held in Italy. There was a rousing hymn, and I watched Carole curiously as tears streamed down her face, thinking how easily emotion can be provoked in her. And I wondered, as I drifted into half sleep, why you were so slow to arrive. It wasn't that far, even on a bike.

And then I got the phone call. I went down the corridor to receive it in the bedroom. It was Eva from the hospital, and she said three words, and the words resounded like a knoll over the night landscape of my heart. 'Olek is dead.' I returned like a zombie to the main room.

Just like that. Three words. You were dead. That meant, no longer alive. I received the message humbly, numbly, remotely aware of its horror. I wanted to disappear under the floor to get away from myself. With ice-cold accuracy I understood Carole's tears. They were for you, and she didn't know it. I should have been crying, not waiting half-asleep. But I didn't cry, I don't think so. They say I beat my head against the wall, but I don't think I did that.

I remember that I froze, and my teeth started to chatter, and they kept chattering as we drove back home, past the police van with its blue lights on the highway, to a home which was no longer our home, but a household rattled by death. A mother who would never see her beloved son again would be wailing. And children who would never again wake up to see their father would be asleep. And I had to tell them. I had to wake them.

Mamushka was wailing, her head in her hands, 'Oich, Oich, Oich!'

Nadya had run out the front door upon being informed by

Mamushka that her father was dead. She ran, ran, ran through the night until she got to the house of her best friend Suzka, and then she dived through Suzka's window and told her. Best friends tell each other everything, they always receive the right response. But this night even Suzka's understanding response was no remedy. Poor Nadya came back accompanied by Suzka, but un-soothed.

Mishka was awake. His large eyes looked black with the awful understanding of what had happened. He was just standing, not crying. He had seen you cycle away, your lights wobbling into the night. He stood there, his white shock of hair visible in the moonlight, and watched you ride out of his present and out of his future. Mishka was seven.

Nine-year-old Jan was asleep. Jan the early bird, always first to sleep while the others resisted going to bed. I lay beside him, trying to tell him, and being desperate not to tell him.

'Jan! Jan!' I was talking softly, to avoid being heard.

'I know, I know!' he said. 'Olek's dead.'

He had heard the commotion, he had heard Mamushka's wailing. How could he encompass such a loss? By pretending it was a daydream and escaping back into sleep.

'My son is dead, my son is dead! Oy yoy yoy!'

He did not want to wake up. He was hoping it would still be a dream, that he would wake up to a completely normal Sunday. Canoeing down the Murrumbidgee with Olek, playing chess with Olek, fighting over who had won the last move, bushwalking with Olek, pitching tents with Olek, learning how to make fires with Olek, stooped together over the kindling flame, blowing, protecting it from the wind, criss-cross criss-cross, small sticks first, feeding the flame.

And now the flame had died.

18

Father genes

'I'll have a brandy and soda please,' I say, testing my feeling of freedom, waiting in the queue with the other bus passengers. It's ten years since your death, Olek, and I'm at the coach stop, en route to Melbourne. And, as I suspect you half-planned, I am married to Voy, who I've left at home.

'You are only allowed to have alcohol if you order a full meal!'

'But this is a full meal!'

'Sorry! A full meal is meat and two veg!'

So that's that for my freedom, so far. A cup of tea, self-served at the canteen by an automatic machine that fills the foam cup to the brim so that it sloshes out onto a gridded drip tray. It's not really tea, it's water in a foam cup holding a tea bag spreading its stain.

I refuse to give up. Deprived of the psychological comfort of a brandy and soda or even a real cup of tea, I'm still determined to test my freedom away from household bondage. I'm on the way to Melbourne for an exhibition of my paintings. I should feel empowered, not reduced by this meagre choice of food.

I try the passionfruit cheesecake. It looks promising. But alas! Being married to Eastern Europe ruins certain things for you, including coach-stop canteen cheesecake. I cannot eat past one mouthful, let alone enjoy it. It's too sweet, it's just wrong. I rinse out my mouth with the cold tea-substitute. Starting with Mamushka, I've been too long with Slavs and good food. But I'm still trying. As the habitual housekeeper I'm off-duty, away from my hearth — far from the ambience, the plots, the sub-plots, the human-bearing space to which I am both attached and enslaved.

Voy is in charge of the family and the house of semi-adults. My unease at this arrangement lessens with every passing kilometre. After all, what is the worst that can happen? The semi-adults will irritate Voy with their messiness, their general insensitivity, their cooking habits, their noise late at night. Voy may or may not express his irritation directly — small or large explosions may occur, or he may just save his frustration up to present to me upon my return. The dishes won't be done, and the garbage may have been forgotten, but this is an expected outcome. Things, I think, could be worse.

But back to the bus, to try and sleep the rest of the night.

I wake, a bit stiff from the cramped position in my seat. My mind is alive with the dream I've just had. Another letter from you, and I had to collect this one at the Department of Immigration office. Immigration? A bureaucratic place for you, the hater of all bureaucracy. Somehow I was in possession of your letters, without having to punch a number or sit and wait for it to be called. A dream of course, but why?

Perhaps the dream was provoked by the fact that I am travelling swiftly into the black night, lulled by the noise of the road. And the road was where your life ended. The road at night. The black highway. You on your bike and a car driven by strangers. The only contact these strangers had with our lives was crashing into you, causing your death. They drove on into the night, leaving our family in agony. And now being on another black highway at night I get your thoughts in a dream letter. There was no return address on the letter, but of course there never is. Which was the source of my unease, during the dream.

And why Immigration? Perhaps because that office is somehow logged in my mind as an obdurate block between people who want to cross borders to see each other. After all, I have spent hours there in that office on behalf of others in exile. So that place has achieved representation in my subconscious.

In dreams I usually float silently and through barriers, like you. Perhaps this is why you write to me in my dreams, because I move the same way, gliding from location to location without impediment. But despite this ease of travel, I have never really found you, even there.

You manage to elude me, having brought me to a certain spot. And in my dream I feel the desolation of an anticipated meeting, which can never eventuate. Is it your desolation I feel? And is it because Voy is still here, with me, waiting behind the meeting place, that you retreat further? Does his presence inhibit you, make you hesitate? You knew him, you introduced him to my life, and then you promptly left. He seemed then, after your death, to somehow have your smell on him – that's what I thought, at first. It was the accent, perhaps, the same grammar, the same seriousness. Of course it was an illusion, because he is so different. But now I have his smell, and yours has vanished, replaced by dreams.

And you, do you remain alone? What can I do to see your face again? We had so much unfinished life together. Yet now I'm with Voy, my life seems complete. He interests me, soothes me. We fight tooth and nail, and in his own thoughtful way he helps to shepherd your family through life. I love him, I get infuriated by him, but I don't tire of him – he's my life's companion. Awake, I feel no desolation.

I want to write back to your dream-letter. I have to tell you what's been going on. Or bits and pieces of it, snatches that stay in my mind. Perhaps I can still make you laugh and cry. Perhaps I can tell you what the children have been up to. They're no longer the little creatures you left behind. A lot has happened, and you seem to have influenced so much in their lives from those early years – through your words with them and through your living example. And because you died, the power of your inspiration magnified – shaping your children's ways and their choices even more strongly.

Nobody really knows how it was for me when you left me, never to return. I don't really know, either. I don't recall the small unravellings of that Saturday, I don't remember what we had for lunch. But each frame of that afternoon and night is exactly and painfully etched into my memory and since then I have never felt quite at ease with Saturday nights. We had seen no need to say goodbye. We were leaving the house separately and then meeting again in a few minutes to watch the soccer.

Nadya was ten, Jan was nine, Mishka was only seven. I was thirty-six. None of them have reached your age yet, but I am way past it. And you continue to make appearances as the children get older. Mishka has a wry smile, it's your smile. A wry sense of humour, your humour. He has your nose, eyes, face, your body, and your capacity for thoughtful endurance. He's stubborn, has your way of walking, head tilted to one side. He has your habits. He measures issues, standing in a certain way. I watch him and it's like watching you. The voice? It's hard to tell when a voice is stripped of its strong accent. He has your compassion, which can extend to unusual circumstances where others may not see the need for any compassion. You used to defend all weaklings and victims, even cockroaches – you defended their right to live, against my better judgement. Quite irritating. I had to poison them in secret. Thanks to evolution, Mishka doesn't save cockroaches. But he prefers to move a spider and its web to another location if it is in the way, rather than destroy it – also irritating when one senses that he may be stubbornly prioritising the spider over the passing of time in a busy day. He has been known to sift through soil with his hands rather than use a shovel so as not to jeopardise the life of a lizard. Fathers and sons.

Jan has your fire, your determination, your abundant energy, your accessible confidence. He never gives up. He doesn't look so similar to you, except for the twitched-up corners of his mouth. His hair, soft features and upturned nose are more like me, I suppose. And, like me, he's an artist. But he has your passion for the bush, for its mysteries, for its freedom. He stretches his arms in celebration of the sky, the trees, the wind. You took him bushwalking, and you certainly taught him that. You were his mentor in the bush. Like you he has flashes of wisdom when you would least expect it. And stubbornness, with that smile, the half-closed eyes, denoting refusal to budge from whatever unreasonable stance he may have adopted. And he is frank, honest perhaps, or maybe just tactless! Yes, that's you! And they have your oversized feet. Both boys. Fathers and sons.

Nadya has your passionate, noble nature, your sentiment, your Jewishness, your poetic rhetoric, your appealing eccentricity. She can also be tactless, in a loud bass voice. Your temper? And she has your nice muscular legs. Perhaps your eyes, too, although people say she's like me. I only see you in the eternal wistfulness of her eyes. And she has your big voice. But she can sing in tune – unlike you, when you broke the teacher's violin bow, she has the gift of pitch. And that's from me! But she is her father's daughter. She surely epitomises the Great Slav Soul. And she's an excellent cook. But that's from Mamushka.

Did you watch over them as they grew up? You must have. Another Saturday night, a few years after your last one, I was lying awake in the dark in the same house. They were teenagers, out for the evening. It was after midnight. And I was listening hopefully for the door to open and shut, for the sound of their voices. Where were they? At three in the morning, was there any sinister message in the wind outside the warm house, was it not more strange and ghostly? And what was that siren, its wail throbbing off into the night?

Sirens are, for me, the sounds of Saturday night. Saturday night should be a night of ease and recreation, but then things go wrong, horribly wrong. Twice I thought I heard the door open and shut, and I went down and checked. Beds still empty. My imagination had pre-empted the sounds of the homecoming, had willed it to happen, so that I could be lulled into security, into the sweet drift of sleep. Then I heard the thump thump of Kasia the dog's tail on the wooden floor, wagging its welcome. My heart beat contentedly with it, knowing that this particular sound was a real sound and no phantom in my head.

The dog's tail was the signal to snuggle into the security of Voy's sleeping back, leaving the night to follow out the rest of its weird passage without me having to be being minutely aware of it. The beds were all occupied again. Familiar forms were under the blankets, heaving a little in the moonlight. Breathing.

19

Going east

Perhaps the stories of Olek's childhood affected me so deeply because when he died leaving his three beloved children forever, they were around the same age as he had been during those war years. Like him, their minds were serious, and schooled by him, they were always aware of some greater purpose of life. I struggled on with them in the way that I knew, always being somewhat in awe of other dimensions the children seemed to have that were beyond my immediate ken.

Olek continued to inhabit my dreams, appearing, or half-appearing, from time to time when I was otherwise preoccupied with my life. And I tried to dream back.

It was the story of your childhood that riveted me, and kept coming back to me, as it seems to me now that so many parts of our life together were born in your childhood. The young kangaroo, injured on the road, which we humped into our car and took home. I was horrified at the thought of nursing a paraplegic kangaroo – I am no nurse, and certainly no vet. It was pissing all over the car and was going to be pissing all over the carpet in our rented house. But you did not hear my objections. And of course the children were in favour of it. You christened him Skoczek, after your partisan bird and you tended his wounds. The children covered him in blankets. It didn't save him from dying that night, and then we had to spirit his body out of the house and dump him in the bush like criminals dumping a corpse, and lie to the children that he was back with his mummy. But somehow both Skoczeks live on, their small legends entwined with yours.

And what about that time you wanted to take Nadya and Jan kayaking down the rapids of the Murrumbidgee and refused to take life jackets for them? 'I will manage, don't worry! I can rescue them if necessary. You meet us with picnic at Kambah Pool at seven p.m!' you had said, as you sped away downstream. And from the un-jacketed ones, 'Bye Mum! Byee! Byee Mum! Byee!'

I waited faithfully at the appointed spot a few kilometres down the river with little Mishka, who was too young to go. My mind was struggling to check its frantic dialogue with fear. As the sun dropped behind the great hill evening became night, and picnic-goers packed up and left, leaving us alone, peering hopelessly into the noise of the river. I couldn't see the face on my wristwatch when you came struggling along, hours later, paddling out of the darkness. We heard you before we saw you, that invincible hero of the bush, with absolutely no sense of time. After all, for our first date you were twenty-four hours late!

I needed to know more about your forest boyhood to explore for myself the landscape of those stories that still inhabited my dreams. They had become a legend in our family chronicle, and a template for your children in their later difficult struggles with identity. It seems to me that the more unusual parts of your personality and story are what they absorbed, and have tried to recreate for themselves. It has not made motherhood easy, dealing with the heroic trajectories set in place by a few remembered words from you about truth and dare and the hair-raising adventures that they experienced with you as their leader.

20

Eighteen years on

It has been eighteen years. Saturday night, 6 May, was your last foolhardy expedition. You cycled off into the night, never to return. Thus it was that our life together was suddenly pushed into the past. You never came through the front door ever again, but the next morning my whole family – parents, brothers, sister – arrived through that door to plunge the house into official mourning, to tidy up. They always tidied up for me, but this time it was tidying up for your funeral, to arrange it. I made a giant canvas and hung it in the courtyard for the children to write to you. I drew a portrait of you and me and the three children. The children added their poems and letters. Guests wrote as well, their own thoughts. That was what we did, while the other arrangements were being put into place. Then we just had to go to the funeral – it was arranged, we had to face the reality. I took the canvas with all of its loving messages and poems and I tenderly wrapped it around your coffin, to make it more ours and less of a coffin. It could go down with you into the cold earth, a bit of us, a familiar blanket wrapped around that strange shiny box with its unwelcome shape that you now inhabited. We could be your shroud.

Nadya, her hair plaited up into coils around her head, came and sat there smiling. And then afterwards she got the giggles.

'Tell her she has nothing to laugh about,' warned one woman whom I didn't know. I understood Nadya – what's the difference between laughter and tears? They both come from the pit of your stomach, the core of your heart, from fear, discomfort, from panic.

It was your small, abandoned daughter, trying to retain her father in whatever way she could. The woman objecting to Nadya's smiling was there out of curiosity – you may have been her doctor, a sad loss for her. But Nadya had lost her beloved, unique, her one-and-only Olek.

The boys refused to go to the funeral. They still believed there was some hope – you were somewhere but not where everyone thought – not dead, never to come back.

The next day. Your clothes remained unworn, your familiar smell still warm in them. I would not allow them to be washed. Your shoes – so big for a short man – still had mud on them. They might hold a clue to your whereabouts. The mud on my shoes was from your graveside.

We, your family, so used to the reliability of our combined existence, were mesmerised by a panic which unfolded slowly and relentlessly, like a great wave, bringing with it a vacuum that sucked us into a fear of the unknown. Almost wordlessly we had followed the rituals of your burial. And then there was the time after.

The autumn chilled to grey winter. Your clothes did get washed and your smell went away, and unlike other smells that bring back reminders of the past, I knew that I would never smell your smell ever again.

The glimpses of life without you seemed to get bigger, each one unveiling a bit more of the unthinkable – our new reality. They kept coming, and were relentless. I dreaded the glimpses because they appeared unexpectedly, often when I felt quite happy. Happiness had always been my habit; I was unused to fear and loss. But now I felt it. Caverns of fear. Pulling me into them backwards. Destabilising me, terrifying the children.

Your patients were abandoned, mid-treatment, left without even a trace of your enigmatic smile, with only a tantalising memory of your thoughtful grimace as you tried to figure out their problems. But I had only an occasional thought about those faceless patients. Their files full of case notes decipherable only to you arrived at the house in boxes, sent back from the unmanned surgery by a secretary no longer employed. I just put them away, sadly. Patients were patients. I had the children to protect from their futile longings, their unrealisable fantasies. And I had myself.

Your habits, your physical presence, your passions, your longings – where did they go? I had one visit from you, when you came through the skylight above our bed and sat beside me, for a few seconds, holding my hand very tightly and saying nothing. I was sleeping with Christina, my sister, and I told her about it. I don't know whether she was skeptical, she was grieving for me too.

Then you drifted around our billabong for a while, in the early-morning rising mist. And that's where I ran in the mornings, to try and be with you before the mists left, making way for the winter sun. It gave me some feeling of communion, being in those mists. And then you went further, behind the hills, the Brindabellas. I suppose they were your very Holy Mountains. And you didn't come back. Your future had disappeared, and we were left with the mysterious caverns of your past.

The children dawdled to school, without excitement, disconsolate, their crisp brightness dulled by the yawning void confronting them upon awakening, perhaps being reunited with you in the sunny moments of their nocturnal dreams. And they kept growing. And having birthdays. And school holidays. And Christmas. And Mamushka.

Voy had come on a journey, arriving so mysteriously. It seemed to me that you found him, brought him and then left him guarding your hearth. He was your countryman. Did you know that your end was near? Had you had a glimpse? Had the gypsy told you what age you would be when you would die? Did you have a feeling, before you left on that dark journey, the journey from which no one has ever returned? Questions like this started to tease me, because the source had gone.

Voy was there that weekend of the watershed of our life. He was with his girlfriend. I did not really know him, but he was significant. He was in the wave that surrounded and then passed over me, a wave of the unknown mixed with the known, taking you – the vital ingredient – as it rolled and crashed away. I sensed in some way that Voy could be part of my future as he had been part of your past. I drank him in with the wave. You said he had a common past with you, he was there in our house after you died. You had kissed him, on both cheeks, he had kissed you back, on both cheeks. He was your friend and your countryman.

He was there at the funeral, pale and solemn. He was quiet, not bothering me with chatter. But he was there and he knew you. He knew your story. The traces of melancholia in his face, pockets stuffed with pens and books, the knitted brow, the sombre look, his strong, heavy body – it suited my mood. He was linking my past with my present.

My energy was still humming, unprepared for the stoppage that occurred. I didn't know what to do with myself. It was like our courtyard grapevine that we pruned in the spring when the sap was rising, and the sap kept running like a gush. Do you remember? Nothing we could do would stop it at the time. Bandages, bitumen, even plaster, you used, scavenged from orthopaedic outpatients! It was all useless. The sap had to go somewhere. I was the vine, cut in spring, outrageously wounded, forced to watch my children suffer quietly. I could not enter their heads where the pain was worst. I was helplessly at the edge of their agony.

They were untutored in what it means to lose a father. They had lost their grandfather Tatush three years before, but he had only been an occasional occupant of their lives.

So I tried to distract them from the strange new awareness that stalked their days and haunted their bedtimes. It seemed unimaginable to them that you would not just come hurtling through the door, arms out, to be jumped on by them, smothered by their welcome. I tried to devise different routines for the evenings, not to miss that one we were used to, the normal one, your evening homecoming.

I tried to fill up weekends with extra activities to divert painful reflection. The season changed from autumn to winter; we went skiing. Then winter turned to spring and I knew that the children knew we were moving away from your life. We were two seasons away and we hadn't heard from you. Nothing.

'I can't see his face,' said Mishka, who had turned eight in October. Christmas was coming up. I found a little poem in his handwriting. Who composed it? Him or Jan? Both of them together? They did everything together.

Before you eat your Christmas pie, think about the man who flies, beyond the hills, beyond the skies, beyond the very holy mountains . . . .

'I don't remember what he looked like', complained Mishka.

I found your photos. And more, photos you had printed in your darkroom, photos of the children, of me. You had let the boys assist you in the darkroom, which was considered a great privilege because it usually meant staying up late at night. Mishka stared at the photographs and I don't know what he thought, I just hope he felt better. He took them away. I followed them, not wanting to lose those precious scraps of the time in the darkroom.

'I don't remember his voice,' said Jan, his own voice breaking. 'I don't remember how he sounds.'

I found your tape, reading them their bedtime stories. That was one bit of your voice, trapped forever as you narrated 'Snow White' and your version of 'The Magic Carpet'. But your conversation was gone, remembered only in snatches, in pearls of wisdom, and the captured voice could not be extended beyond the stories into life itself. So listening to the tape made them cry uncontrollably.

'I will never forget anything he said!' announced Nadya, who had moved her bed into the cupboard for no reason I could detect as rational, and there in her bed in her cupboard she was able to sleep. I pulled her bed back to its spot while she was at school. She pushed it back into the cupboard when she came home. And eventually I gave up and left it there. In the private darkness of her cupboard, bits of your philosophy and pieces of your legend began to sprout seeds. She wrote about you, she sang about you, she moulded herself along the lines she believed had been drawn into her soul deliberately by you.

'Always do what you think is right. Never be afraid to ask why! If someone has less than you, then you must help that person . . .'

She received this advice, along with the boys, and proceeded to apply it even in situations where such brave questioning could only be perceived as precocious. For instance, questioning the teacher on her decisions or classroom strategies. In accordance with the generosity dictum, she rarely arrived home with all her things, claiming when I asked that she had given them to those who needed them more. And having been sworn by you to even risk life if necessary in defence of her principles, she would not back down.

Nadya's soul began its great expansion, leaving logic and smooth dealings as withered orphans in her passionate makeup

I started to paint again. For the first time, landscapes. I had only ever painted people. Now I gazed at the dark hill opposite, across from the lake – we called it Kelly's Farm, that mysterious looming hillside. Its mood changed with the hour and the season. I painted it, working into its proclivities, rejoicing in the subtleties of its profile, pushing its way against the sky with its glimmer of dawn light, or plunged into darkness and backlit by long rays of setting sun, or weighed down by snow cloud, or covered in frost.

The landscape drew me like a poultice. And I drew the landscape. The living room with its glass doors became a litter of paints, turps, brushes and propped-up canvases. I pushed my feelings of fear and panic, of the black vacuum, into the dark areas of the paintings. I learned to mix shadow. I used shadow. The darks in the landscape surrounded and grounded me. My highs embraced the light, the glimmerings and shimmerings of winter sun against a gunmetal-grey sky. Voy was in the glimmerings, he was there in the winter light. Sometimes he stood behind me as I mixed the lights, and pushed them through luminescent kangaroo grass. And I became conscious of him, watching me, watching the movements of my brushes.

Jan started to dig. He dug a huge hole in the garden. Every day after school he resumed the activity. He wanted a fish pond, he said. He dug and dug. He would not stop digging. It looked like a major disturbance in the garden that was beginning, under Voy's occasional guidance, to take shape. But Jan was intent on his fishpond, and I had to support the project because I knew where its energy came from. My heart was soft for him, for his earnest dedication, his serious commitment to the task that he had to perform.

He has to move forward – somewhere, anywhere, I thought.

Mishka lay on the couch, his long fingers delicately stroking the cat, curled up with him, his thoughts floating into other realms. You had photographed him just like that, and developed it, with Jan or Mishka assisting in the little darkroom. Mishka had a bike, which he rode furiously around the paths. He always referred formally to his bike as the Oxford International. You had given him his first stay-upright lessons. Voy took over and taught him how to stop, running along behind, seeing the surprise reaction when Mishka realised he could brake and stop on his own. I stood back watching, satisfied. I was touched and impressed. Could this, I registered, be Voy's first real act as a could-be father? I put the thought away, trying not to tempt myself. But then, I knew, there are some things only men should teach boys. Tears struggled against my eyelids as I heard Mishka's yell of triumph. And then he did it again, and again, and again.

Nadya just hung in with Suzka, her best friend. Suzka's mother had bought her a retired racehorse. So I bought Nadya a pony, a naughty little mare with a long fringed forelock. The two girls went and caught their ponies, which were agisted in the paddock at Kelly's Farm opposite our place. They groomed them, they curled their manes, they prepared them snacks, rode them down through the kangaroo grass to the lake or to the Murrumbidgee River at the bottom of the valley. They brought them back, hosed them down, all the while discussing their weight and condition.

And then when she was alone, without Suzka, when the horses were back at Kelly's Farm and Suzka was summoned by her mother to do her reading quota, I noticed Nadya's face, her grey-green eyes anxious and wistful, and I wished that Suzka did not have to do her reading quota.

Mamushka was like a felled tree, dulled by the loss of her only son. It crowned her life, a crown of thorns – worse than the loss of her husband of forty-five years or her sister and niece in the concentration camps. Your death brought all her losses together and filled her with an accumulated pain that nothing could relieve. No drugs, no painkillers, no sleeping tablets.

I had become more acutely aware of Voy's presence, of his movements round the house, of what he did, the way he chopped the vegetables to prepare the dinner. It was comforting. The dinner was not being prepared by me anymore. We were being looked after. He was making a new routine and I was watching. Everything was strange, and somehow temporary. But a small layer of my being was telling me perhaps it could be for keeps.

I did not want him to leave. One night the children and me slept in the same room as him and Bibi, his girlfriend, piling all the mattresses on the floor, rather than going back to our normal beds and having to face the night again, and the next morning. Bedtime, instead of being a reassuring time, had become a savage gap that none of us wanted to face. We slept in there, all of us, and the children slept without problems.

But then Voy did leave. Bibi left for Germany, and Voy took his rucksack and left too, but did not go too far. He enrolled at the university to do his PhD in anthropology and got himself a flat with a Polish law student, Mariusz. Voy had decided to stay, but not with us. So I was alone with the children, with our empty routines, and it was back to the jagged hole of your unremitting absence.

Once again, nights without your noisy homecoming. The toot of the car, the rush through the door, squatting on your haunches to be jumped on by the children, dinnertime, arguments over whose turn it was to read children's stories, a vodka or two, the last telephone call of the day with the usual complaints from Mamushka checking up on what you had been eating. Me sulking about Mamushka ringing and stirring you, you tempering my irritation using your usual charm. And then our bedtime. That warm routine we had never even noticed particularly became vivid in memory because it had been brutally snatched from our grasp and abruptly consigned to the past.

Winter had set in. A change of season without you witnessing it, or rejoicing the freezing winds, the frosts over the paddocks. You loved the onset of winter as I loved the thick torpor of summer.

Jan's fish pond was getting to be enormous. When Voy came over he called it 'the shark pond', a cavernous hole at the end of our pretty courtyard to trap unwary visitors in the dark. Now it was lined with icy frost. Jan was unfazed by the failure of the pond to retain water, and nobody was going to suggest concrete. But Jan was versatile, as long as the project continued.

'My shark pond can be a herb garden!' he announced. And that's what it became. He read up on herbs, and decided that he wanted not parsley, which everybody knew and would be needing for their cooking, but borage and lovage which, as nobody even knew about their existence, let alone what stew would be enhanced by their flavour, would be allowed to grow unharvested.

'They are,' announced Jan, 'what the medieval knights used to give them courage!'

Jan's courage had always been noticeable. It got him into trouble. He had attitude. He deferred to nobody, and tended to confront people including, once or twice, his teachers. Was that from you? *Always do and say what you think is right and never be afraid to ask why.*

Schooled by your own father in integrity during your childhood, when the truth all around you was suppressed by the new and evil dictums, you were proud of Jan's frank observations and refused to suggest that he mitigate his confrontational approach. But perhaps after you died he needed extra amounts of courage in order to keep trudging forward into the future, to hold to his firm opinions. Jan may have planted borage to boost his own depleted levels of courage.

I slept lightly, waking early. I had been glad when Voy was there, in the house, sleeping the untroubled sleep of a traveller, mysteriously linking me with you and your past. Now he had gone, and I wished he would return.

You and he had had long conversations. About what, I wondered. Do Australian men talk to each other so intensely? Are they so affectionate? I don't know. Affection towards each other is expressed differently by our men, I think. It's how my brothers behave, and my father with his friends, a sort of joviality, a backslapping cordiality. It's my background.

I stole a look at Voy's face. He was physically so different to you, and I was comparing him. I caught myself out. Did I already have plans for him, when my heart and mind were full of you? Voy's face is very beautiful, I thought, and I traced with my mind the delicate asymmetry of his eyes. I wondered about the whimsical tilt of his mouth, if it came from his mother's line or his father's.

Your competent hands, your face sculptured by humour, your thoughts, your mouth with a sudden curl upwards, just at the corners, your habits, bits of bicycle dismembered in the living area against my will and resisting my lament about their presence, your

121

movements, interactions, the phone calls for you, the way you ate an apple right past the core, pips, stalk and all, your sudden bursts of joy, your exasperating stubbornness. Then there was the list of numbers I had where I could find you at your workplaces, numbers that no longer had the power to locate you. They became empty numbers, but they still ring in my head. Your huge life-energy had gone. But where to? Was it trapped somewhere, waiting for its cue to fuel the moody cavities left in your children?

That change was abrupt. Your persona, the memory of your body, your great soul, they lingered, they still do. But the fragile intimacy of our pacts and our flare-ups vanished, unmotivated by action and the passion of the moment, untempered by remorse and sudden bursts of compassion.

And whenever I thought about Voy I felt a twinge of life, a whiff of excitement. Apprehensively I rang him. I asked if he would like to come back. No, he said, but he would visit. I looked forward to the visit. I also found myself changing into something that looked good over my new figure, stripped of its proportions by the refusal of my body to absorb food in the normal way. I put on make-up, viewed suspiciously by Nadya who commented on my efforts to adorn myself. I laid the best china, I cooked my Polish dishes.

He arrived in his usual clothes, the checked flannel shirt with rolled-up sleeves, the trousers with pockets down the legs. Travellers' trousers, I thought nervously. I wanted him to stay, not be a traveller. To have trousers with just one pocket. It was Sunday night. The children had laid the table with flowers and candles. They were pleased, expecting him. Since he had left it had been worse for all of us.

'This is very nice!' he said, looking a bit guarded, sensing a trap.

'But why do you cook this food? It is not necessary to go to this trouble! I could do something in ten minutes!'

Well, I just can't get things right, can I? My mind flashed back to the disastrous night when I had prepared the Polish cuisine for you. Shouldn't that experiment have taught me something?

We clinked glasses and as our eyes flickered at each other the clink rang clear, like crystal.

21

Emerging

So you had gone, leaving pieces of me, pieces of your life, pieces of our life, and three children with the pieces of you in their lives gone missing.

And you left Voy. He came to visit regularly, staying to help with this and that, fiddle in the garden, chop the firewood. A manly presence around the house. Sometimes he talked to Nadya and she listened earnestly, repeating what he said.

Voy understands the complexities of life and lost life, I thought, rationalising my persistent attraction to him. He was rather moody, but in a way his sombre moods were the right backing track for this strange time. And I was intrigued, believing his moods to be the indicators of bottomless depths that I alone could fathom. It presented itself as a sweet challenge. And he did seem to have the capacity to comprehend our ways, our approach, to somehow follow us through the circuitous emotionally charged logic that formed itself around us after you died.

A structuralist himself, he sees structure – or the need for structure – in most things. He does not believe, as I do, that things can just be allowed to meander on and find their own conclusion.

'You see, Kot, one should follow some structure.' I had yet another name to add to my list. Kathy, Katya, Kasia, Katush (although Katush had flown, you had taken it with you), and now, Kot.

And in the interests of securing more of his presence I promised to try his approach. I think that my meandering ways probably did prevail, but I was starting to see more of him anyway. He suggested changing the children's schools so they could go to a local school. I complied. It did seem logical.

I was crossing my fingers that Voy would stay for me. In my life full of grey clouds he was the fleecy lining. He took the children skiing, I watched, and he picked them up out of the snow, one by one, when they were stranded on an icy peak. That was always your job, I thought, as I struggled to stand up myself, slipping and crashing and at the same time attending to the iced snot under my nose, which was starting to smother me. As I watched him scooping up our kids new icicles formed under my eyes, and more under my nose, freezing fresh blubber. A future that might be rosy again?

Please let it be, I prayed. I needed to be whole again, to regain balance and confidence. But I wanted so much – for me, for the children. He helped the children re-measure their skis, to minimise the risk of them getting caught out of control on any more wIndie peaks. This was another of your jobs, the measuring of the skis. I watched nervously from a safe distance as he succeeded in sorting out a fight between Jan and Mishka, a risky business for anyone.

These moments of unity bathed me in their warmth. I relaxed from my ever-present anxiety, and willed the moments to last forever. In the snow country Voy felt familiar and in control. He taught Nadya to make a jump turn and remembered to admire her as she executed the turn.

And then on the way back in the car, the children were asleep, he was driving and I daringly touched his hand as it rested on the gear stick. He closed his hand over mine, thrillingly. We kept driving, silent, staring straight ahead into the night road, into an unknown future.

Voy was hesitant about his feelings. I was nicely shocked by my feelings. The children were very wary. With expert eyes and senses on the alert they observed my growing relationship with the man who was not their father. They monitored my expressions, my way of behaving when Voy was there. Nadya, already acutely tuned in to any flirtatious looks and gestures between us, never failed to bring me to account.

'Why do you have to wear those earrings? You never wore them before! Why are you standing like that? Are you trying to look attractive?'

Somewhat chastened and made self-conscious from being reminded of my flirtatious ploys by my observant little daughter, I nevertheless persisted.

They liked him, they needed him, but their instincts were to suspiciously guard their territory. I found myself preparing them to accept Voy as a father figure, and at the same time I was also trying to school him in tolerance towards children who, on behalf of their own father, put up angry resistance to any change whatsoever to any small arrangement in the house.

'Always do what you think is right, and never be afraid to ask why.' Your advice, so easily delivered, achieved divine status after your death.

The house had to stay as it was – just in case you suddenly returned. Jan led the charge and the defence, and the others closed ranks behind him. Then they would be seen to have done the right thing by you.

PART THREE

———

'You will have two husbands!' The gypsy had told me that when she came to our front door in London, pushing her way in against my gentle discouragements, and convincing me to let her read my fortune for fifty pence. I had stared at my palm afterwards, with the sprig of heather she had left me grasping, wondering what on earth it was in my hand that revealed such a destiny.

22

The second gypsy's prediction

Two years after you died Voy and I got married. The London gypsy's face flashed into my mind, her words ringing in my ears. The words and the random prediction of a stranger, all those years ago, had come true.

Voy's family were not in Australia to celebrate with us, but mine were, in their usual force – my parents, my uncles and aunts, my brothers and my sister, all supporting my new leap into life and hope. We were married in a small chapel at Circular Quay.

Voy wore a suit. It was the first time I had ever seen him without rolled-up sleeves, which carried quite enough appeal for me. But in his formal clothes I looked him up and down with my now-experienced gaze. And it was not just a passing glance of respect and appreciation, the sidelong glance of a woman for an attractive man. It was my man, for life, for as long, I thought, as we both should live. I was content now that this was the man who was going to be a father to my fatherless children. He looked strong enough for all of that.

But then I unexpectedly choked on the marriage vows, which my body knew far too well. Tears blocked my throat, my eyes started to sting. Somehow I got through them, but was forced to gaze into the terrible sadness they held for one anguished moment. And Voy

vowed to take us, forsaking all others. His blue eyes glistened, aware
by now what it all meant. The children, dressed stiffly in their Polish
mountain outfits from the trip we had made to meet Voy's family
and announce our engagement, sang for us to organ music played
by our friend Christopher. But their voices stuck a bit too, and ran
out, as the organ continued to play, and as their hearts and minds
ran with their own thoughts.

Mamushka chose not to attend. But she sent us her gracious
wishes for life. *'Laheim,'* she said.

Laheim! For Life! The wedding party was at the home of my sister,
Christina, and her husband Trevor. We clinked our glasses sentimen-
tally, happy to be on the verge of life together, knowing something
of each other as we did, and sensing adventure in our future.

After the party we got one night off from the children for our honeymoon, one night at the Cross, me and that flirtatious man I had just
married. For once in my life I did not mind leaving a good party.

And then the next day it was back with the children again. The
beautiful suit had disappeared into a suitcase, perhaps forever, and
the rolled-up sleeves were once again at the driving wheel as we
drove back out of Sydney. But Voy and I looked at each other in a
different way. There was a new sparkle of magic between us. And
that's how it was going to be.

23

Papua New Guinea:
Dreams from a winter place, 1981

Now it is 1981 and we have a new baby, Rafal, and with our three bigger children out of school we are all in New Guinea. We have arrived here to live in a bush hut for two years. Voy is an anthropologist, that's why we are here. How unreal it is to be in this place, unlike anything or any place I have ever been. But I get used to it quickly, despite the primitive conditions, despite the intense isolation. Perhaps I've been here in movies, perhaps in dreams.

Is it the partisan stories? I dreamt of you again last night. Perhaps our hut has provoked thoughts of your dugout? The hut is small and dark; it looks out onto forests. There is a little river where we wash. We live on the local sweet potato.

I dreamt that I saw you. You were a child – perhaps in my dream you were Jan or Mishka. You were collecting sap in a strange forest. The image vanished and then I was reading a letter from you, but it wasn't in real writing. I woke up trying to track my dream, and the source of the letter, coming from a grey distance.

Was it from London, or perhaps Hull – that greyness, when our cargo ship pulled into the port through clammy fog in 1969? You were familiar with the grey of real winter.

You strode into the fog and knew what to do. To me it was surreal. I followed, staring and thrilled, carrying eight-week-old Jan tucked tightly into his basket. Nadya's sun-tanned face peeped, curious and alert, from a heavy knitted hat, her cold cheeks jamming her usual chatter as she sat on your shoulders, her chin frozen onto your head, peering into the sombre colours of the wintry English docks.

Then we caught the train and went south, cutting through the chilly white landscape, snapping past cities with snow-topped roofs, until we reached London Bridge. You were going to study and work in the United Kingdom hospital system. That's why we were there – that, and to see a real winter. We saw four winters, and returned with a third child, Mishka.

Now as I try and piece together my dream, which had been sent by you, scenes come back at me.

We sleep here under nets. The jungle is outside our small window, the night rain is soft on the roof of our hut, and if I reach up from lying in my bed I can touch the ceiling. But the incoming dream is chilly like those remembered winters, and there are no warm colours in the place that you write from. There are no warm words either, just rags of words, sounding like regret, a little desolate. A lot has passed. And now as I lie here, snuggled against Voy in this tropical hideout, with a warm baby boy next to me, you still probe me from that strange wintry place.

And what are you asking me? Why have I not been in contact with you and where have I been? Am I with someone else? Is that why we're not meeting? We belong to each other, we never stopped that, but could you return?

Of course if you could you must. But how?

I struggle to respond in my dream. But where are you anyway? It's not a place you write from, it's an atmosphere. You sound bleak and alone. There is no familiarity. But who would you be with, if not us? You would not be wandering on your own without a child bouncing on your shoulders, another running along in front, me with a baby. That was us. And then it wasn't. I have a baby now, Voy's son. He looks like Voy, he's robust and strong. He has Voy's family eyes, but he looks like the others. He's their baby. They drag him around, make him chortle, soothe him when he cries. He's theirs, he's new life, and the underpinnings of our new life as a real family.

During the last autumn you and I spent in London, I remember standing, pleasantly distracted, baby minding, half watching, counting little heads, and my mind was somewhere else. The children buried themselves, screaming with pleasure, in the knee-deep leaves in Hyde Park, their last European autumn. The afternoons were short, nostalgic. The thought of going home before the onset of real winter, to a familiar hot summer, had burned its way determinedly into my mind.

We left at the last moment, and then you remembered that we had not gone through the vaccination procedure, which was a must for returning home to Australia. It was a Saturday. We were due to leave on Sunday. The government doctor at the High Commission was not available. What were we going to do? But who were you to allow bureaucracy to stand in the way of your moves?

'Don't worry!' you assured me, 'I will do forms myself, give vaccinations and I sign against the hard-boiled egg stamp . . .'

'What?' I asked, incredulous, not knowing what you were talking about. Hard-boiled eggs? I was protectively respectful of our customs bureaucracy. It was not the Iron Curtain.

'With hard-boiled egg, onion and coin one can make excellent official stamp. How I got out of Poland, with such a stamp! I can administer vaccinations myself and stamp is nothing!'

Thus it happened – there was no time left to argue with this proposition, and no hope either of changing our rock-bottom bargain fare back home, so I had to go along with the plan. A stamp was concocted from ink, onion, an Australian penny and a hard-boiled egg. It even looked convincing to me, appearing on the official vaccination forms. But the Australian airport authorities were not so easily convinced.

'Eh, what sort of a stamp is this?' they asked us. I blushed and you answered truthfully that it was stamped by the administering doctor.

'Well yers had better come along with us and get vaccinations, I would say!'

And into a room we were herded, ignominiously, despite your vociferous protestations, and delivered of our second lot of vaccinations in the same week.

And that was our coming back. With failed forged documents and doubly vaccinated.

Our families waited at the airport for the extra time, and then we burst out into the summer that welcomed us. We were home.

You finished your studies in Melbourne, and then, when your independent nature rebelled against the constraints of the rigid hierarchy that was the teaching hospital system, and because you loved the hills and the surrounding bush, the bird calls and the sound of wind in trees, we settled in Canberra. We lived just at the edge of the farm country, and could hear the moo of cows announcing the evening. The bush, the wind, the storms, they were so strongly represented in your psyche. How, I think now, could that not have had its origin from the partisans?

Three years ago as we buried you under the falling leaves of the birch trees the old predictions surrounded me, beating me in the head. I stared at the trees in the cemetery as though they were dreams and not real. Why were they there? Where had they come from? In a burial garden full of eucalypts, these two birch trees seemed to have appeared from your past, to stand beside your grave, to watch over it like sentinels from your childhood forest. Did they know? Were they playing their part in the gypsy's story? And now every year those same birch trees, your tomb guardians, they change colour and shed their leaves, like palls, remembering your burial, remembering your last autumn in 1978.

In my dream I see the browning and blowing leaves – they pull at me. But Voy is also with me in the dream, pulling me into the present, back to the Papua New Guinea jungle where we are, to the children who are a little older, and I half wake, and their day is about to begin. Jan springs out of bed, his usual efficient self, and rushes outside to make the cooking fire. Mishka straggles to the door and happily engages in philosophical conversation with an old man who has arrived to score a cigarette. Nadya swathes herself in lap-laps and saunters out yawning, to sniff the latest gossip, and Rafal's cries for his milk join the sounds of the waking day.

Now it's his and mine, this gang. And you stand behind, a spiritual father, removed from rebellions, small difficulties, homework, financial problems, large struggles and the huge rewards of participating in the growing up of the children you loved. Life has mysteriously moved us into another chapter and it just keeps moving.

We're here for two years. But you were around here too, as a medical patrol officer, you would have passed through here in 1964, on your great solo patrol from Goroka to Madang, the year before we met. It's where you always wanted to be practising, Papua New Guinea, but the authorities here had decided against you realising that dream. You had failed their set of bureaucratic questions. So you had to settle for the few months of free choice allowed during medical studies to do a Papua New Guinea jungle stint.

Perhaps you do inhabit the spirit life here, protecting your children in these remote, primitive and often dangerous conditions, but overall do you approve of the experience for them, and relate it to your time here and to your partisan childhood?

Did I feel pangs of doubt in my dream? Or fear? Did I wonder how to meet you? Was there any resolution? My dream mixed present with past, confusing me between two men, and my children between two fathers, you their real father, who vanished in the midstream of your life and love, and Voy, in the midstream of his life, trying to use his famous rationality and ingenuity to unlock the capacity of your children to trust, even love another man.

The dream dispersed gently with the crescendo of the early morning. The noise of pigs rooting and snorting outside our hut joined the bird calls, the soft chatter of Mishka and the old man, the sound of the crackling fire, and the smell of smoke filtering into the moist air. I gratefully grounded myself, clearing the floating strands of the dream. And a few of the strands stayed with me, sewn as they are with you, in the folds of my psyche.

When sturdy little Raf came bursting into our family we left, almost immediately, for New Guinea. The baby and the very challenge of the place we lived left little time to look back. I was pleased when he was born to see the same chest as Voy; that was my first observation. The same eyes. The same moods? Are moods contained in a person's eyes? My brain flickered with this, for a second. His baby routines took all our time. He was endlessly absorbing. The big children played with him, we had him christened early at Mum's insistence, before we left the safe shores for those unknown. To my parents, the childrens' survival – and especially that of a six-week-old baby – appeared to be in the balance. And therein lies that other story that I told in my diary, when we lived in a mountain valley, watched by ancestors.

But even in New Guinea you were there, the ancestor among those other ancestral spirits. You gained prominence by guarding us, your people, in another land, and influencing negotiations with the indigenous ancestors about our fates while in that remote valley.

Mamushka missed us. She didn't want to visit.

'Acch, it is wild place! Olek told me this!'

When I rang her during our visits to town, she lamented, 'Katya? Why you not ring to me?'

'But I'm ringing Mamushka! We have no phone down there!'

'Oich, oich! I miss him, I miss children. Nadya – wot she does in wild place? Katya, where are children? They are dangerous, oy yoy! You okay, you have the face young, you with new man, new child! But where are children – I want to see them! I know such place Katya, I know! Bring them back to me!'

I was left at the other end of the phone without too much to say. What could I say? Everything she said was true for her, and for me too. I did have another man, another baby, as well as her grandchildren. We were in a dangerous place. What could I do? She said she knew such places. Was she talking about your partisan forests? If she was then all of her fierce protective instincts would be reactivated towards rescuing her grandchildren from such dark fates.

How could I oblige her? With Mamushka, replies and solutions are unnecessary, I remembered reasonably. Just allow her, Voy suggested, to let off steam, there is so much grief in the steam, he said, it has to come out. So I mentioned to her in what I thought was a casual voice that she seriously consider having a relationship with a nice man who, she told me on the phone, had begun to visit her. 'Very nice and he has only seventy-two years . . .'

Perhaps, I thought hopefully, the attentions of a vigorous 72-year-old might distract her from her heavy burden of loss. He asked her, she said, to go to the zoo with him for the day. I immediately warmed to him upon hearing this. An animal lover, interested in the external world, not endlessly absorbed by emotional trauma. He could be a good escort. But Mamushka immediately sniffed out my enthusiasm for embracing anything that could lessen her suffering, and quickly reassured me that she would not encourage the relationship.

'What for, to visit animals? I am not interesting in animal, and wiz him? Katya he is old man! What for? One is enough. What for to go with another man to grave? What for?'

And I was left with the phone in my hand, rage in my heart, Rafal fidgeting around on my back, a woman behind me cradling a large grey possum on her shoulder, and at least fifteen people waiting for the phone. And Mamushka wanted the children back. And she thought a 72-year-old too old!

One thing, I reasoned with myself helpfully, she respects suffering, she knows it and she expects us to suffer too. I had tried to reassure her.

'We will come home soon, Mamushka. Please don't worry about us!' My words, sincere enough, having everybody's wellbeing at heart, had no power to comfort her. I trudged back to our hostel.

But come home we did. Yet when we did come, the children were wary of Mamushka's fierce needs – particularly Nadya, her favourite, who, now a teenager, would only visit her with a friend who could act as an emotional buffer-zone. Mamushka did not like the buffer-zone technique. That defeated her whole purpose, deflected her anguish from its target, and left her no relief, no chance to unburden on Nadya.

'Your friends is nothing! Only family!' This was Mamushka's mantra. But what she really meant was, only Nadya.

24

Mamushka and Nadya

There were times, I was telling Voy, by way of explaining to him the Nadya–Mamushka relationship, when Nadya returned from staying with Mamushka for her Christmas holidays in a transformed state. Olek and I would have driven to Sydney to collect her.

She would emerge from the flat at Marrickville laden with presents, instantly alerting the boys to a potentially unjust situation. Semi-hostile to us, her parents, dressed in different expensive clothing not to my taste, visibly expanded, smelling different, she crossed back into our territory, marked with Mamushka's imprint. We got to the car, and Tatush, always reasonable, stood smiling and waving while Mamushka sobbed violently, and thrust a bag of sugared *ponchki* in through the window, hanging on to Nadya, who clung back, through the window, sobbing her response.

'Oich, oich, oich! I can't live without you, Babcia!' said Nadya.

'Don't worry, Katush!' Olek would advise, attempting to soothe me in advance of my certain volcanic outburst. 'We will run her round a bit when we get home. Don't be upset – hush now, Katush!'

At this stage I would not have said a single word. But the visible tightening of my jaw, while sitting in the passenger seat and glaring straight in front, was the obvious signal for Olek to start defending himself from my familiar tirade against his mother and her ruthless advances into my terrain. And the next day I would still be simmering.

'You know, I don't recognise her! She's obese, secretive. She will not take any notice of anything I say! She smells of chicken paprika! She's become *her* creature!'

That was back when Tatush was alive, and Mamushka had Nadya to herself. Tatush remained discreetly in the background, and that is all either of them wanted or needed.

Mamushka's life changed so dramatically after Tatush died, when she no longer had the illegal practice to fuss around, being an efficient and positive force, bustling in her white coat. She sold the flat and moved to the more upmarket suburb of Vaucluse while Olek was still alive. We moved her there. Then, three years later, she lost her son, the greatest loss of all, and the new apartment at Vaucluse overlooking the cliffs and the great ocean, the charm of it all just slid away across the horizon. The morning sun shimmering over the sea, that was just the start of another day of suffering. And when the sun set, and the ocean dimpled with shadows of pink liquid gold, it signalled the beginning of the long night ahead of her. The apartment, with its splendid outlook, became a prison for Mamushka and her sorrows. But she came from time to time, to stay with us, to be with the children.

'She's so agitated and upset with me. I can hear her downstairs – she doesn't sleep, she wanders at night. What can I do with her?'

I was pleading with Voy to advise me on his countrywoman who was bumping and clattering around downstairs, engaged in an obvious effort to disturb the sound and needed sleep of me, a busy mother and wife.

'I do wish she would go to sleep and let us sleep! But she can't, she has lost her son,' I tried to tell myself, as another little devil voice was chanting. 'She is hell-bent on keeping us all awake, because she just has to be the centre of attention. She must make trouble for me! She is furious that I've married again.' And I would start to brew. And stew.

'What can we do for her?'

'Let her spend more time with Nadya,' he advised. 'Nadya gives her life meaning again,' explained Voy. 'She likes to protect Nadya – it gives her an important function.'

'Yes, it's true, but it's making Nadya so elusive. She doesn't like being followed around, focused on and fussed over so much any more. She's embarrassed about being tailed everywhere she goes with trays of chicken wings. She's afraid of being burdened with the weight of Mamushka's grief. She's done her bit – she went to Sydney to stay with Mamushka. I can't just sacrifice Nadya!'

Nadya had been there at Vaucluse for a few days, taking Suzka as her escort. But Suzka was evicted by Mamushka who wanted Nadya to herself, and Suzka, who was declared by Mamushka to be 'false' (pronounced *fuls*), had been forced by Mamushka to go and visit her own Sydney grandmother. So it was that only Nadya and Mamushka came back on the train to Canberra. Nadya was very glad to see me, and Mamushka was being rather remote. What has been going on, I wondered? It didn't take long to come out.

'Katya. How could this be? How? To give me ze child with the lice. How?'

I tried to defend myself. 'Lice are normal Mamushka. They happen to everyone who goes to school! Don't worry about it! I will de-louse her. Don't worry, it's not that bad!'

Of course there was no need to de-louse her, because Mamushka had attended to this herself.

But Nadya told me why the lice had presented as such a problem for Mamushka, her Babcia, who would normally accept Nadya unconditionally.

'Grazyna found my lice at her place and she told Babcia! We were at Grazyna's place, I was sitting on the carpet and Grazyna was brushing my hair because she wanted to do my plaits.'

'"Beautiful hair, your grandchild, Tanya! So long, so much, so blond!" Babcia looked so happy when she said that,' reported Nadya.

'"Ah, Grazyna," she said, "I will show you how she is also clever, the child!"'

'And then, while she was doing my hair, plaiting it and putting the plaits in ribbons, Grazyna found my lice.'

'"Tanya!" she calls across the room. "Darling! Come here and look. What has your grandchild?" And Grazyna showed Mamushka the lice as they appeared.

'Poor little Babcia, she was so humiliated – I felt sorry for her. She went really quiet, then she snatched me and we left. She was really furious with Grazyna, she was muttering all the way back to her place in the bus. She didn't even let Grazyna's son drive us home!'

So then Mamushka was at our place and venting her fury, much more reasonably, on me.

'Lice! Katya. She has lice! *Wszi*! Such shame! Now I would not see Grazyna, I would not bother!'

'Why not? Please don't break such a friendship. It's not her fault! It is my fault, not hers! She did us a favour, finding the lice before they spread to the others.'

'You don't see? Acch, Katya! Who has the lice? So poor people who haven't what to eat! In war they have this *wszi*!'

'Oh, so that's it.' I told Voy about it. He smiled. He often understands Mamushka.

'Don't you see? *Wszi* represent for her wartime, camps, cholera, poverty, pestilence. The things she has fought, left behind, hates, and still fears. And now *wszi* are on the head of her favourite grandchild in front of her best friend, discovered by this friend in fact. And you can't see why she's upset? I would be also upset! Kot, you are so un-European!'

Oh that's it, so it's the war again. Always the war . . .

Her friendship with Grazyna was no longer equal. Mamushka had no son anymore, the prize grandchild had lice. Her bargaining chips in the friendship were gone. Mamushka understood that envy was mixed with Grazyna's praise of Nadya's hair. Grazyna had no daughter, no granddaughter and was therefore envious of Mamushka.

Therefore, Voy explained simply, Mamushka could no longer afford to see Grazyna because Mamushka had lost the edge and would become the beggar in the friendship.

Clued up by Voy, I know now that I was instrumental in rupturing the only friendship that seemed to give Mamushka any pleasure, the only possible competitor to her family members. Grazyna was good at cards, but Mamushka could beat her. She had a lovely apartment, a devoted husband and son – all markers of the worth of a true friend. Grazyna was younger and attentive and she lived nearby. Her son had a car and was happy to ferry Mamushka and Grazyna wherever they wished to go. Grazyna was a generous friend, absorbing some of Mamushka's time that otherwise hung heavy for her.

And she had always been happy to listen to Mamushka's boasting about her grandchild.

'Look, Grazyna! Look, the legs – how she is strong! Look how she eats!' Nadya had stuffed herself with Grazyna's paprika chicken and wanted more. Together they were able to watch with pride as Nadya's proportions swelled.

Now all of that was in the past.

Nadya liked to be able to please her grandmother with the size of her legs, which caused some suffering in other quarters, such as school, where her girlfriends pronounced them to be fat. Except of course, for the loyal and sensitive Suzka, who reassured Nadya that her legs were just cuddly.

'But perhaps,' thought Nadya mournfully, always believing the worst about her body shape, 'perhaps Babcia is right – Suzka is just being *fuls*!'

25

Our birch tree

We had a birch tree, Olek and I, which we planted to start our new garden. We planted it out of sentiment for the nectar from the birch trees in the partisan forest. It was our little *berioska*, and grew into a big *berioska*. We tried to tap it. To see how it was done, to taste the nutritious juice of a childhood which grew such a strong man. To try it on our children, perhaps, so that they would grow strong.

But the tree, purchased from a nursery, nurtured in suburbia, yielded nothing. We checked the tin for a few days while we had the project in mind. Perhaps the tree knew that we had access to other drinks, and saved its precious sap only for desperate exiles living in forests. Perhaps the tree was immature.

Mamushka was consulted. 'What for?' she said, 'to drink such a one! Acch, darlings! You have excellent drinks in shops! Much better drinks, darling, in shops!'

The children agreed. They liked the drinks in bottles at the shops much better than the juice which could possibly be extracted from a tree.

Life was busy, there were many projects, and then we forgot the experiment. He forgot it first, and I said nothing, being a little relieved that I did not have to test the potion on the children.

Years later, after we had returned from New Guinea, I found the tin hiding under the new foliage and branches of the mature tree, and it stopped me in my tracks. Memories grabbed me. I stayed there, spade in hand, touching the tree, as if it were flesh. And then I was thankful once again for the two *berioska* trees that were standing next to Olek's grave guarding his childhood, marking so appropriately the spot of his last resting place.

And life goes on. Our story, his and mine and his as father of his children, which only had a beginning and the first part of a middle, like an unfinished symphony. It ended way before its time, just as the gypsy had surmised. A curious bridge of other exciting realities has woven its way across what seemed once to be an unbridgeable chasm. Olek emerges in dreams, and then retreats back again to his place, and unlike the rest of us he gets no older than his last photo.

And I wake up to my life. To Voy, familiar, asleep beside me, to his look, his smell, his way of getting out of bed, reluctantly, his house habits, his book habits. He changes like I change but is as constant in his own way as I must be in mine. His joys, sufferings and irritations define him as a living man, not honed by the warm sentiment of memory.

Voy didn't know what he was in for, stepping into such a huge role, having to deal with Mamushka, having to be dad to children bristling with the armour of their loyalty to their lost father, as they steadfastly guarded their own interiority, and also their remaining territory, their mother. But the two years in New Guinea built many bridges, some strong enough to weather storms. Mamushka lived, and suffered.

26

The festive season

It was, fortunately, before I met you, Olek, that Mamushka learned to drive the Humber Hawk. In a big effort to free yourself and encourage her independence , you had set about teaching her to drive. In fact, you had bought her a car and forced her to learn to drive, as Tatush, depressed about his dental exams, could not manage to master all the questions required for a driver's licence.

It took many months, but you were determined. Once, as you stood on the pavement shouting at Mamushka about how she should do a reverse park, she accelerated suddenly and the Humber Hawk mounted the pavement and nearly wiped you out. A lady standing near you made the sign of the cross, muttering, 'Jesus, Mary and Joseph' as you managed to leap nimbly onto a garden wall, directing your mother with shouts and hand signals until the Humber Hawk stalled and ground to a sudden halt, its bumper rammed against the wall.

By the time I met you Mamushka was a well-known figure, a diminutive driving presence, scarcely if at all visible behind the wheel of the Humber. You swore that she observed the road from under the curve of the top of the steering wheel and that this seemed to you to be enough. There were sightings of the Humber driving slowly on the wrong side of the road up the steep hill to St Vincent's Hospital, with no driver whatsoever. But we knew better. She was there, not behind, but beneath the steering wheel. And she was on her way to the hospital to visit Tatush who had suffered a heart attack four weeks after our meeting each other.

Anyway, you told me that I should have been happy that Mamushka was so independent, that she drove a car. Before that you had to drive your parents wherever they wished to go, like Grazyna's son.

So, I thought to myself, still being tactfully silent at that stage, things could have been even more intense?

I was never such a great driver myself, and my own family has always ridiculed my driving skills, so I enjoy having my own fun at Mamushka's expense, remembering her in her Humber Hawk. Pardon me, won't you!

I remember moments with you, highlighting pools of memory, illuminated cameos that don't retreat. The time when I was stuck in the snow in our van with the children, on London Bridge. I was so lost, out of my territory, off my terrain, out of my wits. The car was slipping and sliding wherever it wished to go. And I was helpless to prevent it. You miraculously appeared at the window, running beside the skating vehicle. You took the wheel and, familiar with the ice and snow, manoeuvred us all to safety. You came from nowhere. I never even asked how you knew I was there. But the winter was yours, you knew all its icy, snowy traps, and you knew we were stuck in one. Times like that, interludes, fix in my mind, like the incidents with Mamushka and the Humber.

And the other side of love, less fixed but still there, somewhere. Fights about trivia disappear pretty quickly from the forefront of memory that tends to favour the grand, but they can just about be retrieved, minus the fury that would have been their context. Your mother was an expert on stirring – her can contained a few issues, and she could rattle that can effectively for any one of them. Take, for instance, Christmas.

It was around July. We were driving the family to Sydney and had been having a lovely time. We had stopped for a picnic next to a creek, made a fire, and lay across the warm rocks listening to the children play around the creek. Listening as parents do with one ear open for any alteration in the shrill chatter that could signal the need for one of us to intervene, to rescue, to assist. Back on the road, we were going through Berrima, and I was contemplating another stop at the pub, so pleasant was the last stop. And then.

'What are we doing for Christmas, Katushka?'

My body reacted as though it had received an electric shock. Ah, I thought, there has been a phone call. I looked across at you, you had that stubborn, sly smile with the half-closed eyes – the smile that expects some sort of confrontation, and prepares itself.

'Well, I don't know,' I answered cagily. 'Going to Mum and Dad's, I suppose – or to Christina and Trev's.'

'Oh!' you said. 'And what about Mamushka?'

'Well she and Tatush will be invited too, of course,' I answered.

'But Mamushka says she has not been rung yet by your Mum!'

Here we go again, I thought. My antibodies were rising. I tried to keep my voice level. I knew this trap, it had happened before.

'It's months before Christmas – why should she be ringing about it now?'

'Well perhaps you could suggest to your mum to ring Mamushka now?'

I was starting to spurt. Despite all the controls that I had tried to set in motion. My voice was on the rise.

'Because it's unnecessary! Mum wouldn't know yet what they're doing! So why can't you suggest to your Mum that she stops stressing about Christmas and concentrates on something else, rather than making problems?'

The antibodies were circulating actively. A rash appeared around my neck – I could feel it, see it in the car mirror.

'Well you could just ring her, you know, Katush!'

'And what!' I screeched. 'Start pressuring poor Mum? I don't want to spread the hysteria – it's too early. And say what, anyway? They won't have even thought about Christmas! She would have made no plans yet herself!'

'So, Katush', you said, giving up on the whole thing, 'let's go some-where else – Tasmania, Bodalla – where there will be no issue!'

I was not letting you get away with it. My fury was not going to abate. 'But that's not the point! Can't you ever learn to manage her a bit?'

Christmas had stopped being a good word for me. I wished it could disappear from the calendar. The incident subsided. Then, in early December, you raised it again.

'Mamushka says your Mum rang her'.

'Yes, and?' I answered, relieved.

'And, you know, now she is upset, says she won't come.' You cupped your head in your hands. 'So perhaps we should jump across to Marrickville first, for a minute, before going to your parents?'

So that's it. I resigned myself bitterly, once again, to the fact that we would be not one minute late, nor ten minutes, but 110 minutes late to my family's Christmas lunch. We would be there, I reckoned, just as they were all about to open their presents, with their party hats on, the flames having died on the pudding, the pieces of silver having been discovered by the other children, as they listened for the clatter of our feet coming down the path to join Christmas Day. Mum would have saved slices of pudding with bits of silver in them for our children, and nobody really would have minded except me. We were always late, and this was known about us. Especially at Christmas, when it really mattered.

Because you were fighting for your parents, and I was fighting for mine, it seemed that neither of us could really give way. I guess our horns were just locked into place by our different backgrounds.

Christmas is a thoughtless, heartless, uncompromising festival, I thought, making trouble every year for people like us.

'And what are we doing for Christmas?' asked Voy, as his own mood was preparing to deteriorate along with his pessimistic contemplations on the upcoming Vigilia and how it would work out.

Here we go again.

Vigilia, or Christmas Eve, or the vigil of the birth of Christ, to Polish Catholics, means the nuclear family preparing traditional fish and soup dishes, fasting during their preparation, and ending the feast with the sharing of bread blessed by the priest. The bread resembles a sacred host and allows the partakers an intimate wish of wellbeing towards each other. Outside the fogged-up windowpanes, the evening star twinkles its signal in the wintry sky — when to begin the evening's festivities. It is both a solemn and joyful occasion. Having visited Voy's family home in Warsaw I can visualise exactly how Vigilia must look in that apartment. The family portraits would smile wistfully from old wooden and gilt frames, witnessing the frantic preparations taking place as the feast builds up along the table in the elegantly furnished room, its lace curtains delicately obscuring balconies and the shadowy canopies of the giant wintry maple trees in the street outside. The Christmas tree would twinkle with its little candles, family members would gather around the table, the feast would proceed as it has done for hundreds of years, and the evening would end with the family walking through the snow to Midnight Mass.

The whole thing would be a far cry from our table laid for twenty and expecting to have to cram twenty-eight or thirty-two, to eat the fish that has become fish and prawns, and drink not only chilled vodka but also chilled beer in blistering temperatures, the whole occasion ensuring absolutely no chance at all of intimacy in which to share the blessed bread, the *oplotek*, obtained from the Polish church.

In steamy, hot conditions since the time of Voy, I have been trying every year to prepare the traditional Polish Christmas feast, knowing that it would fall far short of his expectations. With the unpredictable amount of people pouring into our house, our Vigilia would be unrecognisable to a Pole brought up within a wintry and enclosed atmosphere. Voy still gets jumpy and moody about the impending travesty of Vigilia, and I get nervous about Voy's growing irritability and the children, now adults, react by secreting in their own special guests in their twos and threes. Voy sees the growing crowd around the table, throws off his apron and threatens to leave to find a family that has a real Vigilia.

But he doesn't leave. He stays and we battle our way to the first star. We have had many Vigilias together. None of them has gone at all smoothly. Olek, who liked Vigilia but was never brought up within its strict guidelines, invited anyone who would like to come. Since then, friends still ring.

'Are you having your Vigilia this year? Can we come?'

'Of course!' I say, and conceal the growing guest list from Voy, the chief cook. He always makes too much food anyway, and I don't want him getting any more stressed than he is. Better to keep the numbers to myself. It's my job to decorate the table, lay the places and light the candles. So I squeeze in as many seats and settings as I can unreasonably cram, and the evening starts to build. With the help of the chilled vodka, the candlelight, the feast itself and the amount of effort and suffering put into it, the celebration gains its spirited momentum in the steamy summer evening.

As for me, I have long since surrendered any Christmas traditions I may have nourished from my own childhood. Glazed ham and roast turkey are consigned to memory, as are Christmas puddings full of money, delicious brandy butter, and presents in pillowslips to be found in the morning after Father Christmas had finished his drunken rounds of the chimneys and consumed all the brandy left for him.

Vigilia and its emotional ripple effect exhausts me so much that, come Christmas morning, I have never once managed to prepare our own culturally dictated feast, let alone organise the pillowslips. Nobody gets presents. And as for the turkey, ham and pudding, I depend entirely on my mother or my sister, should we manage to survive our chaos and arrive at one of their homes.

27

1985 – losing Mamushka

Nadya was just eighteen when her Babcia died on the day of Yom Kippur. The Day of Atonement.

When Mamushka died, people said she was released from her great sadness, and free at last to join her beloved husband and son. I was also released from Mamushka and freed from her unreasonable demands and criticisms, or that is how I thought it would be.

But instead of freedom I was left with a growing sense of emptiness and disbelief. Because I actually missed Mamushka. I missed her emotional pressure, the telephone calls I had been obliged to make from the time of betrothal. I missed her kitchen, her loud complaints. And I realised it was futile to regret my rather tight-fisted and narrow-minded attitudes towards her all those years I did have her, because she was gone.

Could it have been different? I wondered, as I sorted through her effects. Probably not.

Her unattended flat was full of treasures of a kind. Glass and porcelain trophies won at bridge, the old cookery book, *Kuchnia Polska*. It was a sunny day when we went there, to her apartment in Vaucluse. But the atmosphere was sad and dull, lacking the sense of anticipation of high drama and the smell of food, which always accompanied visits to Mamushka.

Nadya tried on Mamushka's mink jacket, but no longer felt the thrill she used to feel when she had paraded in it as a child. Mamushka had collapsed two years after the war was over – a delayed reaction to the traumas endured for her family and the loss of her sibling, her niece and her parents – and the mink was Tatush's extravagant gift to her, to cheer her up, to restore her feeling of being a lively young woman, the woman he had married.

I found in her shelves the Polish beauty manual, *Badz Zawsze Piekne, Be Always Beautiful*. Mamushka liked to remain young and beautiful, and she had many tricks she advocated vigorously, trying some of them on me when I could relax enough to become her guinea pig.

'Before the winkles come you must do this!' she had warned me, smothering my face in strawberries and cottage cheese at the same time as reading incomprehensibly from *Badz Zawsze Piekne*. It was very important, she explained, not to allow one's face to become creased in the first place. As her daughter-in-law, to remain looking young was my obligation. Especially in front of Grazyna.

There was also a massage machine, an electrified strap that if you leant into it would vibrate your bum or legs or whatever part needed to be trimmed or firmed up. And a sun lamp, to give the healthy, glowing look within a few seconds. Mamushka and Tatush always sported an even tan and were rather trim. We took both items to try them on ourselves.

Mamushka's expensive fifties bedroom suite, with its flashing winged side-mirrors, posed a problem. I had always despised that furniture, but now, why was I so reluctant to dispose of it?

There were a few unmarked photographs of Olek as a boy with close-cropped hair, holding the handlebars of an old-fashioned looking bike. Olek as a student in Poland, serious, with thick, wavy poetic hair, and on the deck of the *Fairsea* en route to Australia. Olek in Sydney on the cliffs at Bondi, the sea and sky stretching out cheerfully behind him as he gripped the ground of his new country and looked meaningfully into the camera lens. Cameos from a rather extraordinary life. Now that they're all gone, only I know how extraordinary. There were many photographs of Olek and his family with Mamushka, carefully posed, and a little keyhole shape where the face had been cut out. Why?

'Its because she didn't like her nose,' explained Nadya, who had been privy to all of Mamushka's closest anxieties and worries.

Slowly, as I stared around me at her abandoned ambience, I became heavy with sentimental memories of one of the last of the old-style Jewish mothers-in-law. I knew that part of my life and struggle was over, and I felt real sorrow that I had not coped better with her. I had never really wanted to understand her real motivations, yet now suddenly I did. Too late.

She had outlived her son by seven years. She came and stayed, she suffered, she went back to Sydney and she suffered. Nadya had been hesitant to go and stay with her Babcia – it was not just a *ponchki*-fest any more. Tatush had died before Olek, sending Mamushka into terrible fits of sorrow and loneliness. They had been through vicissitudes together. But all sorrows had melted down to nothing when compared to the sorrow of losing her only son.

Mamushka had felt no compunction whatsoever in attempting to relieve her own suffering by sharing her burden with Nadya. Nadya had eventually reacted by refusing to ever be alone with her. She would only go to Mamushka's house with the boys, or with Suzka, who also had a Jewish grandmother, or Sofie who had a Polish grandmother, another tricky customer. The three girls endlessly discussed the attributes of their respective grandmothers, and Mamushka always came out trumps because she was the one with the strongest accent and by far the most unreasonable. She was the real item, and the others – Suzka's grandmother, Baba, who had no accent at all, and Sofie's Babcia who had an accent but could be reasonable and was neither noisy nor embarrassing, came last and second last.

And me? I had tried to compete with her, to defend myself against her implacable advances. I had, in fact, wasted her, by trying pointlessly to counter her possessiveness, to beat back her powerful emotions. To reason with her.

'Acch! The English! So logic! SO *fuls!*'

'Mamushka, I am not English!'

Here I was, always getting myself tangled up, trying to defend myself against being 'English' with all its connotations of cool falseness and logic, which of course are seen as the reverse side of soulful. The great Slav soul.

'Bugger that!' I had thought, uselessly. 'So why do I try to use logic on her then?' And despite the fact that she had alternately harassed and chided the children for their lack of intimate contact with her, they could not stop crying. For a sense of loss is rarely moderated by reason.

Except for four-year-old Rafal, who just stared at the others, as they were engaged in their crying.

'Babcia is dead, Raf,' they explained.

'Who shot her?' he asked, looking deeply shocked that after all his shooting games, a real person that we knew, our Babcia, had been shot dead. The crying turned to laughter, and then back to tears again.

Barely had I dried my tears than the will reminded me again of her capricious nature. For she had left Nadya the lion's share of her estate; to the boys, a fraction. Nadya, having promised integrity and generosity to Olek, immediately decided that it should be shared equally. So whatever the outcome, I had three teenage children, Mamushka's grandchildren, who overnight and unprepared could wield enough money to follow their immediate whim without any need to consult me. She has completely outwitted me! I thought. And I was right.

I grabbed what I could of the money and against their worse judgement, I bought a house for them, and then waited, aghast, as they discussed their travel plans and what they were going to do with the bit leftover. For your children were good half-Jewish children who were not going to study medicine or law. Not yet, anyway. Because they had the world waiting at their feet.

Not only that, they were armed with the dictums instilled by you and expanded according to their own imaginations. In vain I pleaded with them to study first, travel later. Voy too, he tried. If you had been here perhaps you would have put your foot down. But they did not see that as something you would have done. You had become, in their minds, the spirit of adventure, daring them to go and follow your muse.

They started putting their plans together.

28

Voy's portrait

I'm painting Voy's portrait. He's sitting in the courtyard, holding a book, with an intense look in his eyes. Talk to me, Kot! Don't just *kurva* paint me! One arm is thrown back, over the chair. It was these forearms that I may have noticed first, beneath the rolled-up sleeves of the flannel shirt.

They were strong arms, I thought at the time, worthy of admiration. Perhaps something in me needed such arms to hold us all together. So there may have been some logic in that particular chemistry. Now he holds his ground, for me, for my portrait, so I'm scrutinising his way of being, and thinking of our beginnings together.

He moved into our lives without too much training for child-raising, just a few quickly destroyed preconceptions. The carefree backpacker – serious, intelligent, very European in his manners and sensibilities, always in control of his life. And then, thrown into our family, he was as far from control as he could be. He was anxious to do the best he could as a sudden father, having been seduced by me from his purposeful plans into full-time domesticity. He has dealt with children whose instincts were on red alert against usurpers of their father's position, and has won their affection. He has honoured their memory of you, and encouraged them to keep it alive. Well, I think, he has definitely rolled up those sleeves and involved himself in the scrum of their lives rather than take the easy path and just stand back.

Here he sits now, under my scrutiny, his life revealing layers of itself through my daubs of paint. An engineer in Poland, anthropology was always his passion and that's what he has become, an anthropologist. It suits him, he looks the part.

In Papua New Guinea, where we all went for his fieldwork, he was comfortable amid extreme discomfort. The two years in New Guinea where we braved the elements together under Voy's protection made us a proper family again, with Pidgin as our new common language.

When I was there I understood why you had been so mad about the place, and it was then that I became convinced that you went there following the magic of your childhood in the forest, the real bush, perhaps to listen for the call of your pet bird? To rediscover a band of people living in the forest, depending on each other for survival? With you I guess that search may have been a great hunger, a childhood longing never satisfying itself.

The sound of the bush descended at night. It always made you silent as you listened, remembering. And it was around the campfires when the children were asleep in the tent that you recounted your stories.

I told Voy the story of your Uncle Leon, Mamushka's brother, as he sat for his portrait. I told him the bits I knew, and asked him to explain to me the rest, the Eastern European part of the war, to put the childhood fragments as I had heard them into a context I could understand, to fit it in with history as it is known. Voy was a post-war child, born in 1947, but being Polish, he knows all the ins and outs of the war that ravaged his country, and he often helps me with the gaps. I feel momentarily enlightened, then I forget it again. I get confused about all the alliances, the armies roaming around, fighting first for one side then for another, I keep forgetting which army fought against what enemy, how long sieges went for. There was, for instance, General Vlasov who led an army of 20 000 against his own Russian forces, fighting for the German General von Paulus against Stalin's troops. Why had I never heard of him? Voy finds it hard to believe my ignorance. But I push past his amazement and keep asking him, hoping it will become clear in a solid sort of a way. My historical education had been brief and simplistic. The English, led of course by Churchill, and their Allies were the Goodies; Germans and their Allies were the Baddies. And then the Russians formed the forbidding Iron Curtain and became the real Baddies. And then the Germans were OK again, being on the right side of the Curtain. That the Russians changed sides, split, plotted and dissembled all the way through the war was new to me.

I liked Uncle Leon from what I knew, from his face in the family photograph, the face that did not know what suffering and loss lay in front of him as he stood with his parents and siblings. I had heard more recently about him from reports of my parents who visited and stayed with him in Israel, hoping for a visit to Christian Jerusalem that never happened because of Leon's fear of incident and injury for his visitors.

The family had all broken up, your grandparents were dead, Paula had gone to America, and so had Fanya, and Jakob. The tubby and sweet Uncle Mishka had been killed too, or else he had died of a heart attack. Etya and your little cousin Boubou were dead, you found out, after your mother stood for a long time in offices set up after the war to assist people in tracking down their families. And Uncle Leon had joined Anders' Army, taking his baby daughter with him on the horse. Together they went on this long journey, and he ended up in Palestine.

'What was Anders' Army? Where did it come from? Where did it go to? Who did it fight? How could a baby girl join an army with her father?'

Now I was asking Voy, as he sat there, having his portrait painted. You must have told me many times about the Anders' Army logistics, and all I had remembered was that Uncle Leon carried his baby daughter Ruth on a horse, traveling with Anders' Army.

'Tell me about Anders' Army!'

'But Kot, I've told you!'

'So sorry – I've forgotten! Please tell me again!'

'Well Kot, in '41 Churchill signed an agreement with Stalin against Germany. And this is why.

'Germany had been an ally of Russia from August '39 when they both signed the Molotov–Ribbentrop Pact. Then the Germans suddenly turned on Russia, and advanced into her territory at the rate of one hundred kilometres per day. Russians and mainly Stalin were shocked, stunned, unprepared, Germany was their ally!

'So now those Russians were really thrown back to the Allies. What to do? Well, the Poles were invited by Churchill, who negotiated with Sikorski, the Prime Minister-in-exile in the United Kingdom, to form the army that would fight alongside the Red Army against invading Germans. That was one plan. Stalin, panicking, furious and cheated by Hitler, agreed to release all Poles and Jews in captivity in Russian-controlled territories to expand this army quickly to defend Russian territory against the Germans. General Anders was sent from England where he had fled from Poland as part of the Polish Government in Exile, and he was briefed to marshal the new army in locations as far as Kazakhstan to fight back the Germans.'

'Kazakhstan? Why that far?' I asked.

'Well, because of its geographical location. Look on the map! See where they came from – many from Siberia – and where they went! For months they stayed there, being equipped and fed and trained by the British, preparing. There gathered troops and their families, Poles, Jews, anybody who had papers claiming Polish citizenship at the time of arrest, anybody who could get hold of papers, they were provided free travel to the camp in Kazakhstan and other bases. They arrived from all over, ragged, neglected, a lot of them released from years in Russian prisons, many starved by war in their area, and many families. They needed to be revived, rehabilitated. They straggled in over eight or nine months. Many died, there was a big mortality rate, but finally there were over half a million men including families.

'Then Sikorski and the Poles, always distrustful of Russians, broke from the Russians. Anders' Army was still being financed and equipped by the British, but Russian cooperation was repudiated. It eventually got moving, families and all, and went down through Persia to the Middle East. Some went to India. It took years. Many stayed in the newly formed Israel including, no doubt, Olek's Uncle Leon and his small daughter.'

'Is that because Katyn had been discovered, that the Poles broke off with the Russians?' I asked Voy. Olek had told me about how once, in '39 or 40, Polish officers in the town, including Tatush, who had enlisted in the Polish army as an officer, were all rounded up for something or other, by the Germans. Or was it by the Russians? I don't remember that detail, but I remember him telling me that those who had done the rounding up went along the lines of the Polish men in a big hall, asking them to show their hands. They felt the hands, they felt whether the skin was the soft hand of an officer or the course skin of a working man. Those with soft hands were sent off in a train to Katyn. The soft-skinned Tatush attempted and succeeded in confusing those inspecting by speaking Russian to them, which he had learned from Mamushka and her family. His Russian language saved him, he was put into a room with priests and other soft-handed men of ambiguous occupation, who were then released. Yes, I had heard of Katyn, I had heard this story about Tatush, and of course I remembered it. But Voy was refreshing me, in his usual thorough way.

'Katyn, Kot, was mass execution by the Russians of all the rank of the Polish army. Their graves were not discovered until '43, a year after Anders' Army had left. The Poles and Russians had split, and the Katyn discovery made sure that the split was sustained.

The skeletons were found by Germans in graves, each man shot in the back of the head, Russian style, hands tied with rope, Russian style. You know what they say, that they had been getting rid of those educated ones, preparing Poland for the communist takeover. Still, even after Katyn was discovered Churchill was trying to persuade Sikorski not to alienate Stalin, not to make Katyn an issue. He wanted it kept quiet. Russians were pushing Germans back, they were very important to the Allies and he did not want to risk upsetting Stalin. Churchill did not want to jeopardise the alliance with the Soviets. And of course Sikorski could not agree with Churchill's demands to keep quiet – he wanted the Katyn massacre properly investigated, and the alliance broken. And then Sikorski was killed in the plane crash, a British military plane that crashed after taking off from Gibraltar. Many Poles still blame Churchill, saying it was sabotage, that Churchill needed Sikorski out of the way.'

'What!' I gasped, stopping with my brushes in mid-air. 'Churchill? Impossible! You mean Winston?'

'Yes, Kot, your Winston. And why impossible? War is like that – small sacrifices for big movements. A Polish Prime Minister-in-exile may have seemed not so important to Churchill, who was desperate to defeat Germans. But I don't really go with that theory so much anyway, that Sikorski was got rid of.'

I didn't want to disturb my concentration on the portrait. Winston Churchill won the war for all of us, did he not? With his famous speech about the beaches, raising the flagging morale? That's what we learned at school, anyway. The Anders' Army story filled in a gap for me and I wanted to know more, so I rested my brushes for a moment. We could deal with the Churchill–Sikorski thing later, when I would be more free to fight. I may, I realised, even have to give a bit here, rethink our war hero now, put him in a more critical light.

The subject suited Voy, so I continued. Small chit-chat is never enough for Voy, he likes real conversations. I painted that in too, in the intensity of his eyes, his non-restful posture. In my portrait he sits in a jungle but, I thought to myself, it's really the jungle of his own past in war-darkened Poland – and now, our complex family life which must have represented to him a sort of jungle.

Voy wanted to talk about Nadya. Is it right, he asked, that she wants to do acting? Why not university? Why was she so rebellious?

How, I thought, could I know anything? I was a mere mother. Nadya was always a challenge, for anyone, even for you, when she was little. Always seeding revolutions with her young brothers as loyal followers. Revolutions against, mainly, going to bed. And then, after New Guinea, against even sleeping in a house. How many times had we dragged her and her bedding back in from the outside? She liked to gang up against normal procedures. A fiery creative spirit, scornful of logical processes, she believed in the beauty of impulse. You remember her with plaits coiled sweetly round her head. After your death she cut off her hair, refused to do her schoolwork. She became a tomboy. She wanted to sleep in a cupboard, or even outside, under the stars. She said she felt closer to you if she could see the stars, that you would visit her in her sleep. But as sure as I would adjust myself to one phase another would present itself. Perhaps it was a sort of mourning ritual, combined with the pains of growing up, and exacerbated by her own strong will. Perhaps it was just growing up. Who could ever be sure?

I thought that the wounds of loss had healed. There were periods of real serenity, but that could shatter, almost without warning. Your ways were still familiar to your children, even as they grew. They knew your patterns, your excesses, they were comfortable with you, they knew your body, your habits, your ways of doing everything you did – you were theirs. Voy's ways, until they became patterned in, provoked resistance. But it happened, at first in patches, until they grew to trust the integrity of his body and warmed to his ways.

29

Search for a forest

When Voy and I decided to get married I went to Poland, taking the children with me. We met Voy's cheerful family, who live in a gracious old apartment in Warsaw, and on the Sunday visit to the cemetery plot we placed our flowers on the graves of his parents, and the children were distracted by squirrels running around in the great trees shading the cemetery.

Poland was still languishing behind the Iron Curtain, so Voy could not come lest he never be allowed out again. Kasia, Voy's sister, took us south, to the mountains. We slept in wooden shelters and went on treks, returning in the evening to our bunks exhausted and exhilarated by the different terrain, the intense green of the mountain fields and slopes, the black of the pine forests, and the white summer sky above the craggy ridges. There were walkers and mountain climbers, mountain folk dressed in their traditional oufits, some selling small cone-shaped cheeses, others selling rough grey woollen jumpers. We bought cheeses, and we bought jumpers. There were even nuns hiking, hitching up their habits to negotiate the slope. The Tatra Mountains seemed to be full of dedicated mountain-lovers. And we fell in love, too.

We went a couple more times to Poland, without Voy. We saw the Pope, and immersed ourselves in the frenzy of his visit. The sound of singing in the air grew to a great chorus as Poles lining the city in their millions welcomed back that most famous mountain man of them all, Papa Wojtyła, with rousing verses of the old mountain song, 'Goraly'. Then the communist regime toppled, the Berlin Wall toppled, and Voy was able to go back to Poland.

It was Voy's Poland that I was visiting – Warsaw, Krakow, Zakopane. There were trams, buses, cafes, churches. Before the communist regime fell, the shops were unimpressive, without window displays or any sense of the need to market the merchandise. It was like going back in time. But still none of it seemed to have anything to do with the Poland imprinted on my mind by your stories, the Olek files. And as I wandered around Warsaw, savouring the history written into every bullet hole, every shrine to the dead, as I gazed at bunches of field flowers placed next to walls where somebody's son once crumpled at the end of a German gun blast, my mind inevitably wandered east, to that other Poland, the Poland in the back of my mind, the Poland of your childhood. I had to go there, to follow your past that had become mine too, and had infected your childrens' destinies.

Post-communist Poland struggled into the present. Cafes started to buzz, shops cleaned their front windows to display sparkling merchandise. Arcades appeared. The old Poland was retreating further into time. I had to go and explore the east before it too became part of the western tourist route.

So finally, on my last trip, I left Warsaw and went east looking for a forest –looking for that very forest, your childhood playground, your dream territory, that wartime hide-out you could never forget.

Voy saw me off at Centralny, the main Warsaw station. He was instructing me like a mother sending her child to school by itself the first time. He checked my bundle of tickets, explaining each one to me, so I would make the right connections and hear the appropriate instruction from the guard. I was going to his friend Edek who has a weekender there near that great forest, the Białowieza.

The journey was long, the train slow, and when I changed trains to an old train it got slower. The terrain changed, the towns changed, we passed Nurzec, Nowy Nurzec, Dobrowoda, Czerenica . . . did these places feature at all in your cosmology or were we still too far west? The train slowed, stopped, letting people off in fields, copses, unmanned sidings. Each time the train stopped the guard, who most of the time sat near me, would don his cap and adopt an official expression, blowing his whistle and waving the train on. I peered at the little towns, which seemed trapped in time, wondering at their nature, looking for clues. Their shuttered eyes were lowered discreetly against an outside world no longer to be trusted. They told me nothing, but I knew from their expression that we were moving east.

The train rocked me into a trance.

Could this be the same river that flowed under the bridges where you crouched, hidden with the partisan men, trembling finger at the detonator, eyes so serious? Could these clumps of birch trees be the beginning of the great forests that concealed your group? There were no other forests on my map, and only one river. We must have been approaching.

Eventually I arrived in Hajnowka. Edek greeted me. Tall and distinguished, he stood apart from the locals. With him were Konstanty and Ignacy, his little boys. It was night and we went to a restaurant, a cosy haven of bustling hospitality in the unfriendly dreariness of the town where I disembarked. I ordered a vodka, sipping it, no longer throwing it down as I had at my first Slav party, but letting it slowly warm my being in order to fortify my spirit for the venture into the forest of dreams and memory, the haunt of your childhood.

The next morning at the back of Edek's house I saw the forest across the fields and past the windmill – the edge of my journey. I was sure it was *the* forest, the beginning of the great Białowieza, the oldest forest, extending deep over the Polish border into Belorus, which was also Poland before the war.

I put on a warm jacket and packed drinks before entering the forest – I didn't want to depend on the sap from birch trees. And because I was approaching the territory of another little boy I took Edek's boys – they shall be my guides, I reckoned, and their presence could alert me to clues.

The black limbs of the trees intertwined gracefully like lace across the sky, whitened by the eastern sun. The lace was tinged with a light green quite foreign to my palette, which is keyed into the grey-green and khaki tones of the Australian eucalypt. This green was a pure green, the first colour of spring, a green that is full of yellow. It looked tender, optimistic, perhaps trusting the warmer weather not to dash its jaunty beginnings.

The ground was carpeted with white daisies. Did you ever mention them? Was this the same forest? Or had I just forgotten about the daisies? I gasped at the forest's innocent beauty, and peered into the layers that stretched like stage scenery, retreating into the misty distance, leaving me a mere outsider, secretly looking for a trail of a certain childhood in the thickening mists of the forest, and of time.

The chatter of the boys kept me in the present. They climbed on top of mossy fallen tree-trunks playing King of the Castle, and looked for treasures such as sticks and leaves, chattering to each other the whole time. That's what boys do. They create their world, wherever they are.

Could it be, I wondered, that I am really looking past these contemporary boys for a small, scrawny urchin with a soldier's jacket, *valenki*, a shorn head and intense gaze, with a wing-splinted bird called Skoczek perched on his shoulder? And would my eyes meet his, if I met him on one of these tracks? Would he know about me? Or would he run from me back into his past, into my dream, the forest closing around him, and leaving me standing there, a stranger, a tourist woman, older than his whole present and future?

Was I looking for a dugout? Those I had seen did not look even remotely habitable. The thought of living in such a hole during winter ejected itself from my mind. It did not seem possible to live in these dugouts for a day, let alone two years. There was something wrong. In my mind, in remembered descriptions, the dugouts were cosy, inviting and homely, with beds and candles.

And was I looking at the river, the Narewka, the only river in the forest? Rivers go on, but not the people who have drunk from them, crossed them, played on their banks. Or detonated their bridges. Konstanty and Ignacy were squatting at the edge of the little river. They cast their sticks into the rapid stream, and raced to the bridge to watch whose stick won, whose got stuck and stranded. Then they started again. And again. They were unaware of time, of the beauty around them, of the chilly wind whipping their cheeks red, and of me standing watching them.

The sounds of the forest intermingled like a symphony, the wind in the canopies, the birds, the gurgle of the river – voices of the forest that had borne witness to so much life, so much destruction, and in particular, to two years of one childhood that was burning brightly in my imagination, the life of little Olek.

The hunting parties of Tsars charged through these forests in troikas, their furs flying and bells ringing. The great bisons and major roebucks were marshalled for the convenience of the royal huntsmen who, trained as nobility, and therefore not expected to exercise patience or cunning, could take pot shots from a clearing and be sure of hitting their prey. When Goering first saw this forest, he declared it should be preserved as his personal hunting ground. The British timber companies raided it to furnish their noble dwellings with oak floors and doors. Partisans hid in it, German soldiers searched through its undergrowth for their human prey. And yet the forest prevails, calmly changing its seasons, seemingly oblivious to the history enshrined in its depths.

The voices in the trees may have whispered of this past and that past – great royal hunting parties, sleds, bells, picnics, cruel slaughter of its animals, the ravaging of the great oaks. But to me they whispered of one little boy with a bird on his shoulder who loved his forest home more loyally than any princeling loved his palace.

PART FOUR

———

It was 1989, and we were living in Sydney. Voy was completing his PhD thesis, and I was painting and exhibiting – and running an extended and unruly household with what I hoped was calm nonchalance. Mamushka's bequest had scattered plans for orthodox study. Nadya, Jan and Mishka all wanted to leave for somewhere else, to see the other worlds out there across the seas. All three left, and our large, chaotic household became small and quiet.

30

Journey to the truth

One by one our children left, as each finished school. Nadya to Poland to work with a singing theatre group, and then Paris to study acting, which we all believed to be her calling. Jan took off for South America with no particular plan in mind. His stated idea for travel was 'to discover the Truth'. We disagreed on many issues, and his journey to discover the Truth was one of them. It made little sense to me and gave me no confidence in his return. In vain I plied him with logic – his mind was made up. And, if Jan ever made it, Mishka was going to join both of them in Paris, with me, when he left school, and then the two boys were plotting to cross the Sahara. This was going to be, I hoped, the last leg of Jan's journey – but unfortunately, the first leg of Mishka's.

Perhaps Voy was their inspiration for this Sahara crossing. He had crossed the Sahara, and they knew his stories well. They knew your stories too, but being partisans in the White Russian forest was hardly an option open to them, so I think they settled just as happily for the Voy template. Voy's own African travel heroics blended conveniently with your stories of survival, and my pleadings for their staying and studying were not even under consideration.

Perhaps it was their eternal search for you that fuelled their quest for a rich spiritual life, compelling them to explore other realities.

Or perhaps these voyages of discovery were a natural rite of passage, as Voy suggested – the need to exit from boyhood in the most dramatic way possible.

I flew with Mishka to Paris, taking the eight-year-old Rafal who had to say his goodbyes to the big brothers who had been his companions since birth.

Nadya and Jan met us and took us to their abode in Avenue Félix Faure. They seemed to be comfortably ensconced in a beautiful old apartment in this rather good part of Paris. I was thrilled. Past the boulangerie we went, past the smelly fish shop, past the delicious aroma of the patisserie next door, past bossy mothers ordering well-dressed children along the footpath, and then we entered their building by pressing a combination of numbers on a side panel. Wonderful!

My room had been nicely prepared – bed made, flowers on the bedside table, and a candle. My window looked out onto converging grey Paris rooftops. My cup of happiness was full.

But when the light failed to turn on in the evening and the gas didn't work, and the glamour of the apartment with its marble fireplaces and gilt-edged mirrors revealed no bathroom whatsoever, just a toilet, basin and bidet, we sat around by candlelight and the truth came out.

They were squatting. My euphoria evaporated, and was replaced by fear and apprehension, mixed with embarrassment. My kids in a squat? But much worse. Me in a squat! This is not something I had contemplated, not at all. What, I thought, would these very respectable French neighbours think? Me, at my age? Squatting? And anyway, what about bathing?

'Oh, Mum,' they told me, 'it's cool! Don't worry! Jean-Luc is in charge of this apartment – he is our friend! And you can wash in the bidet. You wash in bits and pieces ...'

It was fine, they said, the place was abandoned, they had cleaned it, someone had died there and his girlfriend had died too and there were no owners and the neighbours were grateful to have such nice young people living there and keeping the place clean and their friend Jean-Luc who lived upstairs had put them in there, and there was nothing at all to worry about. Nothing.

Worry I did – of course I worried – and very soon, after being frightened by a uniformed chimney sweep talking to me in rapid French on the stairs, and thinking he must be a gendarme after me, I moved with Rafal into the small Hotel Best Western next door, which had a bathroom. After observing one night from the window of the Best Western a van full of actual gendarmes, not just chimney sweeps dressed like gendarmes, entering the next door building, and knowing that the suspicious neighbours exhausted by my children's loud noise at night, by their Australian way of clattering up the stairs, knocking skateboards, banging doors, would have called these gendarmes, I eventually managed, by dint of cunning persuasion alternating with threats, to persuade the squatters to move.

At first Jan refused, citing the Parisian Squatters Rights Law – which the gendarmes had kindly explained to them – that squatters could not be evicted from November to March, the winter months. I alone was aware of the consequences of the full fury of the neighbours.

Having won the Battle of the Paris Squat, all of us together, including four of their schoolmates who had arrived on the scene, moved to the Three Ducks Hostel up the road, in order to advance the preparations for the Sahara.

The boys planned to drive from Paris to Lagos, along with the four school friends who had decided, against the will of their parents, to join the expedition.

Nadya, Rafal and I travelled with the Sahara party as far as Chartres, where we visited Bernadette, our au pair from our days in London. They drove away without a backward glance, leaving us waiting, from that moment, for the next news, for any news, from where we could only guess. I watched them go, strangely calm and numbly accepting my fate, bound as it was so inextricably with theirs. Was this going to be my last sighting of the two sons of yours and mine and now Voy, who had occupied my thoughts, fired my pride, stirred my anxiety, for so many years of my life? I pushed such thoughts from my mind, but they kept returning to plague me as I stood there in the early morning in the fading wake of their exhaust fumes which polluted the crisp winter air.

I committed them to your care, Olek, I prayed and hoped that you were taking notice. What else could I do? It made me feel a scrap better, not to be the sole one responsible. And anyway, you can cross borders and see into other countries.

The noise and chaos in the hostel was replaced by a set of empty, stripped bunks in a large bunk room. Overcome by our loss, we quit the place and went to find a cosy little family hotel. Rafal and I were going home in three days. We stayed within grey walls and counted the days and finally the hours until we had to say our goodbyes, leaving Nadya on the underground metro station, her face more forlorn under the weird shadows of the fluorescent lighting.

From his seat in the train Rafal watched anxiously, seeing her face getting smaller and then being snapped away by the train turning into the tunnel. This parting was different, it seemed more callous, because we were the ones leaving, and she had nobody of her own. No gang, no friend, no family. Only the acting school she was not comfortable with anyway. It was a mime school, she was a voice. She was no good, she said, at being a piece of chewing gum or a sheet of crumpling paper.

Now she was left, I was sure, with nobody to talk to. Where was she going to live? The boys had been exuberant to be driving south, and we had been sad. Now nobody was exuberant. Nadya looked lost, huddled in her large winter coat, with the strange European fog wrapping round her, reclaiming its grandchild. I hoped she would find that friend she thought she might have made, that she might share a place with, and that the friend would become the replacement family she craved.

Olek, I really asked you then to come with the fog and warm it up, like a secret blanket, protecting your creature. For sure you would have preferred me not to leave her. But she's twenty-one – I kept saying that to myself. But so small, young-looking. And she wants to study there. Or does she? Was Mamushka's bequest going to turn out to be a curse? Had it sown the seeds of a disaster which had already started its inexorable course? We had to go, we had a plane to catch. Why is life so brutal?

It was the last day of autumn in Sydney. Still and clear, and tinged with the sense of loss that comes with the sense of something good that's passing forever. The winter lurked behind the pink city horizon, and I was actively savouring the taste of the drawn-out early evening.

Nadya was still in Paris studying at L'école Jacques Lecoq. I was thankful she had not also gone to the Sahara. Abby, Ruth, Chris and his girlfriend Anne had gone with Jan and Mishka. Our household was small. Me, Voy, Rafal and a couple of lodgers. To me it seemed suddenly quiet.

Three weeks, Mum, they had said. Ring you when we get to Lagos.

It was already ages since they had left. I had made a rare decision to free myself from my months-long telephone vigil.

'Over to you, Olek,' I thought, as a way of tricking myself into some sort of security. You're closer to them from where you watch than I am here in Australia, so far from everywhere.

'Waiting for news from the Sahara,' I thought, 'is a thankless business, and I cannot tell a soul that this is how I spend my time.' It would seem pointless to most people to have let them go in the first place, let alone then having to stay permanently within reach of a telephone, forever scanning the map lying open on the table beside the phone, hoping it would tell me something, which square centimetre they were in, if they were alive.

Warding off anxious calls from the other parents had become one of my newly acquired skills. My boys were the instigators, their travelling companions the innocent victims of the Mamushka bequest. And nobody, none of us, had a single clue where they were. Voy was against my oft-suggested Foreign Affairs intervention scheme, saying that this would defeat the purpose of their journey, that the journey was, after all, a journey of self-discovery, which would not be helped by a search party sent by an anxious mother at great cost to the taxpayer.

The fate of my children was of greater importance than saving the taxpayer. I was simply consumed with anxiety about them and the fates that awaited them in the great, fearful Sahara Desert.

Where, I wonder, would you have stood on this? Would you have sided with Voy, supposing that such a situation could be possible, where you could have been in consultation with him about their fates? Would you have taken the idealist's stance that young men had to brave adversity and encounter bizarre adventures in search of themselves? Or would you have been the anxious, protective parent, prepared to call in any force to return your sons? I was trying to see your possible point of view, via Voy, so as not to just be the mother smotherer.

Whatever your view, I know you would have been waiting for news and out of your mind with anxiety. Do you remember when you decided that Jan and Mishka should go hitchhiking with Voy and his friend Marek, when they were visiting travellers, and I was talked into agreeing? Jan was nine. Mishka was seven.

'Let them get hitchhiking out of their system!' you had said. 'They will be safe with these guys! I trust them! Boys need adventures!'

Was that your childhood asserting itself in yet another situation? That boys need real-life adventures? I doubted that.

But you won, and off they went, little fellows that they were, each accompanied by his respective guardian. Jan, confident and equipped, with Marek, and Mishka, small and incredibly trusting, with Voy. Different hitches to different places. Nadya was jealous.

'But I'm the oldest!'

'But you are girl!' Olek said, and I agreed wholeheartedly, resisting the urges of feminism to make girls equal. To let the two of them go was crazy. To let three of them go would have been too much.

For two days I waited for phone calls while you rang me constantly from your surgery, your voice tempered with jovial casualness so as not to alert me to your own anxiety.

Voy rang the next day, and every day after that. Mishka, he said, was fine. I heard nothing from Marek for five days. We read that there were floods up north. But is that where they were?

Was I crazy, asked my mother?

'Have you both gone mad, to let your two little boys go off with complete strangers?'

I could not tell Mum that this was your idea – she would have written you off as a lunatic. So I shouldered part of the blame. Mamushka, of course, never knew that they had left.

So, did your theory that boys need adventures also lead in some way to the fact that your young sons were now lost in the shifting sands of the Sahara, with their school friends Abby and Ruth? The other two in the expedition, Chris and Anne, had bailed at Tamanrasset and gone to Italy, to Rome, to luxuriate with Chris's parents at the Australian ambassadorial residence. Lucky parents, I thought. We had heard that much from the expedition.

I ate my fears. I restrained myself. Boys need adventures, I told myself, and mothers just have to cope. Well, I was left with no other option.

That particular day in autumn I had decided that they were resting up in some small town, dining on dates and coconuts, and riding on camels. I went out, happy with my fantasy solution. I went shopping and enjoyed the expedition. I heard the phone ringing as I came back up the lane towards home again, and I nervously fumbled for the key. The phone kept on ringing, and I knew what it was. It had a special sound to it.

'Is Mrs Kathy Golski there?'

The call had been preceded by a little pip signalling that it was from far away. But I had known that it was my call, even while I was putting my key in the door. Should I tell him it was me, and risk hearing what was to follow? I had no choice.

'This is Pat O'Brien here, Mrs Golski, from the Australian Consul, Lagos.'

My body shrank, and then started to seize. This caller was a Bad News caller. I hesitated, collecting myself for the next bit. Bad News calls have been programmed into my being since the call notifying me of your death.

'It's about your son, Mrs Golski.'

I knew it was about my son, or my sons, both of them. His voice was careful, considerate, even kind.

'Oh, yes, you can tell me,' I said.

'It's your son, Jan. He's in prison. In Lagos.'

Relief flooded me. Only in prison. Not injury, not death. Prison in Lagos.

'Phew!'

But, hang on a minute. Thoughts of Amnesty International suddenly crowded my mind, tempering my initial relief that he was not dead.

Prisons in third world countries. Drugs, scapegoats, bars, chains. Torture? Oh my God, please no. AIDS? Amnesty International? Uggh! My brain had gone numb. My teeth had started their spontaneous chattering.

'Oh, I see.'

I was happy for the news to stop right there.

'Well, Mrs Golski,' he continued, his pleasant voice careful and measured, trying to keep me calm.

'He was arrested in Northern Nigeria while crossing the border, with no passport or money. It seems that your son deliberately burned his passport, claiming it was for religious reasons.'

'Oh!' I said, and relief started to grow again, cautiously.

It wasn't drugs. He hadn't run over a Nigerian. He wasn't set up. He had simply burned his passport. He would not be hanged for that. Even in Nigeria. But what were the religious reasons? Should I worry about that? The relief started to shrivel. Panic was expanding.

My intuition had already informed me that Pat O'Brien would have assessed the situation, distancing himself from it sufficiently by noting that this problem traveller had a foreign name and was therefore not really one of his own, a grandson of Anzac, behaving after all in this most un-Australian way. Would a true Australian ever burn his passport? Perhaps this erratic and emotional behaviour might even disqualify him from the sort of diplomatic protection that would be the basic right of any true descendant. I made an instant decision to go for the common bond. I had to establish myself as being the consul's kinswoman, despite my foreign name. This could help. Same background, same Catholic school tradition, well, with a name like O'Brien, he would have been Christian Brothers, whereas I had the nuns. But basically, nothing at all suspicious, except that I had erred in turning my back on my reliable countrymen by marrying a foreigner. An erratic and over-emotional Continental. That's what we called them, Continentals. They used too much Brylcream and practised flirtatious tricks on women.

And now I was reaping the wind that I had sown. Those unreliable Continental genes. It's true, they're your genes that sent the boys careering off into the Sahara. And perhaps Voy and his Sahara stories? Not my genes, I don't think so. All my instincts as a mother would have said 'No' to that.

Anyway, now I had to also distance myself from such genes. So speaking to Pat O'Brien, I put on my most Catholic High School accent, easily abandoning all Slavic veneer, as I mouthed the next question.

'And what can you do for him? Is he okay, Pat?'

I went for the Christian name, a bold move, calculated to bring me a step further into the soft underbelly of a common past.

'It seems, Mrs Golski,' he went on, ignoring my first-name, old-mates tactic, 'that your son, when he burned his passport, claiming it was for religious reasons, said that he was, in fact, a spiritual voyager, needing no earthly documents to cross man-made borders.'

'Oh, I see!'

But what did I see? My vision of my daredevil, hot-tempered, cognac-swilling, marijuana-loving son Jan in jail in a highly religious frame of mind was not something I could really see, let alone understand. He had been a bit wild, and very self-willed, but there had been others much worse against whom I could measure him and his excesses. And he had always been a great communicator.

'Did he mention the tarot pack?'

I was anxious to blame something tangible, for myself, if not for the consul. I had suspected all along that the tarot, read by Jan to an excessive degree in Paris, was influencing their direction. Was that the same tarot used by gypsies? I feared it was. Carmen, I remembered, had kept cutting tarot cards in her moves towards the tragic fate that overtook her. I wanted to leave gypsy premonitions, get them out of my life. They seemed to be stalking me again, this time in the Sahara.

'Er, he did offer to read my tarot when I visited him in the prison. I refused.'

A bubble of anger rose in my throat, as I imagined the pragmatic, practical Australian consul, dressed in clean tropical gear, well-fed, in control of his life, smoothly declining the kindly gesture of my poor Jan, a mere prisoner but his countryman, struggling to keep his dignity and sanity in some hell-hole African prison.

This vision of the consul refusing my son's noble offer suddenly outraged me. How dare he? What right did he have? Who pays the taxes to keep him there? No, but I had to keep the consul on my side. Careful, keep calm.

My mind flashed back to the last few weeks with Jan in Paris.

I had been helping the boys prepare for their foolhardy expedition, wishing all the time that they would call it off, and knowing they wouldn't. My role had been reduced to assisting them to at least prepare adequately, or rather, comply with my requests.

Insurance.

Spare tyres.

Proper registration for the two cars that they were busy purchasing.

I negotiated with clerks in offices for the different cartes that were a compulsory part of travelling in cars bought in France. Voy was offering advice from Australia.

'Tell them,' he cautioned, 'to take a bucket of vaseline for the windscreen in case of fierce sandstorms.' And a few spare tyres, tanks of extra fuel, tanks of extra water – the list went on. And they only had the two Peugeot 504s in which to cram themselves and all this gear supposedly necessary for their survival.

Who was paying? Mamushka, of course! If she had thought that they were going to use the money wisely to study medicine or law she would have turned in her grave. And spending it on their friends? That hard-earned money that she had scratched together over two countries, and assiduously saved, being carelessly spent on a crossing of the great, fearful Sahara Desert.

I was cursing my lack of influence and authority. They eventually did buy six new tyres and chained them to the roof racks, a huge tin of grease to cover the windscreens during dust storms, containers for extra petrol and the water tanks. And last, but not at all least in importance, they took the pack of tarot cards. Their direction-finders.

Jan had painted the cards himself. I thought they were beautiful, tiny works of art, painted in Jan's meticulous, naive iconographic style. I tried to tell him this, emphasising his talent, to show him a possible direction other than the one he was on. To Jan, any artistic talent represented in his little paintings was peripheral to the magical power contained in the ancient imagery of the cards.

To him, and to all of them, the cards were so much more than art. They carried the secret knowledge of gypsies through the ages, they knew the future, they could read the fates of those for whom they were being read.

Were they going to replace a map? I asked, not really wanting to know the answer. I was becoming uncomfortably aware of the relative importance of the cards in their scheme of things.

'Perhaps, if the map does not help us. What is a map, anyway, Mum, when you cross the Sahara? There are no maps for sand, Mum!'

The more faith they had in the cards, the less secure I felt about them. Now this reasonable man, my type, to a certain extent, my age, a man with whom I shared common ground, was telling me that my son was in prison, a fate no doubt predicted by the cards. Jan had offered to read the tarot for the consul. It would have been a generous offer, an attempt to put him, the ragged prisoner, on some sort of equal footing with the consul. I imagined the consul's words.

'No I don't need my tarot read!'

But he also said that Jan had read the tarots of the prison guards and that they, the guards, were impressed.

'Oh my God – he is crazy, isn't he!' I gasped over the phone.

'No', said the consul, 'not crazy. Not at all. He looks very well, considering what he's been through. He's been in five different prisons. But he is thin, and he appears to be extremely religious.'

'Religious! Him! Which religion?'

'It seems that he has taken on a mixture of all of them'.

So is this, I wondered, his discovery of truth?

'Well, so, what can we do?' I asked the consul.

'I can get him out of prison for you, but what then? He has no passport. He burnt it. You realise he has committed an offence in doing that? Destruction of Government Property. It is an offence.'

I was trying to conjure up a picture of Jan burning his passport. Had he made a ritual bonfire, and sacrificed the document? My mind was presenting me with several scenarios, none of them

Photo: P. McCulloch

Photo: Niki Zubrzycki

TOP Raf joins the *Moka* dance, Papua New Guinea, 1994.
BOTTOM Rafal – mood and music displaces football stripes, 1999.

TOP Indian wedding, Delhi. Voy and Kot bless the bride and groom, Jan and Bem, 1992.
BOTTOM Nadya and Franco on the Moto Guzzi, 2006.

ABOVE Kathy in her Sussex Street studio with rainforest paintings, 1993.

TOP Nadya and her gypsy musicians: Rafal Dabrowski, Sam Golding,
Daniel Weltlinger, John Maddox, 2007.
BOTTOM Two imps after a pancake binge – Indigo and Tally, Sydney, 1999.

Photo: Rafal Dabrowski

Photo: Bem le Hunte

TOP Raiden, Indigo and Abraham, 2008.
BOTTOM Kashi, Tally and Rishi go camping, 2008.

ABOVE Voy and Kot, Canberra, 2007.

ABOVE Watercolour landscape by Kathy, 1995.
OVERLEAF Kathy's portrait of Nadya, 1988.

reassuring. What were the others doing while he was burning it? Were they standing round chanting? Were they egging him on? And who suggested it? Was it the tarot? The Hanged Man? The Queen of Cups?

Which of the gods over the Sahara were working their strange power on my boys there, those mere pilgrims in time, small specks of life in the great merciless desert?

'I don't have to charge him with the offence, but I should send him home. I think he has travelled enough, anyway – and, of course, he has no passport.'

'Please send him home, please! I shall organise a ticket for him, and, thank you very very much, Pat and also, if you don't mind, try to keep an eye on Mishka and the two girls.'

'Well, Mrs Golski, I can make a suggestion, but beyond that —'

'Yes, I know. But please make the suggestion sound more like a command, if you understand what I mean.'

The consul had spoken to Mishka. He was refusing to even consider coming home. He wanted, he said, to traverse the Sahara himself now, from south to north, hitching, with only his camera for company. He wanted to take photographs whenever he wanted without being restricted by the needs of others. That's what he said.

The phone call ended. And I was left, sitting there by the silent phone. Voy came in.

'Any news?'

'Jan's coming home next week. Isn't that exciting?'

For Voy, I realised, this news may not have represented such high excitement. He had planned his week, and it did not include the return of a young, triumphant Sahara hero. And I had not even filled him in on the rest of the story. I did not know how to tell it, or perhaps I did not want to tell it for fear that the telling of it would make it cold hard fact, whereas it still had a chance of remaining as a figment of my imagination, if I just kept it to myself.

I was distracted during dinner. And in bed I lay awake wishing the night would pass quickly, but each time I peeped out the window at the welcoming light of dawn I realised it was still only the streetlight, and dawn was hours away. I thought of Jan in his humble, filthy cell. I wanted to tell you and I tried, but that did not work for me. You didn't come to me in any dreams. I was desperate to share my fears, but I didn't dare tell Voy in case he compounded them with his own pessimistic predictions. And then the weight of the whole thing would have sunk me.

I touched Voy's warm shoulder, for reassurance, and he grabbed my fingers in his sleep and gently kissed them, putting them firmly back again, not to wake him further. His tender gesture made me collapse into silent sobs. I wanted to wake him, to tell him everything, and at the same time I couldn't. I didn't want to make the thing more real for me, by throwing it into the ring of discussion. I didn't want to hear him say, 'You see what a mess you've created, with your method of child rearing?'

I only wanted reassuring words from him. I knew he had the power to soothe me, but I had to pick the right moment. Like when he had had a good night's sleep and breakfast as well. In my undistracted company.

I lay there, staring at the black shadow of his back in the dark, longing to be part of his comfortable oblivion, and feeling hopelessly alone. The night stretched before me, as my mind and body became a trembling shell filled with raging fear.

I tried desperately to contain it, and to overcome the sorrows that crowded my head and pushed at my eyelids. Olek, are you there with Jan, in prison? And why is he in this prison anyway? What legacy have you left him that you failed to warn me about? Did the gypsy also tell you that your oldest son would go to prison? And were you too afraid to tell me that during our campfire talks? Or reluctant to admit the old prediction to your consciousness as you watched your little boy, lying innocent and vulnerable, asleep in the tent? Who will ever know?

I tossed and turned, and then I started to wonder where Mishka was staying, in Lagos. Was he with the two girls, Abby and Ruth? I wished the consul would invite them to his house and make them a nice roast dinner and insist that they have a bath, and sleep in beds, and get Jan out of prison and make him have a wash too, and just play daddy to them. And then tell Mishka that he was commanded to come home.

Did he have children, this consul who had entered the soft linings of my life in such a strange way? A nice, warm family who would welcome pleasant young visitors from Australia in such an outpost?

My sudden fantasy made me feel better. My own traditional culinary background cradled me as I became fixated on the idea of a roast dinner for my children, the Sunday roast, where family members should gather and relax together. Their vegetarianism did not present itself as an obstacle. I was going to make it all happen.

I left my bed of insomnia, and went downstairs to the phone. I had decided to ring Pat O'Brien and try him with my suggestion. He, the consul, had to become a mate, and our night was his day, after all.

His secretary told me he was out, visiting the prison.

Prison! A thud crushed my fantasy, the roast was forgotten, as I suddenly felt the prison doors clang shut on my hope. I waited for the morning, for Voy to come down the stairs. I had to tell him. Everything. But where to start?

31

Nadya in Paris

It was eleven in the morning. I was in the studio with my apron on, paint on my hands. Jan had been released from prison and was about to embark on his homeward journey. I was called to the phone.

'This is a reverse-charge call from Nadya in Paris. Will you take the call and accept the charges?'

'Of course!'

I accepted all those charges because I always did and I was automatically aware that at this time of the Sydney morning it was 3 a.m. in Paris and therefore the phone call must be some sort of emergency. I braced myself. At least it was she who was calling, and not somebody else calling about what remained of her or something like that.

'Mum!'

'Nadya? Everything OK?'

'Not really, Mum, I've been bitten by a monkey!'

It sounded like she was in Africa too. With the boys? Or had a casual job at the zoo. But I responded calmly.

'A monkey? Really?'

'Well he just bit me on the leg, right up the thigh and it's really sore and swollen.'

'Nadya, can't you be normal? You're in Paris, the operator said!'

'Look, he just leapt at me and bit me – I only smiled at him and said hi!'

My mind tried to encompass the scenario. Nadya, monkey, Paris. And crazed monkey bites friendly foreigner. So what, my mind shouts, about rabies?

'Mum, just a minute. Hang on a minute. Sorry, Mum – got to go. I don't like the looks of those types outside the phone box!'

The phone went dead. And I was left, sitting at the desk, dazed, head in hands. The girls in the office above my studio where I took the call came over to me.

'What's wrong, Kath?'

My eyes, fixed still on the receiver, were focusing on the scene that had just frozen my day. Paris, 3 a.m. Mist swirling round the yellow sulphur street lamps. A young woman, looking even younger, standing in a callbox. Probably wearing that pink mohair jumper I bought her. Small, with a monkey bite somewhere on her person, right up her thigh. Perhaps already brewing rabies?

Suspicious-looking predators outside the booth, more than one of them, hats disguising their evil faces, coat collars turned up, patrolling the streets, on the point of catching a naive, tender, defenceless Australian victim. My mind was on my next conversation.

'Hello, is that Interpol? Err oui monsieur, ma errm fille, qui errm habite er, in, je ne sais pas exactement l'addresse . . .'

I realised I had no idea where Nadya lived. Somewhere in Châtelet, but perhaps she was not ringing from there. Interpol would not be interested unless I could give them exact details and was certain of an abduction. Anyway, their interest in my small predicament would be minimal.

One has to be able to rely on some authority in times of emergency. But who was this authority? Was my only option to wait and sweat until I heard some news? I might never hear. And then what?

'But Kath, perhaps she hasn't been abducted. She probably just went home to her flat, or met some friends. You know, Kath, kids

189

unload on you, then they feel better and off they go. And then you're the last thing on their minds. She'll ring in a few days when she needs to talk again. Go back down and do your work.'

Work is often distracting. I couldn't ring anyone anyway, for fear of blocking up the line. I had to keep it clear, for a call that may never come. I returned to my canvas, painting with heavy strokes, a workout, saving bits of light in the dark landscape, bits of light in which my daughter could hide, be warm, seek refuge. It made me feel a bit better.

Should I tell Voy? He could help – perhaps he could soothe me, or distract me. He could say, 'Kot don't worry. It's not wartime!'

He often had to remind me of this fact, when I felt insecure, when I asked him, 'Where are they? Where do you think they could be?'

On the other hand, what if he chose instead to concentrate not on Nadya's extremely dangerous situation but the ever-touchy subject of the phone bill, swelling with reverse-charge calls from Paris?

'And Kot, tell me, how are we paying for these phone calls?'

Yes, Voy could have made it a lot worse. I decided not to tell him. And he wouldn't get to see the phone bill anyway. He wasn't curious about such household expenses unless he happened to open the mail and see them and then he would really start to make trouble and lay blame. I would make sure that I got to the mail first. I would have loved to be able to confide. I had to tell someone. I rang my sister. She's always practical and reassuring. She was not even amazed that Nadya had been bitten by a monkey in Paris.

'She must go to the hospital and have a check-up for AIDS and rabies!' she said.

'Oh yes, of course! But where the hell do I find her? Supposing that she's still alive!'

'Oh my god, Kathy – you and your daughter! Look, don't worry about her. she'll be okay – just make sure she gets that AIDS and rabies test, when she does ring. Look, Nadya is a very resourceful girl. Even if she's been abducted, she'll have her abductors in the palm of her hand by now. They'll drive her home, buy her supper, find her hot-water bottle for her. We're talking about Nadya! Just go back to your work, and stop panicking.'

Prussian blue, Payne's grey – I was mixing them into the shadows, giving the darks their own mysterious life. And then I found the beginnings of a cold dawn light. I pushed some red into the cold glimmer. That was better. It was the beginnings of daytime now in Paris. The terror of the night was over. Light would be seeping into all the little dark nooks. Perhaps even a watery sunlight. Sometimes, I thought, it must be sunny over there. It was four days after the phone call, but I was still fighting my way out of the fear it had induced. She's probably having her morning coffee, oblivious to my unreasonable fears. That's what I told myself. I was winning at last.

The phone again. It was for me. I was being called to the phone.

'This is a reverse-charge call from Nadya in Paris. Will you accept the charges and take the call?'

I gulped at the phone, my heart pounding with relief. It was four days later, and she was still alive.

'Of course I will accept and pay the charges!' I was more compelled than ever to accept, delighted to pay the charges.

'Mum! You there? Mu-um have you heard from the boys? I'm worried about them!'

Nadya always seeks reassurance from me no matter what situation she may have got herself into or however the evidence presents itself. I usually provide this reassurance, despite my own misgivings.

'Mum, I'm so worried about them!'

'So what's happened to you now? With your monkey bite? And with those suspicious types outside the callbox, Nadya? I've been so worried about you!'

'What're you talking about, Mum? What types? Who? What callbox?'

'Oh forget it, how's your monkey bite? The boys are fine, Jan's on the way home, Mishka is okay. Have you had an AIDS test for your monkey bite?'

'Don't worry about the monkey bite, yes I went to the hospital and they gave me this and that test, I'm okay, but Mum, I've had the worst time at school I really don't want to be there any more!'

'Nadya, what is going on?'

'Mum I promise you, that acting school, honestly Mum, it's the biggest wank, all those Americans there, turning themselves into bits of chewing gum at Monsieur Lecoq's instruction. Mum, they're wankers! Look, it's really not me! I can't even turn myself into an aeroplane, they all just laugh —'

'For god's sake Nadya, you are making no sense. Please stick it out – you must stay with it! Get that bit of paper!'

'Mum, I don't actually need a bit of paper. I can turn myself into a bit of paper – that's the one thing I have learned at Lecoq's. You don't understand! I'm really a singer – I know it from my soul, Mum. I've met all these musicians and I sing with them in a basement. I've found my voice again, after all these months at mime school. And, well, there's this really lovely sax player, Didier, and we really get on well together. He looks a bit like Jan, with curls, and he's quite serious – sort of spiritual – and, well, he's Algerian. I sing with him. That acting school is soulless! I've been there long enough. And I'm not allowed to even open my mouth. It's destroying me!'

I could feel my blood rising. First of all had she, or had she not, given up acting school? What did she mean, all those wankers? Wankers compared with whom? And this Didier? What on earth was going on there? So spiritual indeed. A spiritual Algerian. Bit of a worry? Have to ask Voy about that one. No getting out of that. Probably a fanatic. Isn't it enough that Jan's gone into some strange religion? How much should one mother have to bear?

'Well, anyway, Mum, Didier says that I should only sing for the praise of Allah, and not in public. Do you think he could be right? What do you think?'

Why is she even asking me? What does she expect me to say? Control yourself, Kot, calm your anger against Allah, against Didier, and most of all against your daughter. Why does she do nothing the normal way? Try to sort out a rational rescue plan for her. Send her a ticket home. Olek, help me. It's your daughter, she's so young, small, alone in Paris, so impressionable – it's your fault she's there, and she's so yours! I'm here, so you please be there! But I keep pleading, trying to invoke logic.

'Nadya, please Nadya, first of all, go back to school, and get that one thing finished. Please do that. I don't know Didier. But I'm sure you don't have to sing for Allah. I mean you're half-Catholic, half-Jewish – isn't that enough without bringing Allah into it as a third party? And what about money? Will Allah pay you? If you're a singer you have to get paid. Look, please, where are those nice normal friends you had, Megumi and Nils? They sounded such fun. Please, no fanatics, for god's sake! Islam is, look, believe me, possibly the last thing you need now. Anyway, have you looked up that Charlotte woman? She would help you sort things out a bit.'

'Oh, her, Mum, she's a snob. You know when I went to see her and took some friends from acting school, she really made us feel unwelcome – just because one of the guys had green hair. She made us feel like real street trash. I'm never going there again.'

Well that's that, I knew nobody else in Paris. What could I do? That Nadya could have met some Muslim Svengali while in acting school – and endure a monkey bite – was the last thing that would have occurred to me.

I was beginning to wish that I was still waiting for the call. It seemed that now there were simply a whole range of new problems, quite apart from the impending return of the much-changed Jan, and the fact that Mishka appeared to have gone missing altogether. Nadya was quitting the school she had gone to so much trouble to get into, after I had done all that running around getting references about her talent and her character. And now she was turning Sufi

Muslim because she'd fallen for a sax player. I sent her a ticket home, and until she arrived, I begged.

'Olek – take control, will you?'

32

The vegetarian and the carnivore

We were walking up Oxford Street, me and Voy. I had tucked myself under his armpit to ward off the cold. Just as we were passing the blank shopfront of the TAB I blurted out the whole story about Jan. I told him everything. About the burning of the passport, the prison, the reading of the tarot, the consul, and that Jan would probably be arriving home almost immediately in some very unusual state. I imagined Voy's response before he made it. For a year now we had had control of the house, free of jostling, ego-driven teenagers and their friends. We had lived our own life. And it was about to come to a sudden, jolting end. But Voy laughed.

'He must, you know, be going through his spiritual phase. You know, Kot, every young man should have this period of suffering, like me in my ashram period. For two months I just stood on my head in a cold ashram in India and only ate once a day. I had lost my mother. After she died my heart turned to wood. Don't forget, Jan lost his father. This is a harsh loss for him still, very harsh. He has to go through many agonies. But he will be all right. Don't worry about him.'

My surprise at his response, and the relief that burst through my veins, almost melted my body. I was cured. My two fears were dismissed – the fear of Jan's strangeness, coupled with my nervousness about Voy's response, turned to exhilaration in expectation of the homecoming.

My dear Olek, my latest communication to you. Your first-born son returned as a mystic, with dreadlocks. It was Voy who spotted him first at the arrival lounge. He who had left looking so smart, with a new backpack, the latest T-shirt, was now walking slowly, his socked feet in thongs, his clothes ragged. He was holding all of his worldly possessions in a cardboard box, balanced on outstretched arms. Spread across his face was a beatific smile, which he turned on us calmly.

'There's your son, Kot,' Voy said, and I went and stood in front of him, to be sure. I looked, and he looked at me, my changed son. But he was there, still there, somewhat disguised, but there. We rushed to each other, ambushed by joy rather than thoughts, and then he disengaged and delivered his prepared homecoming words to me and Voy.

'Hello, Mum and Voy. I have come home to look after you, to pay you back for all those years when you looked after me.'

If he had pulled a gun on me I could not have been more amazed. I was transfixed with relief at seeing him, but taken with complete surprise at his new humility, the way he looked and spoke, so humbly dressed. But my tears of happiness joined the ocean of arrival-lounge tears. The tears of joy, of having waited and worried and been rewarded. There was definitely moisture in his eyes too, but his old exuberance remained corseted behind his newly drawn angelic smile. His story? What was it all about? Did it even matter, now that he was back home?

It took a long time to leak out, but he did want to talk about it, and it came in bits. He had been in nine prisons. What? The consul had told me five. One of them had been a cage in the bush. He had survived intact, meting out the densely compacted essence of his strong boy's soul to endure the external hardship, ever-present danger and loss of freedom that had become his lot.

The Nigerian police had not worked him out, the spiritual voyager with no passport, no documents and no earthly possessions. They had no blueprint for Jan. And he had no tools, weapons or allies to defend him other than his innate boyish wisdom, which resonated more profoundly than the signals given by his loincloth, his dreadlocks and his main possession, a pack of tarot cards.

And you. Were you at his side, silently being there, an eternal presence, hovering and protective of your first-born son?

Jan was ensconced in his old room, which, having been occupied by various guests, had been hastily cleared out by me, the contents stuffed under different beds. He remained in a meditative state, cleaning the kitchen, reorganising the cupboards and cooking our meals – crusty, decorated vegetarian pies that excluded the stimulants of onion and garlic – which he started to prepare for us early in the morning, rising around 5.30 a.m. to begin his kitchen routines.

It was very strange for me, and no use at all comparing him to you. You could only, I think, boil rice, and that you only learned to do before going to New Guinea. This careful and long-winded preparation would have been far from your area of kitchen competence.

Within days Voy grew tired of the bland pumpkin pies. Jan's attempts to convert us to his style of cuisine were doomed to failure. I was fine with those bland pies, if eating them meant peace in the household. Voy was not fine with them. He wanted to cook his own pies and add whatever he felt like to enhance their flavour.

Danger signs were in the air. You couldn't enter the kitchen with the intention of cooking, only to eat or talk. Cooking for myself would have been a lot easier than being cooked for by two men in competition with each other, but this option was no longer available. I used to do the cooking, it always seemed natural. But now Jan was trying to outdo Voy, as I had tried to compete with Mamushka.

I would have happily starved for peace. But far from starving, I was being served two sets of meals. Intensely aware of the tension developing between Voy and Jan over the food preparation issue, I started to lose my appetite altogether. My only wish was to avert an open battle between my son the vegetarian and my husband the carnivore, both of them dedicated to preparing their respective cuisines, neither of them willing to give an inch.

The kitchen was becoming a place of nail-biting tension, with the two of them likely to arrive together at the stove at any given time. But then just as the great eruption was imminent, between the meat eater and the meat spurner, Nadya returned home from Paris on the rescue-plan ticket I had sent her. A noisy dispersal of tension. To my immense relief Jan forgot all about cooking. Voy resumed his comfortable dominance of the kitchen, preparing a welcome feast that actually included his version of a vegetarian dish. And Nadya set about the business of stirring Jan out of his new and unfamiliar holy state.

'What are you doing with those ridiculous dreadlocks? . . . Jan, can you stop meditating and say hello to me?'

'Mum, this is ridiculous, someone has to organise him a girl-friend . . . . Mum, it's urgent!'

33

Lost in the Sahara

Four weeks had passed since Jan had come home, and Abby and Ruth had returned, but I had heard nothing from Mishka. Once again, I never left the phone unattended in case of a cry for help, in case I had to act quickly. It was getting on Voy's nerves, my obsession with staying near the phone. For sure you would be just as nervous as me, asking me every ten minutes, 'Has he rung?' But you must have a better view than me from where you watch and wait.

I dreamt one night that you found him. He was lying, sick and alone in the sand. You picked him up, helped him walk, put him on a truck, you had your arm around his thin shoulders. You sent him back to the land of the living.

And then I woke up and I knew all over again that Mishka had not been found.

Once again I stared at the map, as if a clue would appear to me from the Sahara. The map just kept on looking huge and hostile, the Sahara region covering three of its creases. I folded it back. I had no idea where he was. I returned to the sink. Dishes always await my attention, a sort of primitive therapy often available in a house with enthusiastic male cooks.

When I asked Jan if he thought Mishka was okay, he lectured me on young men and the need for them to be given challenges and independence. I could get no further than that with Jan.

'But what about the season? Isn't it the season of the wind and windstorms? Isn't it difficult to get lifts during this season?'

'Yes, Mum, you may be right. It's just about impossible, but Mishka knows what he's doing – stop worrying about him. He is eighteen, you have to respect that.'

'But how do I know that he's even alive?'

'You don't have to know, because it's irrelevant. Mum, why don't you learn to meditate?'

'Would that help find Mishka?'

'It would help you to understand!'

'Understand what?'

I was convinced that Jan was hiding something from me, and was trying to prepare me to accept something unacceptable. I didn't want to explore that area of my frightened mind.

Another four weeks and still nothing.

So, full of suspicions, I went to a house in Jersey Road where a colourful photograph of the Maharishi of Beatles fame presided over the sotto voce patter of the meditation teacher. I was given my mantra and I learned to meditate, to commit my outrageous fears to a spot in my head where they spilled slowly out and drifted into the atmosphere, like coloured smoke.

And then I got the call. It was preceded by the long-distance pips.

It was a haw-haw English voice.

'It's Mrs Baggott here. I'm ringing from Arlit, Agadez. Your son Mishka is here staying with me.'

My eyes searched the unfolded map in front of me for Arlit. I found it, and my heart slowed. Mishka still had miles to go – he was not even halfway. Disappointment curdled in my veins like a poison. But for the moment anyway, he was alive. My son was with Mrs Baggott. Mrs Baggott was the saviour.

'Oh, you lovely woman,' I stammered gratefully. 'Can I speak to him?'

'He is a very sweet boy,' she said, reassuringly.

'But how is he?' I waited, thanking Mrs Baggott over and over for protecting Mishka, for being the Good Samaritan.

And then I heard his voice, steady, recognisable, but weak, despite his attempts to project strength.

'Mishka, you're sick.'

'How do you know I'm sick?'

'Well you sound sick. And I haven't heard from you, and I knew that something was wrong. Have you still got malaria?'

'How come you know I've been sick?'

He was persisting in this vein. Perhaps his mind was slowing down? I was getting nervous again. I asked him about his illness and about Mrs Baggott.

'I've been staying here with Mrs Baggott for six weeks. She's really nice to me. She's married to an Arab, she's English. I haven't been strong enough to hitch any further, but she's been getting a doctor to come and see me. He gives me quinine. I feel a bit better.'

And how did you find this saint, Mrs Baggott?

'I was lying there, in the sand. I had lost all my strength, and thought I would die. And then I heard a voice, calling me back to life. It was the truck driver, I had been travelling in his truck. He came looking for me. I got up and went, I was weak and he helped me. I got onto the truck again. And the next stop was Arlit, that's where I still am, someone brought me to Mrs Baggott. She's been really good too – she's so good.'

So, I thought that might have been you, in my dream, speaking as the truck driver, helping your son back to the land of the living, not claiming him for yourself to keep you company. Did you decide that he had to keep on living? Were you not tempted to keep him? I didn't tell Mishka. Of course I didn't. I didn't want to confuse him, I wanted him to keep coming home to us. So I tried, like an air traffic controller communicating with an injured plane, to talk him back to base, suggesting manoeuvres.

'You are insured, you know Mishka. You can actually get out of there on a plane and it is covered by the insurance – you can even get all the way home. Let me organise it for you!'

But the injured party was resistant. Too injured to cooperate.

'Mum, I don't think you realise how remote this place is. It's difficult enough to get a truck passing through. Nothing comes here – no planes, nothing! I'm waiting for a truck to go to Tamanrasset, but I'm still too weak to sit on top of the canvas roof, which is where you have to sit if you're hitching.'

In vain I tried to persuade him to use the travel insurance that guaranteed to provide a plane to evacuate the injured and sick to a reputable clinic. I told him all of that. He was unimpressed.

'Mum, you're dreaming. There are no planes around here. Don't worry, I'll ring you from Tamanrasset. I may need more money when I get there because I'm just about out. Can you send some money to Tamanrasset?'

And that was it. Mrs Baggott eventually rang to say that they had put him on a truck. The next town, Tamanrasset, several thousand kilometres away. Get some money sent there. That is something I can do. And he's got malaria, but he's having quinine. A bit old-fashioned perhaps? I'll ring doctor–brother David and check. But what then? I can send money, but I can't send the latest drugs. Just more waiting to hear news.

Day after day in the sandy corrugated desert lies poor Mishka, sick, shivering with fever, and clinging to a vibrating canvas truck-awning. You had malaria once – you were such an expert on it after New

Guinea. Now he has it, that little boy you left behind. Look after him, Olek, watch over him as he bumps across the thousands of kilometres of lonely hostile desert, help him again to survive, send him back to me. I'm here on the end of the phone. That's all I can do. Be on the end of the phone.

Voy agreed with Jan – I was still not allowed to call in the external forces. This was Mishka's 'journey'. I was just a poor ignorant woman who wanted her son back safe and sound or unsound, in whatever condition he survived, if indeed he did survive.

I waited another three weeks, and then another call came. My heart jumped a little when I heard the pips. It was Mrs Baggott. My heart fluttered and sank. Why Mrs Baggott again? Had she heard some news?

'Mishka,' she said, 'was turned back from the Algerian border because he has an English passport and they're having a blitz against the English.'

So he had returned to Mrs Baggott, ready once again to be nursed and cared for in the smooth, cool order of her household. Why had he not rung me? Why was I the last to hear the news that I craved, from second to second? She told me that they had put him on another truck and this time he was carrying only his Australian passport and she wanted to post me his English passport. And he was somewhere out there, once again in the cruel desert, in the season of the fierce winds, returning to Tamanrasset.

So if Jan could burn his Australian passport for religious reasons, then why couldn't Mishka burn or bury his offending English document for practical reasons? Why did he have to go all the way back, thousands of bumpy kilometres, only to return again, perched like a sick monkey on the canvas top of the speeding truck?

Did he feel so sick that he just wanted to lie in Mrs Baggott's nurturing environment for a few weeks longer, making no decisions, being fed and looked after? Was his power of decision-making impaired by illness and weakness?

Mrs Baggott knew no answers, she just told me that Mishka was a lovely boy, so polite, and that now he was on his way home again. But how far from home?

We had to wait another three months for further news. It was not until Mishka arrived in Morocco that I got the phone call. I nearly jumped out of my skin for joy and relief.

From Morocco he went to Germany, where he collapsed. We got a call at 2 a.m., and Voy sprang into action. Voy rang Bibi, his old girlfriend who had been visiting our house at the time of your death, to ask her doctor husband Manfred to rescue Mishka from a railway station in Hamburg. Mishka could no longer move.

The German hospital cured him, and he continued his pilgrimage, to India, where he resided with a hermit in Rishikesh.

And then he arrived just as he had said he would, the day before Christmas. No phone call heralded his arrival, we just went to the airport with the faint hope that he would arrive on the ticket that had been booked for him a year before. And he did. Disguised somewhat, wearing a purple turban. But, yes, there was Mishka's face and smile, distinctive even beneath the turban. Our household was complete. I gave you a special and hurried thanks before rushing forward, arms out.

PART FIVE

———

The children returned and filled the house once again. Their lives and activities took over, pushing me and Voy back into a rather smaller space.

Nadya started her first band, a jazz band, which rehearsed in the living room where she also taught singing. She embarked on her first singing tour of the Pacific, managed by Mishka. In a moment of passion she married a charismatic chieftain from the Solomon Islands , but the marriage ended abruptly. Since then Franco, a creative Calabrian blacksmith and sculptor, has been the love of her life. He matches her fire as skilfully as he operates his forge furnace. And her music has become gypsy.

Jan fell in love with Bem, and finally found his Truth. Together they set up an in-house writing and design business. They made plans to marry in India, the home of Bem's Indian mother, so we travelled en masse to India to proudly partake in their exotic Indian wedding. Soon they welcomed a son, Tally, and then a few years later another, Rishi. The writing–design business inspired other creativities. Bem began writing novels and Jan became an architect. He designed a treehouse deep in his beloved Bodalla bush for their family.

Mishka, a photographer, also repaired many Valiants outside our house, bringing parts and tools in and out of the house and irritating me and infuriating the neighbours. One Saturday at the market, the ingenious Rachel and her mercurial two-year-old daughter Indigo stole his attention, and two boys later, we had another marriage in the family and a coffee business.

And Rafal became a part of Nadya's gypsy band, and studies film making.

34

Welcoming hearth

You struggled, at least your parents struggled, to get another house-hold going after the war. Every family needs somewhere to go back to at night, to cook, to sleep, to wake up, to hide from the world. The household you and I built together was more than that – I wanted it to be the most welcoming place I could ever imagine, I wanted it to exude ambience. And with Voy the ambience continued. There was more food cooked in our house, more messes cleaned up, and as the children grew up, more temporary lodgers, than anyone could imagine. There was laughter, there were arguments, doors slam-ming, tears, broken hearts, love counselling, making up – all in our courtyard.

And when Nadya became a musician there were also musicians. There was the African drummer who asked to stay for a week and was still there three months later, so deluded by his alcoholism and other excesses that he wanted to evict the family. He claimed that our house was not our house at all but his Temple. He called me 'Mum' and made a gracious exception for me, saying that I would be welcome to remain with him in his Temple.

One Saturday afternoon we watched aghast as Jan, with boyish determination and typical tactlessness, asked Mojojo to leave and to give back his key. And off the drummer strode, dreadlocks bouncing, taking with him the lingering scent of musk oil which had been the aura of his increasingly annoying presence.

Voy tolerated Mojojo because with Voy, the tradition of hospitality had to continue. But none of us were sorry to see him go and we were relieved to be rid of his Rastafarian ravings and the scent of his musk oil. Voy solemnly congratulated Jan on his brave incentive.

Before the war there was largesse in your mother's family home. The extended family gathered, there was always food and music, and people played instruments. Then there was the war, and it all crashed.

After the war there would have been so much need for the survivors to gather to soothe the scars and repair the badly damaged social fabric, to discuss endlessly, to argue in lowered voices about the new system of government, to grieve for the losses of relatives and of freedom and to celebrate small gains. Your mother would have always been there, preparing soup, *pirozhki,* bustling, laying the table, clearing the table, chattering, trying to reconstruct something that had been lost – the memory of which had created a strong habit and a longing.

You would have liked our new house in Sydney, its interior partly inspired by collections of our youth, partly by Voy's ideas and his possessions, and his amazing gift for creating a romantic garden in any space whatsoever. It houses – not without huge clashes – everybody's hobbies and incipient professions. It's a house with cosy corners and charm, a little verandah, hidden lofts and spaces, two fireplaces, a courtyard where we have transplanted the grapevines that were planted by your Italian patient, and which already display the gnarled twists of middle age.

Today things started off well. I thought to myself: today is the day when things will get finished. I saw that the sky outside the window of our loft looked bright and optimistic. Voy was already up, having planted a prickly kiss on my cheek, responding to the call of his triple-crescendo alarm clock. His work as a teacher of anthropology suddenly disappeared, with even the tenuous short-term contracts dwindling as funds from the universities for humanities such as anthropology dried up. He was miserable about it, trying not to be bitter, but turning himself to other things — native title, private clients. There was still a lot to do, just less space in which to operate.

'It's black times in a country,' he complained, 'when universities are able to sacrifice humanities, it reminds me of communist Poland, engineering, engineering and more engineering. Are so many people talented in business here that they need so many courses? Humanities keep us human, give thinkers something to think about, talkers something to talk about, writers something to write about, providing oxygen! So we can breathe! Without humanities there is nowhere to hide, nowhere to rest from reality, which can be too harsh.'

And then to add to his gloom we discovered rats in the house. Things were nibbled in the morning, bread left out was tunneled. There was a hole in the flour bag, flour sprinkled everywhere throughout the food cupboard.

'Don't worry!' I said to the swearing Voy as he complained that we must be the only *kurva* house in the area with a rat problem.

'I have caught the rat in the trap! He's already dead!'

'Ah, Kot. You are such optimist! Don't you know? Don't you know? There is no such thing as lonely rat?'

That's an old Polish saying. I've heard it before, it's typically Polish to look at the dark side. Voy goes straight for the dark side. If there is one bad thing, he will see a proliferation of its negative aspects. So, far from celebrating my skill in catching the dam rat, he was ruminating upon all the live relatives of the deceased rat that would, even as we spoke, be planning their conquest of our house and particularly the flour bag. This was Voy's current grouch. His life had just lost that major structure, the university day, and he was free to observe all the shortcomings of our household. And for sure, there was no such thing as a lonely problem!

Preparing courses, lectures, reading and marking essays, caring for students – all of this used to keep him on campus for long hours. Armies of rats could have passed through the house unobserved by him. And shortcomings would not have caught his attention. Straggles of yawning youngsters blinking their way into the midday sun, leaving their things everywhere, raiding the fridge, leaving and slamming the door till the house shook . . . they too would have gone unobserved by Voy.

When he was no longer there in his familiar office on campus to counsel, assist and discuss, a gaggle of his bereft students followed him to the house. When one of them was due to arrive the house was checked for vermin and other things that Voy considered unsuitable. Visitors, singing lessons, cooking and music – they all had to wait in the wings. Youngsters about to wake had to stay in bed. Oddments shoved under the stairs, Valiant car parts covered with a rug. Chairs positioned, fire stoked. The house could always present its serious face, especially when Voy had to make room for an extra chair in his overcrowded study.

35

Patch war diaries

It was six months since Voy had done any fieldwork. The current contract had ended, and for the time being he was here at home, with all his stuff, wrestling with his feelings about losing his university life and the burning desire to pursue his commitment to anthropology. An anthropologist loaded with knowledge, fieldwork experience and teaching skills, he had cubic metres of notes, journals, mind maps and books. And they all needed to be catalogued and organised. And they all needed space.

I always had the downstairs space, the living room, just inside the front door. That was my territory, shared territory – I would paint, or write, or chat with callers in. Voy was always upstairs in his study, or else at the university. It worked. Now, confined to the house, all his books and lecture notes, field maps and documents had returned. His Cancerian nature, his profession, and a natural passion for the written word all joined forces to cram his study with papers, books and grey metal filing systems.

Needing to expand, territorial gain was uppermost in Voy's mind. Seizing the two or three days while I was away in Melbourne, he made a bid for my space and, therefore, the social space. He ensconced himself in the living room. I entered, and he greeted me shiftily. He had lit the fire, his fire now of course, and I saw that he had installed himself on the couch, covering all the adjacent surfaces with newspapers and paper clippings. Printouts were draped over my paintings.

He had put on two pairs of glasses. He looked determined to stay there. He had taken his coffee cups there. He was not going upstairs to his room anymore, except to bring down more stuff. He stated that he would not answer the door. If I answered the door he told me he did not want any visitors, and especially any children. He asked me to please keep my voice down when answering the phone. In my absence, Voy had taken over.

Rage rose from the pit of my stomach, going right to my burning cheeks. I could feel my eyes darting around in my eyeballs. War clouds were brewing. If Nadya answered the phone and started her giggling gossip he exuded fumes, and muttered loudly about idiotic conversations. He told her to shut up. She told him to put in his earplugs.

'Ooaah!' I hovered in the kitchen waiting for an ugly explosion, devising ways of avoiding it, knowing that I would fail, knowing that I was going to have to go to war for my patch. But I had to try.

'Sweetheart!' I said, working to find a voice that did not sound false.

'Let's take Kurtz for a walk!' Kurtz is our dog. I tried a smile, which was supposed to be casual and inviting but I could feel that my smile was looking, as Mamushka would have said, *fuls*. It was too late anyway. Voy's glasses were down on the end of his nose, focusing his ire on Nadya.

The newspapers were forgotten; my friendly suggestion was ignored. He was as easy to distract as a dog approaching a dogfight.

'Why are you here, anyway? Have you nothing to do?'

Nadya looked amazed, innocently surprised at the aggression she had managed to provoke. But unhappily for me she was not backing down either.

'Do you mind letting me finish my phone call?'

'Just go and make your *kurva* phone call somewhere else!'

I emerged from the kitchen, where I retreated to devise a subtle and confrontation-free strategy for removal of this new enterprise from the living room. Dishes always wait for me. That is a constant in my life, a curse and a comfort, an excuse to withdraw, an opportunity to vent anger. I clattered and banged the dishes more expressively than usual. It was a most legitimate retreat. I had a tea towel draped over my shoulder, Spray 'n' Wipe cocked in my hand, ready to use it if necessary to chase this aggressor out of the occupied territory. I had decided upon a plan of action.

The door slammed. Nadya had left, theatrically offended. Voy, having won the territory, continued to fume, muttering about what a deficient parent I was, that my children felt free to come and go whenever they felt like it, and occupy the living room.

'Anyway, why aren't they all at work?' he demanded.

Yes, why? I thought guiltily, and then resumed my position of attack and defence.

My responses were more or less ready, non-original and were guaranteed to add petrol to the furnace that was erupting. The dishes got mentioned, his newspapers, the burgeoning proliferation of junk in his study, and this outrageous expansion into the living room, which I was not going to stand for. Out it all came again.

And then it was his turn.

'You're just mother, and now grandmother!' he started, his lips curling with a jealous snarl.

What about him, the husband? Neglected! Children children, that was my life now. And grandchildren! He was a husband who was fed up.

'Let's forget the whole thing!' he said, then continued, 'If it's not your grandchildren it's the telephone!'

Why did he bother to dream about a life together with me when he could see that I was totally unsuited to anything beyond being a mother cat?

'You smell on milk!'

'*Of* milk, you mean!'

I was being a cat and I felt catty, really catty. My responses had become primitive. Attacking his English grammar? I had lost all sense of decency. I was that furious. And I was not giving up – he just had to retreat to his own space. But I ducked back around to the kitchen, Spray 'n' Wipe clutched defensively. Deep breathing. Regaining composure. Think, for a change. How could I, a laidback Aussie with little war experience, out-fume a fuming Pole whose name means 'man of war'? I couldn't – I could only outwit him. This man, my beloved, had invaded my space.

He explained, more quietly, that in the living room he felt different – almost like it was his muse. Victor Hugo, he continued, could not write unless he was standing up, in a darkened room, surrounded by the smell of pears.

Well, I was not surrendering the territory. I did not give a fig about the need to stand in the dark and smell pears. I was determined that the living room was not going to be annexed, even if I had to squat in it all day long. There was no longer anything subtle about my campaign. It was all there, out in the open.

His eyes told me that he was prepared to go even further than that. Perhaps all night as well.

'I'll bolt the door!' he threatened.

'Well, I'll get some bolt cutters!'

We had guests coming in the evening. How could we possibly repair ourselves to the extent where we could present as the relaxed, hospitable duo, Kot and Voy? Oh! So glad to see you again! Come, sit down, have a drink!

At this moment we were on the point of mutual extermination over two metres of sunless living room. We were both still there, he, infuriatingly, reading again, not even pretending, but actually turning the pages slowly, taking notes. He seemed to have the ability to read and concentrate even when fighting a campaign. How could he?

He was occupying the whole couch, and had his legs on the coffee table. Totally incensed, I was nevertheless confined to the edges of the room, having to pretend I was also occupied. How could I? I could neither get at my desk nor make a phone call – and even if I could make a call I would have exploded on the phone, into a mess of sobs and wails, no matter who was on the line. Was I really a woman in her fifties? Brawling like this? I think most people would tone down their behaviour in middle age. Was this normal? Standing in my trench, armed with Spray 'n' Wipe, and Voy in his trench exuding chemical repellent?

I peered at him to see whether he was really concentrating on that boring-looking article. He was. He was making marks with a pen. Damn him. How could he! If it were bedtime he would go straight to sleep and leave me fuming and sleepless. But he wouldn't go to bed now, even at bedtime, lest the enemy seize advantage and occupy territory.

What about painting? I could have brought that canvas in. Painting soothes, it draws anger into the dark spaces, into the black clouds behind the hills. He thinks he's allergic to the smell of my paints. That would be the equivalent of bringing in nerve gas. Not fair play. Since when was I one for fair play? I just wanted the space back, like it always was. I wanted it to revive and breathe, like a creature, with air coming in and out of the door, like lungs, letting life ebb and flow.

It was not going to become a den, forbidden territory, dominated by a grouch. But I didn't bring in the canvas, and neither could I read, write, or talk on the phone, ring any of my usuals to have a mutual bitch. Because he was there, listening.

So I paced and fiddled, placing letters and bills in one pile and then in another. Sifting through them. And taking surreptitious glances at the scholar who looked more stubborn and entrenched than ever. I felt like snatching those papers, tearing them up into tiny little pieces. Once I would have. But not now. I was, after all, in my fifties. Damn him, for squatting in my patch. And damn Nadya for being insensitive to his hyper-irritable presence.

He went upstairs. Then he came down and went to the bathroom.

Ooh, good! Perhaps he's going out, I thought, seeing the chance to quietly sneak all his things back upstairs and rearrange them in his room. Yes, he smells of aftershave – a good sign, I thought. He's not just popping out for half an hour. Time to make a move.

I started to plot. Perhaps after moving all his stuff back I'll even offer to have Tally round for a couple of hours. The grandchild. We can make a few pancakes and then I will send him home and clean up. Then I will fix the dinner, not Polish cooking, and he will never know that chaos reigned while he was out, or that I have been stuffing more grandmotherly duties into my over-full life.

I planned to light the candles, prepare dinner for the guests and make the little room orderly. Brush my hair. Change out of children-stained clothes. A little eye makeup would do wonders. Light the fire and the candles to make the shadows dance around the walls of the room, and the evening would absorb the aggression. He would be thankful to see the living room restored to its former self, and forget that I'd won the patch war. I prayed for no knocks on the door, heralding unwanted youngsters intent on their own agendas – I didn't want the door to be the lungs of the house any more. Not tonight. The guests were a good excuse to clean out the living room. I knew I could win this.

The evening began well. Voy must also have been thinking of a truce, as he came in with a bottle of red. I sat him down next to the fire and fetched the bottle opener, four glasses for us and the guests, and some bread. He opened the wine, looking rather appealing with a twinkle in his eye, and wearing a decent shirt. We clinked our glasses. *Nazdrowie!* To our health! And we had the first sip alone, sitting on the couch.

A knock on the door, and I hoped it was not one of the kids. For kids never travel alone, but come accompanied by an assortment of others who trail in, make a mess, and trail out again into the night, banging the door or leaving it wide open.

It was the guests. The evening passed, we discussed certain well-trodden issues, with me weaving secret strategies underneath the conversation, preparing myself for the tricky time when they would depart. The door closed on our guests, and it was just us. Voy offered me another glass of wine, which I sipped obligingly, waiting for the turn of the evening, hoping for the truce. And then all the fighting, plotting, childminding and cleaning must have exhausted me, as the sip of wine coursed through my veins as strong as hemlock. I felt my eyelids getting heavy.

'*Kurva*, Kot! Don't sleep! Talk to me!'

I couldn't say to him Well, Voy, I am exhausted from having to deal with your outrageous expansions in the house – and with grand-children, and preparing the dinner, and cleaning up, and moving your office back up the stairs, and scraping up pancake dribbles . . . because this would have brought it all zooming back again. So I just leaned over, put my head in his lap and allowed sleep to take over my exhausted body. And I heard him sigh in despair.

'Once again I have lost her, this terrible Kot!'

36

Kids no longer

I think of our house as a living creature, with lungs, oxygen, life-blood – and even feelings. When I tidy it I know it to be patient and never complaining, no matter how overworked it is. Returned from all of their travels, the kids move in and out – out when they have a place of their own, back again for the interim, which can last for months. Bedrooms are switched around to adjust for swelling families, partners, small children being born and, of course, dogs.

Nadya moved here and there, to Bondi and back home again, until she and Franco, our soulmate–neighbour blacksmith and sculptor, struck a flint, and we all sighed and smiled. For Franco knows what to do, he knows how to tame fire, so it works. Together they moved to his small house where the artistry of Franco's blacksmithery, his curling whimsical balustrades and coffee tables, sit creatively with Nadya's life. Musicians visit at all hours. Piano accordion, bass, violin and voice try to muffle their sound so anxious neighbours can sleep, and family members with their children pop in on winter days to sit by the open fire and match their hunger against Nadya's famous cooking. Raf sits around at odd midnight hours getting his briefing from Nadya and Franco on the creative life into which he is embarking, and of course, whether he wants advice or not, on his love life. The household is warm and exciting, until the periods when Nadya slips off to Paris to perform with another gypsy band, taking Raf, now her keyboard player, and her bass player to tour the European summer festivals.

Jan and Bem have another sort of household with their children, who now number three because of the determined arrival of a new little dark-eyed, curly-haired boy sprite, Kashi. Jan, now an architecture student, has used his artistic skills and his undefeatable spirit to extend a little terrace house into an expansive home that reaches out to the sunlight, and up to the top branches of the Moreton Bay figs on the other side of the road. The house welcomes many people up the hall and into its warm ambience of food and children.

Their backpacker- and family-assisted renovations proceeded apace, with the family remaining intact, balancing on struts and joists, masked against flying plaster and piles of rubble. The intrepid Jan, covered in white plaster dust to his eyelashes, directed operations, and Bem, power tools roaring around her, calmly continued with her novel, stopping from time to time to wipe the builders' dust off her laptop screen. How it got called *The Seduction of Silence* is one of life's mysteries. Jan, as always, is still the cook, still a vegetarian, but now his role is undisputed by Bem and more importantly, by Voy, who can go there as a guest to enjoy the cooked meal.

Mishka and Rachel moved to Newcastle with their three children to start a coffee-roasting business, Suspension, named after the Sahara cat that had found a secure home in the suspension of the Peugot 504 until 2000 kilometres later, when its meowing was detected. Once discovered and named, Suspension had survived luxuriously inside the car on leather seats until and after the car was sold. Suspension Espresso the coffee shop also struggled valiantly on the outer, only to be eventually written up as the best cup of coffee in Newcastle. Once again, Mishka's capacity for endurance and in this case his obsessive focus on roasting techniques were rewarded, and are now being extended to Sydney, along with his roaster. So our house has opened its lungs once again to breathe them all in, as they try to establish themselves in Sydney, and see if they can provide the best coffee Sydney has known.

Raf, the youngest, occupies a charmed position. Handsome, thoughtful and mysterious by nature, nobody is ever quite sure where he lives – he too may have a drop of gypsy blood. But he spends a lot of time with his Indian girlfriend, Sakshi, argues with her about the cricket, and pops in on all of us, absorbing what he needs of the creative life and trying to work out the difficult balance of those two most opposing of forces – survival and creativity.

37

Grandparents

I believed, my darling
It was so naïve of me,
That we are like two shores
Of the same most beautiful river
(old Polish song)

Our beautiful river has flowed through rough territory. It has forked and divided. Now that little boy on the platform who lost his father's instruments for a hat with a red star on it, now he is a grandfather. And there is a little grandson who would also lose his bundle for a red star. It's Tally. As for me, that young woman figuring in the gypsy's prediction, I am a grandmother. How did that happen, Olek?

As far as getting work done, being a grandmother is like having brakes permanently applied. Sorting out fights and falls, scraping up mess and sheer vigilance grabs precedence. And here I am making pancakes again, and they're helping me – Tally, Jan and Bem's child, and Indie, Mishka and Rachel's child. I've pulled two stools over to the stove. Tally and Indie are intent on the activity, as children always are, watchfully competitive with each other, oblivious of the pancake mix dribbling between the bowl and the pan and my uneasy consciousness of the growing, sticky puddle on the stove dribbling via the stools onto the floor.

Voy comes down the stairs.

'Oh, Kot? *Krasny ludky* again! You just can't live without them!'

Krasny ludky are little people in Polish, sort of leprechauns. That's what Voy calls the children. Perhaps he's right. Perhaps I can't live without them. For me and Voy there has never been a time without children. Did we have a honeymoon? Yes, but with the children!

Here they are still, and it's the next generation, continuing the chain of life and chaos. I open a drawer, and it bulges with photographed images. They spill out in disorder, some ripped, some stuck together with old pancake mix no doubt, others faded, and I know I must rescue them. Our children, yours and mine, our whole family, you and me, you and me and your parents, my parents, you with the children, you running across the sand ducking your head against the wind, braced to keep a child on your shoulders with one crooked arm, the other children running behind you. Where am I? Holding the camera?

And then you're gone from the photos, you've disappeared, and the children and I are pictured with Voy, who has one arm around them and the other around me. The photos show a happy family, giving no hint of the bleak, pale wintering of the soul that followed your sudden disappearance from our lives, and the sickening confusion it brought into the sunny lives of your children. And here there's another child, Rafal, and we are all looking at him.

Then there's a studio photo of Voy's parents, humorous and elegant, his mother's mysteriously twinkling eyes telling secrets of a life I can only imagine, in pre-war Poland, before the ravages of communism drove society underground, disapproving of its existence. They are, of course, Rafal's grandparents, but they died years before he was even thought of. Life rushes on in a hurry, leaving little time for reflection.

The photos continue. Captured here are our two years in New Guinea with Voy, a bearded and slim anthropologist on his field trip, the children liberated from school, happy in the jungle. And baby Rafal, looking bigger. He's become a toddler. He's there, white and pouting, on the tightly knit shoulders of a black warrior, who poses formally with one hand clutching Rafal on one shoulder, balancing an axe on the other.

And there's our little hut in the jungle. The boys with feathers in their hair. Voy with local chiefs, notebook, tape recorder. The anthropologist at work. Me, girlish and dark-haired. Nadya carrying a huge net bag on her head. It must have been during these two years that Voy became a real father, away from our normal world and the pressure of place, habits, memories, old friends, and above all, preconceptions about what children should be like.

Then home again. Now Nadya is posing seriously in studio shots taken by Mishka, the photographer. Her lips are pursed and dark with lipstick, she is being moody for an acting career that changed course and became a singing career. She's a small diva with a big soul and a huge voice. Shots taken at gigs show her clutching the mic, face contorted, skin glistening under sweat.

Here is Jan with close-cropped hair, here he has a mass of curls, now in this one he is serious, purposeful, with sacred dreadlocks. He's become a Rastafarian. There he is with a backpack, going somewhere. To Africa. Always on the move. And when you left he was such a little boy, like an elf.

And here is Rafal again, sturdy and small, dressed in his football stripes, perspiration and grime part of the flushed gaze of victory. You never even met him. He stands with his trophies. Here he is again, this time with cousin Jake – you didn't meet him, either. They're on brother David's boat, and Raf's going for yet another seafaring adventure with his uncle and cousin.

But now in these shots Raf's a young man, taller than any of his siblings, with the same thick dark curly hair as Jan. And there's no football, no grime. His gaze is internal, his expression mysterious. The beginning of the pains of manhood. He's just turned nineteen.

And here is young Chrissy Mac, who semi-adopted us when he

was nine – you never even knew him – occasionally appearing in between the boys, but turning his face as if to hide his tragic past from the camera's sharp scrutiny. And here are newer wads of photographs of Jan and Mishka, our sons proud as young fathers, with their dark-eyed women, the mothers of these grandchildren who have mysteriously appeared. When you left us and so carelessly rode your bike away from the house, into that fatal crash and out of our lives, more or less as the gypsy predicted, you were forty. I was thirty-six. You had no idea of what you had started or of what you had left. Or of what you were going to miss. Neither did I. We parted then, without warning, with no alarm bells, in the warm rapids of our lives, when even a week's separation would change things between us.

And where are you now?

Twenty-two years have passed steadily and surely, like a river, which perhaps you watch from the bank, following only certain swimmers. The children are in their twenties, thirties. Nothing stays the same way for long enough.

Voy, having just gotten used to being a father, has had to suddenly face the shock of being a grandfather, taking your place. A *djiadek* with its implications of benign age. Poor Voy. He was such a boy when we met him. And now he's an accelerated grandfather. I was scarcely prepared for it myself. But as usual, Voy thinks everything through. So he has thought about his role as a grandfather, and put it into a context acceptable to him. A natural teacher, he announced his role in advance of its happening. If one of the grandchildren ever wishes to tackle him on mathematics, metaphysics, philosophy or history, he says, then he can become seriously involved and will take over from me. And my pancake sessions can be retired.

So until that time comes, if it does, I tell him stories about the children, and he laughs and is surprised and occasionally moved, and then he discusses the stories and how the little incidents, fights and resolutions relate to theories on child behaviour formulated by a Swiss man called Piaget. And also, how the part played by each child traces the patterns of their future respective characters.

He endures their noisy presence with the help of his earplugs and experiences the children via my stories of their exploits, which fuel his theoretical mind.

Sometimes I feel wary of such extrapolation. Why does he have to contextualise these innocent tales? Why can't they come from nowhere and go to nowhere? Like the song of a bird? Bringing joy and momentary reflection. And why should their little fates be locked in by theories?

'Who is this bloody Piaget, anyway, that you always mention?' I say.

'You don't know Piaget? Ah, Kot! Piaget's life work was beautiful. Research into development of the child's mind, the moral conscience emerging, tempering atavistic impulses, the beginning of reason, the notion of justice and proportion.'

And whom, I wonder, did he observe for these findings? Feeling irritable, I imagine Piaget as an intrusive and unhelpful academic, perhaps similar to Voy – a husband and father who in all probability used his own children as subjects, innocent informants of his field studies, yet he would never think of bathing them, putting them to bed, finding their shoes or scraping squashed bananas from their lunch boxes. And in this mood I shut down the conversation and stalk out of the room.

At other times I'm interested, and grateful to Piaget for his precious research and to Voy for his imaginative interpretations that provide me with food for reflection, a welcome and creative extension to sheer childcare drudgery. So, feeling affectionate towards both of them, I cautiously tell Voy my suspicions about his mate Piaget. Would he have simply observed his own children while they were creating chaos and mischief, and done nothing to help out? Would they have been objectified in order to serve as subjects of his field studies?

After careful scanning, and detecting no malice in my question, he admits, 'Well, yes, I think you're right, Kot. Yes. And I think he used his grandchildren as well, but not only his own. Many many other children. It was Freud who used his own children for his research into early stages of sexual development.'

My irritation then swings to Freud, who must have been quite an annoying father and husband, preoccupied with analysing his children's innocent gestures. That is a challenge that must be far far off for us. None of the children seem to be anally retentive while I'm in charge, so perhaps there would be nothing for Freud to sort out and their parents could deal with that when the time comes. Piaget and the child's moral universe will do for the time being.

But back to Voy. Despite the chance it would give him to observe a primary source, like Piaget, he lives in wary expectation of over-exposure to the source. And I tend to hover in the slipstream of his apprehension, pre-empting his reactions by occasionally not inform-ing him at all of the children's presence, in the hope of course that thanks to his earplugs and noisy window rattling airconditioner, the visit may pass unnoticed by him. My sly approach succeeded only once. Usually the secret is blown. Neither of us gives way – I can't, and he can't either. He says he needs the time for him and me. That's what he fights for – time alone, just the two of us. He says that we deserve it, after all these years of children and not so much as a honeymoon. And, of course, he's right, and I'm probably at fault.

But I'm still looking forward to the future when one of the grand-children seeks out Voy for serious enlightenment and Voy waits, expectant and ready to share his mind – like me with my pancake mix. Then we'll all be happy at the same time.

38

Pull-ups

A knock at the door. So early? Bem, Jan's wife, flicking back her long mane, swept in with the little boys, for now there were two brothers, Tally the Lively and little Rishi. I called the younger one Rishi the Wise because his dark eyes contained worlds of wisdom, and his speech was in proper sentences formed only after deep consideration.

'Good news,' she told me importantly. 'Rishi is toilet-trained. No more nappies! He now has pull-ups!'

Well, I had grave fears about pull-ups but agreed to mind the boys while she went mini-skirted and funky to a meeting with her business partner Jan. Potential clients. Potential clients was the magic phrase for me. Money coming into the family. Off they strode with their portfolios. I watched them from the gate, a carefree couple, swinging jauntily down the road, hand in hand. For a moment I had a vision of the dreadlocked Jan, burning his passport, Jan the spiritual voyager, Jan behind bars. Now here was this exemplary young husband and father swinging off to work. Was I not after all a very lucky mother to be rewarded in this way, to witness such normality? Or was our son destined to be on this trajectory after a few compulsory dances with danger, in order to comply with the dare-fate template set by you and your story?

But there are duties, as part of the mother's golden rewards. And the role of grandmother allows little time for contemplation. Tally the Lively had begun his usual activities, one of which involved tying the dog lead to the skipping rope, looping it round the top branch of the camellia bush (which, subject to his regular attentions, was unlikely even to bear blooms), abseiling up the skipping rope to the top, where he perched like a small bird on the branch, coiled up his rope, hung it on another branch and prepared to sit and watch the street. Voy came down the stairs.

'Is that child safe up there?' he asked.

'I don't care,' I answered. 'He's up there, he's very agile and I know where he is – and no one ever really hurt themselves falling down from a camellia bush. Anyway, he's made of rubber!'

'But what about poor fuckin' *kurva* bush?' he asked, suddenly aggressive, and, ah, I saw where his concerns really lay. Voy the gardener.

Who cares about a bush, I thought defensively. It's given up on producing camellias, perhaps it looks forward to Tally's visit, to have a function again.

'Every living thing has to have a function,' I said to Voy, who remained unconvinced. As an anthropologist, I said to him, he should be convinced by functionalism. Anthropologists, I have observed, relate to isms. He was preparing breakfast for me. He replied with his usual wit that this gave him a function. It looked like a ceremonial breakfast. He was throwing chilli onto eggs and dill, he put the toast into the toaster, sliced the tomatoes, peppered the slices. I wished I was hungry, and I wished he wouldn't throw all that chilli and dill onto the eggs, and I wished I hadn't slurped up all that leftover dinner when I got up.

Now I had to manage a second breakfast, eggs with chillis, otherwise he would surely see me as a woman without an appetite – one of Voy's pet hates. I knew I just had to wolf down the breakfast no matter how stuffed I felt in order to prove my appetite – and suffer from indigestion all day.

This day was not meant to work. And neither, it seems, was I. The portrait I was involved in remained unattended. Voy laid the breakfast on the low coffee table, with the cups ready for the coffee, and went to get the plunger. Well, it was no longer a plunger – the thing in the middle had disintegrated, it had become a plunging jug without its plunger – but we still grandly referred to it as the plunger. Meanwhile, the freshly toilet-trained Rishi, in his greater wisdom, had seen his chance to outwit the system. Wrenching his pull-ups down, he saw his chance, grabbed his willy and manoeuvred it in the direction of the coffee cup.

'Wee wee!' he announced proudly, filling the cup.

'Good boy!' I whispered, slipping the cup away before Voy returned with the coffee. I emptied it into the toilet, popped it into the dishwasher and adroitly returned another cup to its spot. We sat down to our eggs with dill and chilli, and coffee, my second breakfast. So were these the problems of peacetime? Too many breakfasts? And the ingenious invention of the pull-up?

39

Back to New Guinea

When I'm painting river landscapes I like to work on a river's curve – it's the Australian river, deep in parts, sometimes rocky and shallow, and often just dry, a riverbed curling through stony country. I imagine when I paint that the river has a long love affair with the ground. The river nourishes the ground, and it distresses the same ground when it floods, angry and out of control. It neglects the ground when it shrinks, because unfed itself by the rains, it can no longer provide nourishment for its mate. But the ground never leaves the river. I think I feel like the ground.

But enough of this metaphor, Olek. Your gang, plus one, a new baby, four kids in all, went with Voy to New Guinea to live in the remote Western Highlands. There was no school for the kids, just life in the jungle. Like you, living in the forest with the partisans. I understood your partisan experience with a greater clarity while we were there. Our New Guinea experience bonded me to your recollections, making them more precious, because New Guinea, in a way, was our partisans' camp.

The physical hardship, being cut off from the world, living with a different people, with the elements, and the same incredible sense of cosiness emanating from the tiny home in the bush, was the beginning and the end of each day and each excursion. That must have been the same for you. And in a way New Guinea was your 'second partisans', because you went there on patrol, probably in deliberate search of the things that we experienced.

We woke with the dawn, and when the jungle became black, before the moon crept up the sky throwing its strong light over the mountain, we slept. We knew the passage of the day and we witnessed the coming of the night. If there was something happening at night, if the sounds of singing filtered through the night to tease our ears, we grabbed Rafal, the baby, and went to investigate, walking along forest tracks and navigating only by the full moon. We were aware of the season changes. We lived much of the time on the produce of the local gardens. We washed in the river. And we had a pet bird, not for long. But Mishka had a pet possum – it lived on his shoulder and was called Malu Malu.

Then after two years we returned home, to normal city life. And a few years later we went back for a visit. I was overcome by amazement that I had lived there for two years, in this spot in the jungle. I just stared around me as my memories and fantasies about the place were replaced by the small realities, the petty discomforts, rampant theft, shortage of food, illness, the constant pressure of people needing, wanting whatever we had or didn't have. I wondered how we were going to survive the three-week visit.

Perhaps if Mamushka had returned to the scene of their partisan camp she would have felt the same. And you? I wonder how the forest would have looked to you if you had happened upon it ten years later. Would it have matched up to your fantasies?

Returning for me was difficult. Almost immediately, I became ill. I got diarrhoea. The only toilet was an uninviting hole in the ground located through the vegetable garden and over two pig fences. The forest was drumming with rain – it ran off all the branches, and into my eyes and my soaking clothes. I was aware of Voy's reliable arms guiding me over the two fences and down through the wet, spiky pandanus. I was aware of him holding me, half the night, over the horrible hole with its malodorous depths. I was dependent on his soft voice reassuring me inside the constant drumming of the rain that I wasn't going to die. I was so weak from shitting I would have fallen into that hole with all its horrors.

This is not at all how I had remembered our two years. I had forgotten the hard part, recalling the softness of the valley, and the highland mists, the smiling faces, the laughter round the fires. I remembered my body glowing with strength.

Now, lying on my hard mat in the hut, struggling to sleep, folding clothes under my head to substitute for the provided pillow which was the customary long narrow log, ignoring a live network of itchy spots, I felt as if I was living the past, and it felt nice. I was trying to recall it, but the itches were keeping me in the present. I thought about love, and how sometimes I measure it by small acts – like, I thought, being held over a bush toilet in curtains of rain. I reached out and touched Voy's hand, crystallising that moment. He squeezed my fingers, through sleep. And then I put my head on his upper arm, nicer than the log pillow, more sweaty than a heap of clothes. It was a hot night, hotter than I remembered. I had no memory of sticky heat – just cool nights, snuggling under a blanket. Now we were there again, I thought wakefully, in that place from our own past. Together. With Voy I could revisit a past I thought had closed on us. With you I could not. My past with you cannot be visited except in thoughts and dreams, stories. Secret tears burnt my eyelids as I dropped gently into sleep, but they were not tears of sadness – just tears of reflection.

Going back to the spot where we had lived those two years was an unexpected challenge. Had we really lived that life that had receded into dream territory, following memories of my life with you? The valley, the people, the timeframe, the ages of the children – I remembered it all as distinct and separate from our lives, like a wartime experience perhaps, or like your memory of the partisans. Framed by forest, by distinct seasons.

The food we took in with us on this visit – the sacks of rice, the boxes of tinned fish – was quickly consumed. Numndi's tribe, victorious from their recent war, had moved from their previously fertile ground in the valley to high country, where their food gardens had not yet yielded the first crops of taro, yams and sweet potato. After our own rations of rice and tinned fish had disappeared we became dependent on our hosts who, being tough mountain people, were used to making do.

So we waited with empty bellies for a daily meal of boiled sweet potatoes, served once a day in a mushy pile on a tin plate. Hunger is the best sauce, and we looked forward to the otherwise inedible lunch, or breakfast, or dinner or whatever it was. And then, when I got sick, my portion seemed like a waste of valuable stored mushed, watery sweet potatoes. And when Rafal got sick too it seemed worse than a waste, because we had all been stashing bits and pieces to feed him, the child member of our family expedition.

Lying in bed at night meant being squeezed onto the floor, six of us together in a hut where the snores, grunts and coughs of our hosts sleeping in the adjacent section only stopped to meet the dawn calls of birds, the peeps of light filtering in through the bamboo walls, and the murmuring sound of talk around the fire. Fleas were devouring our tender white winter flesh, starting an extra sound, the sound of fingernails sleepily scratching the bites.

Is that how living in the partisans was for your parents? Fleas, rats perhaps, being crammed together for warmth? Sharing common food, and not enough of it. You did not remember hunger, but they must have been hungry, the adults, to have to go and get the sap from trees and catch horses belonging to other people – even resorting to stealing from gypsies. In peacetime they would not have dreamed of such excess. In war it was a struggle for survival, and niceties including observation of the laws of property were irrelevant.

We had arrived at the point where the truck could go no further and as we bumped to a stop, we were pulled down by swarming

Gamegai tribesmen and women. We trekked through the forest, led by Numndi, Pella and many others from the tribe with whom we had lived ten years before, and they recounted in bits and pieces their recent family tragedy. Numndi's daughter Sana, the mother of a new baby called Nadya for our Nadya, was grieving the loss of her young husband. He had been brutally slain by his brother. Was it possible we had just arrived on the scene of a recent family massacre? It did not seem real – we were still being greeted with smiles, hugs, and tears of joy. Or were they tears of grief? Tears come from both sources.

Why? We asked. How? How shocking! How did this come about? We were asking, but searching for our presents at the same time, it seemed that trivialities were still relevant.

The brother went on a rampage killing not only his sibling, but his mother as well. It started with a brawl between the two men. Sana's husband barricaded himself in his hut for safety. The aggressor, furious and frustrated, aimed and fired an arrow into a gap in the hut wall, and it killed his brother. Their mother started screaming and hitting her son, who then struck her with a rock on the head, committing the crime unthinkable to most societies including theirs, matricide.

After the killing frenzy the murderer brother escaped his wrathful clansmen, running through the bush and hiding out until he could find the police in the nearest town and lie low in jail until the mood of revenge subsided.

'And what then?' we asked, thinking, the notion of actually finding police to protect you for having murdered two people was a new slant on crime and punishment.

'Ah,' said Numndi, always the wise one. 'His family will be sorry that they have lost so many, and will not want to lose him too – he's a young man, he's needed for war and for building gardens. He will just come home again when his jail sentence ends. He is safe in jail. Their anger will be gone. And they will be glad, because he is their clansman.'

Once again, I thought, anger disappears quite quickly. The long-term survivor is love, the feeling of having lost.

A funeral feast was planned. But apart from this not too much special attention was being paid to the young widow, who quietly attended to her baby, and sat in the back of the hut now occupied by Numndi and Pella. And us. She had moved back home to Mum and Dad. Any huge shockwaves from the recent carnage were not apparent, as village life flowed on. Did she feel as I had felt, when I lost you? Her face, bent towards her baby, was inscrutable.

The transition from dream territory to the reality of actually being there and having to cope was difficult. The familiar smells, the pig grease and sweet potato mingling with sweat, the guttural noises of the language, the sound of rapidly running water, of pouring rain in the forest, the birds, the coughing of the old men and the grunt of foraging pigs. The same old demands on our resources, medical supplies, expertise, money. And also of course, the latest gossip, illnesses, injury, and who had died, who had had babies, who among the elderly still lived.

And the war. Who were the victims? The trip back to Papua New Guinea also made me aware that I was older. In dreams one is always young. So, coming back, it was not only the grey in my hair, it was my failure to insulate myself from elements that previously I must have dealt with. No water, no privacy, insufficient food, insect bites, the recent family slaughter. I remembered the wailing and singing from before. It was suddenly familiar, the scent of a part of my own life.

Our emotion at seeing them all had overwhelmed us. We had been so preoccupied with the logistics of getting there that I had not given a moment of thought to the meeting and what it would be like. So I had just sat quietly in the back of the truck, allowing myself to be mesmerised and preoccupied by the shocking beauty of the sunset piercing the high mountain mists, shooting like lasers through the foliage.

And then they appeared through the bush, those people who had been so close to us for so long, they were running over a stony creek towards the truck. We were seized by them and by laughter and tears as we stumbled through the creek bed. My Pidgin was hopeless and muddled itself with bits of Polish but it didn't seem to matter. They cried and shook their wrists and shouted their surprise. 'Kayeeah! Kayeeah! Kayeeah!' The fact that Numndi and Pella had not changed at all reinforced the strange feeling of visiting ourselves at another point in our past lives. We gradually adjusted to it, as we talked and laughed into the night, remembering old times.

We arrived in the middle of a *moka* ceremony, whereby one tribe gives pigs to another. That could have been dreamlike except that it was familiar to us. Painted faces, body decorations, beating drums. The heat, the chaos, the noise. Most people were painted up, their faces unrecognisable. Then Rafal was selected to be painted up and to dance with the men. After all, he was, they said, their boy, having spent his entire babyhood in these forests, with this tribe, and much of it in Pella's bilum.

So, ten years later, he was being led away to partake in a ritual that his infant eyes had witnessed uncritically as part of the natural rhythm of his baby life. The droning sounds of the sing-song chant, the rhythmic boom of the *kundu* drum, the smell of the pig grease on thronging bodies, the made-up pigs, the peering faces covered in the red and white Hagen tribal colors would have been as familiar to him as sitting in a supermarket trolley is for a city child.

But. Pants must come off. And he was no longer a baby, but twelve. That was a problem. More so than the elaborate patterns being painted on his white face and the hot, heavy crown of feathers burdening his head. He did not want to go out with his thighs on display, sprouts of leaves covering the crack in his bum, and a grass panel over his willy.

But seeing no way of escaping this embarrassment, Rafal heroically submitted to the preparations, as his brothers had done ten years before. Numndi and two men advanced upon him, undressing him, first his shirt, pulling the *komak* (bamboo *moka* beads) round his neck, and the strings of black beads. Then they tried the armlets on his upper arms, but they were all too big, being used on the bulging muscles of grown men. For Rafal they had to pad out the arms with soft ferns to make the *pas pas* fit. Then they tucked the green tufts of fern into the bracelets around the upper arm muscles, to emphasize the biceps. After that, the *skin dewi*, the bark belt, doubled around for such a slim torso. And then the *tanget* (cordyline) leaves, also supplemented by fern, were fitted into the bark belt over his backside.

Pella painted Rafal's face while Numndi held the mirror in front of them. The last bit of the procedure was the construction of the feather crown. Numndi had to stuff the *het bilum*, the woven hat, with ferns to make it fit onto Rafal's slippery, non-fuzzy, non-springy hair. Then the feathers were taken, ever so gently, one by one, from cardboard splints, first the little red parrot feathers that made the front band, then the long black tail feathers, which were inserted one by one into the stuffed hat. Then lastly, the yellow bird of paradise, the huge central piece, which was flattened and mounted onto cardboard backed by a page from the *Education Gazette*. Anything that could be harnessed into a headdress could be used.

Now he was ready. The whole process had taken two hours, and as the sun mounted in the sky I tried to smear sunblock onto his reddening white shoulders. But Pella smilingly and firmly negated the process by re-smearing the shiny pig grease into the shoulders, to give them the right gleam. I had to give way to her greater knowledge about what was a good look, and accept that my young son was going to get horribly sunburnt. I spent a second wondering whether your mother had ever felt the same, completely helpless as you were led off by the partisan men to blow up a train. Could my experience even compare?

Led by two fully dressed men, Rafal was taken to the moka ground, where he was fitted into the line of dancing men, being placed between Councillor Pri and Dokta Kewa. His slim white arms were linked into the experienced, muscular biceps of the older men as they taught him the ancient rhythms with their own bodies.

The *kundu* beat dictates the dip of the legs, making the skirt over the bark belt flick forward and then the whole line of skirts ripple in time to the off-beat of the drum.

The men were perched on the edge of a misty abyss, and the slow, rhythmic roar of their chant started to swell the valleys below, echoing and re-echoing. The line of women, standing at an angle about twenty-five meters away, were also dipping and incantating, their deep wail offsetting the roar of the men. Over and over, a pause, and then the beat of the *kundu* again, and the chant. The forest trembled with the roar and the drum beat.

Rafal caught the rhythm immediately, his skirt getting the right outward flick with the bob and push of his knees. The onlookers were murmuring, impressed. *Kung Rapus*, Boy Rafal, he's one of ours, really, they told me. 'He was our baby, so now he belongs here,' they said.

It was midday, and the sun was beating down through the dust. After two hours of the knee-dipping movement Rafal's legs were beginning to waver and lose the rhythm. His eyes, staring out from the gaudy paint surrounding them, looked droopy and red. They called for help.

'Shit!' His eyes were saying directly to me. 'Get me out of this, will you?'

Would it be normal mother behaviour to rescue her ailing son when he is becoming initiated? What did your mother do when you were being taken by the partisan men to engage in mysterious missions? Did she protest loudly? Try to pull you back? Cry as you were led briskly away from the camp by the saboteurs? I knew very well that I was expected not to interfere or to attempt any rescue, and Voy backed me up on this when I checked with him. But I suffered watching my weakening child, and being absolutely unable to pull him from the roaring, dipping, relentless line.

Numndi came to watch. He was gleaming with pride at the prodigy he had been able to produce and display. Voy rushed backwards and forwards with his zoom lens. And then a young, heavily painted girl was brought along and placed in the line beside Rafal. Her handsome face was coy and demure beneath yellow and white paint. She had a possum fur crown and a matching breast plate. Her look would have graced the cover of *Vogue*. She linked arms with Rafal, and Numndi explained to me that this could mean love, when a girl dances beside a young man in the *moka*. Her rhythm was wavery and uncertain and she looked to Rafal to guide and tutor her.

But there was no tutorship left in Rafal, and little pride. His exhausted eyes were blind to the planned love match. He just wanted out. At the next break he left the line. He said he'd had enough.

'Wah! Go back!' they shouted. Numndi tried to fix the feather crown, to make it more comfortable, less heavy, to stop it sticking into his ears. Someone brought him a Pepsi. I gave him a banana. Numndi gave him a slice of pineapple. He ate his refreshments and returned obediently, linking arms with Pri and Kewa, as he became lost once again in the roaring crescendo of their chant.

At night Rafal collapsed and ran a high fever. The next day he was even more sick, and after he was diagnosed as being sufficiently ill he was exempt from further dancing and his feathers were passed on to another dancer.

He was lying flat on his back, his face still painted garishly, his eyes painted to their rims, and he was burning with fever. I dredged from my mind the treatment dose for suspected malaria, and treated him, hoping that whatever illness it was would not be made worse by the strong drugs recommended for malaria.

And then I got sick myself. We lay in the hut like two stones, I was thankful for the cool darkness. Voy had left early in the morning to do the long walk over the mountains to Rulna, our old home. Pella came from time to time with grubby tin mugs of water. Around us the noise continued, the snorting of the pigs, the crying of the babies, the deep muttered exchanges of the men. From the next hut came the sound of Nadya's cassette, played over and over again on the tape recorder we had brought for Numndi.

It had become a maddening jingle, played on a half-dead battery

239

with no break, on half-speed. 'Haiwei Driver! Haiwei Driver!' It made me feel worse. I regretted giving them the tape recorder and the cassette of Nadya's now-famous recording in Pidgin English. The bird noises should have been enough, and the snort of the pigs, the deep, warm voices of the women busy with their babies, making their fires.

The next morning Rafal was up and playing football with the local boys. Seeing his recovery, I felt better. I got out early from the hut, to test my own strength. The sky was a little dark, and I noticed that the soil looked rich under the purple clouds. The colours were more vivid. The greens of the banana leaves and the muted greys of the *yar* trees give the highlands their predominant colours, the softest grey-green, as muted as the swirling mists. Only the red lilies and the yellow marigolds in the garden were breaking the grey-green. The mists, sweeping through a large clearing seemed to bring with them the warning sound of a drum, which got louder and then disappeared, retreating. Just as I thought I must have imagined the sound, it came closer again, and more insistent, marching out from the dream world of night and the dawn.

I grabbed my paints and paper, and followed the sound up the clearing. The roar of chanting male voices had already joined the drum. With daybreak the *moka* started again. I settled into a shady spot and looked out through the trees at the pink dawn creeping over the misty mountain.

And then there was the funeral feast. We had been there five days, our food had been consumed without us noticing, and we were hungry. There seemed to be no abundance of sweet potato as there had been when we lived there before. Anyway here we were guests, without firewood to make our own fire.

We had to walk for two hours through the bush, across the river, to the delegated spot for the cooking of the meat for the funeral. Weak with hunger, I could think of little else except the pig meat, cooked in the ground oven, which would be raised, spread on banana leaves, and divided around among the mourners.

I fantasised about it. I smelled it in advance. But it was a two-hour walk and I was still weak. My legs were buckling under me, I followed Voy on the narrow track as he strode ahead, never tiring, his anthropologist's brain on fire, all traces of melancholy gone. In his element. How could a foodlover like Voy not even notice that he's hungry? Food consumed my thoughts.

Shamefully I felt no sorrow or sympathy for the mourners. In my mind I was falling hungrily on my portions and relishing the familiar taste of the gelatinous fat on the pig, flavoured by the fern leaves mixed with taro and tasting of smoke.

Intermittently aware of my own callous attitude, I absolved myself of guilt, figuring that I had not even known these in-laws who had all killed each other. It must have been like that for your parents in the partisans. Survival and hunger can be so strong that they sublimate the normal decencies and courtesies.

We arrived weak at the site of the feast, hot and exhausted. After a brief but futile search for a modicum of shade, we flopped down under the equatorial sun in the middle of the treeless area, cleared brutally of any foliage in expectation of such eating ceremonies.

Finally the meat was raised from the ground. The hot rocks were lifted out of the hole with bamboo tongs. The aroma escaped with the steam, tempting my nostrils. And the sharing of the different cuts began. Names were called out one by one and the portions, served on banana leaves, were distributed in order of importance. Back at Numndi's house it was going to be slim pickings again. I hoped we were going to line our stomachs for the next few days.

We were given the lumps of meat with a thick layer of fat, the honourable portions. And we tucked into them in complete silence, gnawing and concentrating on the pleasure of the flavour as I for one had never done before. Even Mishka, the vegetarian, showed his true survival instinct by eating the taro and sweet potato cooked in the same oven as the meat – something he normally would have declared contaminated. But voluntary vegetarians are unknown in these parts, despite the fact that the normal diet is mainly limited to the products from the mountain gardens. Pigs were killed only ceremonially, and not as part of the day-to-day diet. Meat hunger is always part of the ceremony.

And it was worth walking to satisfy that hunger. It demonstrated to me yet again that tragedy, joy and desire – and in this case, the need for food – are not a separate entity, to be dealt with as discrete units, but part of the whole process of life. Life is the great river that keeps on going, carrying bits and pieces collected from its banks, merging them into the current, turning them around and changing their form.

40

Kitchen rights

This may be the greater picture of our lives, but even in the greater picture there is always the secreted detail that in peacetime, for the most part, dominates. Being fed by Mamushka, for instance – a trial at the time – has become a wonderful memory when remembered within the context of my life. I'm no longer trying to match her culinary skills, I just remember them with great warmth. And now I'm being fed by Voy, who jostles for kitchen rights – and that is the detail. Voy wants to cook, to feed me in his style, which he considers to be superior. And therein lies the problem.

I'm used to Polish food, it's become part of my life. Mamushka's kitchen occupies such a cheerful place in my mind now that she is no longer there to force-feed me. Memories of her table trigger salivation. It has become one of the great treasures of my sensual memory. I occasionally try to approximate it, even laying out the white, gold-trimmed china on a white cloth, although Mamushka favoured the embossed plastic table cover.

Voy, however, has the feeling that cooking strictly Polish food is for nostalgic migrants pointlessly longing for the homeland, and he would like to dissociate himself from such forms of nostalgia. The anthropologist in him makes him skeptical of what he calls useless and mushy sentiment about the homeland. Therefore he varies his cooking along the lines of what he has eaten during his long travels. A bit of this and a bit of that. Pork? No. Schnitzel? Unhealthy. Just fish, and fish, and fish, and shellfish. Very un-Polish. He is skeptical of my occasional efforts to cook the full Polish meal, considering it regressive behaviour and arguing that my time would be better spent painting. I secretly think that he just wants the kitchen to himself, but likes to present a selfless rationale for his motivations. My health. My career. What could sound better?

'Why you bother with this ridiculous work, making *golomki*? Fiddling with fatty mincemeat and sour cream. So unhealthy. Have you nothing better to do with your time? Go and paint. Leave cooking to me. I am quick, never more than ten minutes to make anything. And you will be healthy.'

And healthy, touch all the wood in the world, I am.

But I still resist. Though at times I perversely dream about those delicious unhealthy lunches of Mamushka's, I don't always like to stop what I'm doing and be fed. The sour cream covering the *golomki*, served on the white china plates with their gold edging, on a creased tablecloth, and Mamushka's eager eyes, watching, to see if I had a keen appetite, perhaps the situation has transferred itself – different cooks, same lacklustre devourer of repast.

'Would you like lunch?' Voy asks.

'Yes, I would love some lunch. What is it?'

'Don't ask me what is it! It is lunch!'

'Well, can I know what I'm going to eat? I feel as if I've just had breakfast!'

'So don't have any *kurva* lunch then. Don't!'

'If I eat anything now I feel as though I could burst!'

'So you will burst. Or starve! You choose your way! Who will hang will never drown!' Another Polish saying.

My appetite is returning.

41

Valentine's Day

It was seven a.m. on St Valentine's Day. Rachel was having five-minute contractions, and Mishka was confident that, thanks to his daredevil driving skills, they would make it to the hospital in time. He was dying to have just one legitimate speeding ticket, to grace his long record of indefensible speeding charges. Could I meet them there, as a birth assistant? Who, me? I was flattered – and terrified.

I passed the responsibility to Jan and Bem, who had more expertise and enthusiasm for the process, and I offered to look after Tally and Indie who were also invited to be present.

The presence of the children at the birthing centre quickly got the better of everybody, as they pelted the atmosphere of intense concentration with bits of gravel and flowers from the pot plants outside the birthing chamber. When they leapt into the birthing bathtub with wild glee, I hastily withdrew them from the main event and took them to the beach to wait for news there with a mobile phone.

By nightfall we were all crammed into the hospital room, peering at the face of Raiden Valentino as he lay curled up, eyes shut tightly, resisting the harsh lights of the world he had burst into after his huge effort.

Not one of us could suppress tears at the sight of Mishka bending over his new son, his face lit from within. A boy with a little boy,

I thought. Another grandson for you, another cheeky mouth with upturned corners? The corners were so compressed between the chubs of cheeks, I couldn't yet tell.

The following day I brought Mishka home from the hospital for a well-deserved sleep. Nadya had her apron on, a scarf on her head. Her cleaning-lady look. There were buckets everywhere, and rubbish bags.

'Guess what, Mum? I've done a huge clean up. We have de-cockroached the place, I've done all the washing and we've even cleaned the fridge!'

Mishka stood there, frozen mid-gesture, his glow turning to ash.

'You didn't, by any chance, as you were cleaning the fridge, you wouldn't have thrown out the placenta, would you?'

'Oh shit, Mishka, what does a placenta look like?'

'Nadya, it looks like liver or something. It was – hopefully still is – in a plastic bag.'

'Oh no. A bit of liver? Oh shit, Mishka. Yes, I think I did throw away something like that. I was doing a thorough job, you know?'

Mishka's glow was gone. The most reliable spot in the world, our fridge – the fridge that was cleaned out only when bulging ice prevented the door from shutting, and even then only by me – that haven of reliability, had been devastated.

'Well, I hope it turns out that you haven't!'

I sensed from Mishka's intense interest in the fate of the placenta that this was important to them. But now this precious treasure may have disappeared, fallen victim to Nadya's rare frenzy of house-wifely activity. I know about placenta ritual, something ignored by our generation. It's often kept for all sorts of reasons by the next generation who variously bury it under a new tree, eat it to benefit from its rare nutrients, or burn it and sprinkle its nutritious ashes over the garden. Which of these, if any, Mishka and Rachel had in mind I wasn't sure, but it was clearly important for the three of us that this item should be recovered.

The following day was garbage day. It was a stinking hot night, and I was sitting out on the street with the garbage bags, and wearing my rubber gloves. Everyone was asleep. While Mishka dreamed about his new son, I tried to find the lost placenta. I was very glad Voy was in Poland and not here telling me what an idiot I could be. Because I knew that in this particular instance he would be right.

Instead of sleeping, like the rest of the city, I was looking for a bit of deteriorating liver that may or may not have been the placenta. Kurtz the dog was sitting beside me, looking mournful. He was jealous, perhaps because Mishka's attention was elsewhere. Kurtz had been eclipsed by Raiden Valentino. Or had he? It was a steamy night, and rain had started to descend gently, like a soft mist. The streetlights were quite bright, but I was mainly guided, as was Kurtz, by the smell.

As the saying goes, every dog will have its day – and that day, Kurtz had his way. While I was contemplating what to do with the soon-to-be rescued placenta, Kurtz convinced me that he was the solution. Because he was, after all, Mishka's dog. I found what may have been the placenta, gave it to Kurtz, and he devoured it, licking his fangs. I re-tied the bags and took Kurtz for his midnight walk, hoping against hope that my decision would be acceptable, but somehow fearing that it wouldn't. The fear lodged in my heart and started to mushroom.

The next morning there was a terse telephone message in Mishka's voice: 'Mum please make sure that the placenta does not get thrown out, no matter what sort of condition it's in.'

Was this his idea? He is stubborn, adventurous and has strong ideas mysterious to me. Or was it Rachel, the Buddhist? The plan, whatever it was, must have been devised by both of them. Why, oh why, did I make that decision to give it, if that's what it was, to Kurtz? Why, oh why, did Nadya for once in her life want to clean not only the house, but the fridge as well? Who could have guessed that she would embark on such an uncharacteristic activity?

My mind raced through a few alternatives to actually admitting that Kurtz had eaten the placenta. It was becoming clear to me that the something that I had discarded, or allowed the hospital to discard, so easily four times over, along with the rest of my generation, was some sort of major player in this child's birth. I had clumsily thwarted an important plan. Trouble was going to erupt if it was not produced, trouble between the young couple. And I would be the cause. Me, the mother-in-law. A classic.

Jan and Bem had buried their placenta in our courtyard, in one of our pot plants with a miserable amount of covering earth. Perhaps, unbeknown to us, that placenta met the same fate while we were peacefully asleep, and Kurtz was on night watch. At the time I had thought their decision strange, but as they were on their way to the airport, to begin a three-month trip, I couldn't ask them to bury it in their own courtyard. With no warning, no preparation ceremony, the burial was performed while I watched from the kitchen, not even trying to relate to the process; and making a mental note not to include it in my news of the day for Voy, not to have to listen to his diagnosis of such a ritual.

Sometimes anthropological explanations are just redundant. What could he say?

But neither would I tell him about my current dilemma. I considered executing a very cunning plan to obtain a placenta from a maternity hospital and present it to Mishka and Rachel as their own. Of course this plan failed while still in my mind, on several counts.

Even if I obtained a placenta, I could hardly pass it off as Mishka and Rachel's. What if they wanted to eat it? And what if the hypothetically obtained placenta was diseased?

So I didn't do it. I was not capable of executing a scheme involving so many unknowns. The plan, I decided, was heavily flawed. And for a second I had a fleeting glimpse of the bizarre workings of my own mind.

Armed with flowers and my sketchpad, I bravely entered room 18 at the hospital. I had intended to soothe my agitation by doing studies of the father–mother–baby love story. I faced them heroically, snuggled into the cosy corner of their life with their new baby boy, gazing at his hands, his feet, matching his foot size with your line, Olek – remember your huge feet? Surely you do. The boys all have them.

They looked at me. Where was the placenta? I thought they were thinking. Nothing else, I imagined, mattered to them, the other part of the happiness corner.

'I have a terrible confession to make,' I said, waiting, my heart racing. Fearing not that they would turn on me, but worse, that they would turn on each other, due to the well-meaning act of the mother-in-law.

'I gave your placenta to Kurtz. By mistake.'

How brave can one get? Silence. They stared at me. Incredulous. And then they started to laugh, first her, a huge belly laugh from someone whose belly had been under such stress, then him. I was off the hook. Off the meat hook. Or rather, the placenta hook, the latest hook to enter my life. I didn't laugh, I just sat clutching my paints and paper. Relief was tearing through my body, burning my face that was about to contort with a huge buildup of anxiety and relief, joy at the sight of the baby boy, the recent tenant of the placenta, and gratitude to the enigmatic Rachel for deciding to spare me.

'Good on yer, Kathy!' she said, recovering from her laugh. 'After all, Kurtz is part of our family!'

Her compassionate womanliness dissolved the phantom of my anxiety. Relief started to seep out the corners of my eyes as I hid my face, bending over my paper and making the strong watercolour seep into the crumpled curves of the baby's sleeping face, the round curl of his little hand and the long fingers of the mother cradling his head against her elbow. And then her face, the point of the brush feeling for the delicacy of this new but time-old relationship between mother and son.

42

The green-eyed monster

One night, home alone, I was paying the price for starving Voy of sufficient conversational opportunities and gritting my teeth, trying to cope with the fact that he had gone to the theatre with one of his ex-students – female, of course. Tired from a day with grandchildren, and having seen two dreary performances of *Waiting for Godot* in the past, I had refused Voy's offer of an evening at the theatre seeing a show directed by his friend. So the ex-student adroitly slipped into the breach and as I suffered pangs of remorse at home, she would have been sitting in my seat next to him. And most annoyingly, enjoying the performance, or at least, I thought suspiciously, faking enjoyment.

Anyway she would not have been snoring as I no doubt would have been, and she would be agreeing with his observations over several glasses of wine at interval instead of the less festive, wowser-ish water I now prefer, since wine has become, for me, the supreme soporific.

'Why not go alone?' I had said to him, peeved when he told me of his plan to invite her. 'Why with her? Why go at all? Don't you ever get sick of *Godot*?'

'Because, Kot, we have been given two tickets and you don't want to go and I must go. Besides, I want to go – I love theatre. I really don't know why you have a problem with this, Kot!'

Ever since he left the university he's been followed everywhere by these ex-students, all women, arriving at the house at different times – in groups, in couples or alone, seeking help with their theses, with their lives, their plans for the future or whatever. This woman would be one of them. That's fine, absolutely fine, I argued with my other self. But going to the theatre with her? Was that fine? I analysed my thoughts, trying (and failing) to induce feelings of calm indifference towards what was probably an innocent and intellectually based outing.

But that's the problem. No intellectually based outing is innocent. Voy really gets off on that sort of stuff. Serious, thinking women – he loves them. I railed to myself against her, for manipulating me into a position of such disadvantage. I mean, because I didn't want to get involved with Beckett, she did. Of course! She would be all eager ears, intellectual antennae on alert for the post-theatre discussion. He would be thinking: If Kot were here she just would snooze off . . . And it's true. I would, and then I would have to be revived after the theatre, and I would be no good for discussion about the play because I would scarcely have experienced it. Especially, I admit to myself but certainly not to him, after slogging around parks with small children. If I have three children for the morning I try to pretend I only have two, if I have two then I try to pretend I have only one. But Voy is onto me. He can count. 'Ah, Kot,' he says, 'there is, you know, no such thing as lonely rat!' That old Polish saying again. Well, surely there is another saying for my predicament.

So what was I going to do? Put out some glasses of wine, and a candle on the table, for when he returned? I could do that, but then the warm expectation of his coming home would be mixed with irritation and jealousy, which would quickly get the upper hand over the quiet, rational self-control I knew would be the better course. My welcoming gesture would then appear *fuls*. Perhaps this is what I had become now? Having spent a great part of my life becoming attuned to Slavic excess, I was going to have to call on my logical Anglo blood, and re-learn calm artifice. Learn to be *fuls*.

'The English!' Mamushka used to exclaim in wonder. 'So logic! So *fuls!*' No screeching, no door slamming and no running into the dark night in a fit of pique. That is the Slavic way. The British way? Just strategy. So I was going to have to call on the forebears.

'Sweetheart, tell me about your evening.' This is what the wise strategic woman would ask if she was exercising her British genes. And then she would continue her tasks, clad in a tight, enigmatic smile – not plague him with a hysterical build-up of questions. *That* would be the Continental way.

The latter option of course had immediate appeal, with emotions brewing. I pushed back tears. Snatches of a recent conversation, benign at the time, started to activate in my head. I was livid but still fighting with myself, trying to keep in mind the British option, and remembering Voy's ruminations.

'You see, Kot, we could be a bit different, unconventional – you are artist!'

'What! Us? That's outrageous! I feel no different!'

At the time I gave his observation not much thought, merely dismissing it as somewhat insulting. But now I was thinking, perhaps he was generously including me together with himself, in some elevation of a new morality based on not being part of the masses but rather cognisant individuals able to formulate their own moral codes? Well, pigs to that.

'Look, Kot! We had a good evening and a great conversation! You know, you never seem to have time to talk – and I love to talk. I'm interested in her subject, it's good . . .' That's what he would say. I could guarantee that.

And here was I, thinking who is she anyway? A pretentious flatterer. And neurotic, for sure. I could imagine her, agreeing with his every thought, praising his brilliant observations. And he would be at his most gallant and charming for her, opening a car door for her, instead of sitting in the driver's seat muttering impatiently as I flustered around doing last-minute chores.

Perhaps, I thought, I should inform this female impostor what he's really like. How, for instance, would she like to put up with Voy when he's in one of those stinkers! And the amount of books and journals, how would she cope? I was re-activated, remembering old conversations.

'Monogamy is like monotheism. Monotheism is the justification, the social rationale, for monogamy. It helps keep society easy to govern.'

Did he once say that? I remembered his voice saying something of that nature. Such thoughts would never occur to me in a million years. And it was coming back to me. So why, I thought, did he say it? Was it that he was gently trying to explain something to me, masking it in academic metaphor? My heart started to tremble. My eyes were stinging. Now I felt like hitting him when he came in. I had worked it all out. The British cool in me had all but disappeared, replaced by Slavic fury.

What do you think, Olek, I asked you. Did you ever do this to me? Well I wouldn't know, really – the hospital was another world. You never had to pack up all your instruments and patient notes and X-rays and stuff them into the house. You had your world, I had mine. We shared early mornings, evenings, occasional holidays and most weekends.

When Voy was at the university we had separate worlds. Now we shared this small space, me and him. His world had to accommodate mine, and mine his. All of our subplots were exposed to each other. His adoring students, my children, my adoring grandchildren, weaving their noisy way through the underworld of the furniture, demanding my attention from beneath the table, or from behind Voy's desk, pinching his paper clips and scissors and sticky tape, stuffing their pockets with his rubber bands, dribbling pancake mix in slippery rivers over the kitchen floor, as I tried to pretend they weren't even there! The two worlds tended to clash.

Voy did, of course, come home from the theatre in a good mood.

And I had been brewing. No drink ready, no candle. No *fuls* welcome.

We took the dog for a late-night walk. Going down the quiet, dark street, I started to fire fretful questions about the theatre date, the pitch of my voice escalating. I was going against my cool judgement. Cool judgement always wins. I knew that, but I was about to lose. I had let myself be overpowered by feelings of humiliation, anxiety, loss of divine status. I had become the complete victim. I was going to lose control and the questions were spilling out, despite my attempts to curb them.

'Did you go to our cafe with her too? Why didn't you ask me to come? Did you take her home? Why? Is she so helpless? How pathetic can a woman get?'

Unwise women exercising unbridled passion lose out. They lose themselves, they become insecure, shaky, unrecognisable. They lose weight, become bores to their friends, to themselves. They are victims of panic. The prey of the green-eyed monster. They wake the neighbours. And I had become one. Overnight.

'Hey, would you guys mind just shutting up?'

A voice from the window. I hope they didn't recognise us. Everyone around here knows our dog – he makes sure of that. He goes to people's garbage bags, makes holes in them looking for snacks, and leaves the contents strewn around the pavement.

'He's a menace in the street!' one man told me when I was walking Kurtz.

There is a lot of the unwise woman in me. Impetuous, hysterical, jealous, possessive. I scrutinised myself in the mirror for evidence to support my case. Is it what I see in the mirror that he loves? Is it a face to be loved? Hardly possible! And less likely, I decide, with every month that passes. I've adjusted my face in the mirror so many times before, nursed it through different haircuts, and I have liked what I have seen. I've practised confident smiles, different expressions, and strutted out to meet the world feeling great. And, more recently, I have morbidly inspected new wrinkle maps, trying to smile my way around them. There's a new line there today, ready to join up with another line, presenting a perfect scowl. I'm trying gracefully to adjust.

'What's wrong with you today, Mum?' Nadya had asked. 'Stop looking so stressed!'

'I'm not stressed at all. But anyway, how about doing the dishes you used last night? And don't leave your clothes draped around the living room!'

'There, I told you you were stressed. Go and do some yoga, will you, Mum – and get off my case! Concentrate on someone else for a change – the boys, for instance. They never do a thing!'

But back to this other woman.

'Look, Kot, I deserve a conversation and we have topics to discuss —'

'Oh, I see! Then that must be all right, then, as long as she's clever! I used to be so clever too. I was the clever one. Now I'm clever if I understand and agree with your new theories of monogamy equalling monotheism for the real purpose of having girlfriends!'

'Kot, what are you talking about? I have no girlfriend and no intention of having girlfriend! Is one woman not enough? Kot, will you stop raving? Please?' Voy remained calm. But I could not let it drop. I just kept harping on about his theatre date.

'Kot, I admire you and adore you!' he protested. 'But you are being *irrational*! Try to understand, you have your children, your grandchildren all *kurva* time. I must have occasional conversations, exchange ideas! And so what if it's a woman?'

'Yes, exchange of ideas meaning total acceptance of your ideas, a blind acceptance of your views. Right?'

'No, I do not mean this! Kot, please stop! Now! Whole street is waking!'

But I was on a roll. I had a few things on my chest and I was going to get them off my chest no matter who was forced to listen. Sorry, street, I thought, it's not my fault. The street must have been wide awake. Paul on the corner, Richard opposite, that nice family four doors down, the school teacher over the back fence. It's a quiet street, an early-to-bed, early-to-the-stock-exchange type street. Orderly families, small white dogs on proper leads. Occasional children, properly dressed with decent, recent equipment. Unlike my grandchildren, who always seem to be covered in pancake mix and without their shoes.

We turned around and went home. Perhaps I'm spreading myself too thinly, I thought. Yes, I know I am. Thin is the word. Voy does like full attention when I'm with him. And I tend to slide away from this need of his, having many demands on my time, all seeming to be equally urgent.

The next day I was painting, still preoccupied with Voy's theatre date and how it irked me. He'd been sitting inside musing, I thought, on monotheism and monogamy, and then came outside towards me. A shockwave passed through my body and my face flushed. I turned away from him, towards the canvas. Sometimes I'm glad I have a brush to steady me, a canvas in front of me. My old friends, the canvas and the brush. I felt like splattering him with a great big dob of blue-black.

The smell of the paint was supporting me. I thought, I'm going to do it! Splatter him! My hand was trembling. Splat! Splat! The canvas received the blue-black blob kindly, warmly and patiently. Straight on, thick, dark, to hell with all those delicate marks, my being wise and elegant marks.

'The English, so logical, so *fuls!*' Is that me? Hardly, I thought.

The splat went slithering along the elegantly worked canvas, along with my English blood. Thanks, canvas, for taking the punishment and being so nice about it. I'm often grateful for my tiny world that mirrors my feelings – it looks after me so well.

Voy saw what I was doing. He must have seen the fury in the

back of my neck, in my angry movements. He tried to laugh. I caught
his laugh, held on to it, and pushed the unwise woman back down,
very hard. He tried too. We laughed together, a bit stiff at first. He
moved his chair closer, removed the brush from my hand as though
it were a very dangerous weapon, he put it down and held out his
hand to me.

And I just stood there and dissolved. How stupid, to melt like
this! Laughing, crying, rage, love – they're all the same. But they
shouldn't be, should they? My dammed-up river started to flow,
at first as a trickle, and then as a torrent. And I knew that I would
paint in the water, moving again, flowing as it should. But not until
the next day.

43

Dream-catcher

In 2003 Mishka and Rachel married. The celebration took place in their festively decorated Newcastle barn, led by Nadya and her tiny gypsy *orkestra*. So, I thought, they are the first couple in the family since Mamushka and Tatush to dance to gypsy music at their wedding.

They went on their honeymoon, leaving me with their three children – for suddenly there were three of them. There was now a small fellow with thick hair that stood vertically, as blond as flax, and he was named Abraham. So after the lively wedding festivities I suddenly found myself alone with the children at Mishka and Rachel's for ten days.

The children missed their parents, and did not understand why Mummy and Daddy had had to escape. Their trust in me wobbled and wavered as evening approached, and when night fell, they didn't want to sleep. They were on watch. They were unused to honeymoons.

'What is one?'

'A honeymoon is when Mummy and Daddy can love each other very much.'

'But they love us, too?'

'Why didn't we go with them? Wahh wahh!'

I tried to explain, as I half-dragged, half-bribed them to their bedroom. My explanations were futile, failing to penetrate even the outer layer of their logic. The sight of their beds provided a new rush of energy that waxed as powerfully as mine waned.

I tried stories, but I was yawning before I began. It had been such a long day and I was desperate to sleep myself. But there was a seemingly insurmountable obstacle – getting the children to sleep.

Oh my God, I hope they return from their honeymoon, I thought, suddenly alarmed that I could be there forever. And then I guiltily excused my selfish thoughts and prayed humbly for the safety of the parents. And then I began my usual tale, the tale with which I have bored children to sleep so many times over.

'Once upon a time,' I began, 'there were three bears.'

I was yawning, my eyes watering, drifting into the netherland between reality and dream world. My eyes closed, and I struggled with the three bears and their bowls of porridge. It is really a very short story, after all. But I was scrambling the story, mixing it with my dreams, and could hear their voices objecting to my version.

So I begged for a short break, before progressing to the bears going up the stairs to discover that their beds had been slept in and finding Goldilocks slumbering sweetly on Baby Bear's bed. They did not wish to grant me the break. They told me to stop snoring, I had to stay alert, they didn't want to stay alone on this honeymoon . . .

'Kaffy! Don't sleep!'

Raiden was prising open my left eyelid. He had climbed out of his bunk and was lying beside me. Through the forced slit I saw his face, earnest, anxious, terrified of being awake with me, the adult, having slipped away, abandoning my post of responsibility. I lazily pulled him under my arm, stroking his head bristles with my fingertips. He wriggled, he tormented my eye again as I started to snore.

'A bad dream will get me!' he said.

Dear, dear little Raiden. How dare I go to sleep! I goaded myself into guilt. I must stay awake to catch his dreams, stop them from getting at him. I don't want his dreams to get him, I thought to my sleepy self. But wasn't the warmth of my adult body next to him enough to keep those dreams away? Did I have to be awake for this task? He thought that I should. I forced myself into wakefulness and resumed the story. The bears had arrived back in their house, deeply shocked that their porridge had been disturbed . . .

Meanwhile, Abraham was standing in his cot, still dressed as Batman, hood and all, despite my sincere offer of pyjamas earlier in the evening. He was, I noticed, looking refreshed despite the fact that he had been awake for almost fourteen hours.

'I want to do my pooh!' He told me in a tone of command. Up I got again. No arguing with that one. I would have to wait with him, stay in the toilet with him, guard him from the Baddies. The pooh took its time and, stupefied into obedience, I waited.

But Raiden, unwilling to stay alone with Indie, who had deserted him in sleep, followed us. He had forgotten, he explained seriously, to clean his teeth. I generously told him he was excused from this chore, but he shook his head. He was, no doubt, remembering Mummy's last instructions as she shot out the door in her bridal outfit. 'Don't forget,' she yelled, 'to clean your teeth!'

In her absence the command had become a sacred duty. Compliant and without the resources to go against his wishes, I offered him a toothbrush with a koala on the handle. 'It's not the right one,' he explained, he needed *his* toothbrush.

'It's red with a blue koala.' The one I had offered him was Abraham's.

Raiden couldn't find the red brush with the blue koala. He was looking everywhere for it, and I was just waiting, transfixed with exhaustion, sitting on a chair, unable to exert any willpower over the boys.

But finally, they all dropped off. I woke up from my hard spot on the floor. Once again I tucked them in, draping blankets over their shoulders and hands. The intensity of their tightly sleeping faces projected me into wakefulness as I thought of their futures and felt pangs of wanting to protect them from uncertain fates. I whispered a fervent prayer for each of their precious lives. Finally I crawled gratefully into Mummy and Daddy Bear's bed, pulled the blankets over my own body, my shoulders, my hands, and started to snore.

The next day. To the local swimming baths. In the Valiant, with *Just Married* scrawled all over its windows in indelible, iridescent pale-blue paste. Streamers and tin cans popped out from under its back mudguards when the engine started to zoom. The children would not allow me to remove these trappings, saying that they were Mummy and Daddy's wedding things.

What a spectacle we must have presented. The driver's seat sagged and leaned back, supported at a certain angle by wire and hessian, and my body had to be propped up by living-room cushions in order to see over the dashboard and get my feet to the pedals. I felt like Mamushka in her Humber. But then the cool breeze rushed through the open windows of the old car, I extended my hip and put my stretched-out toe to the floor and for a moment I got a flash of one such summer in my youth.

It was not a Valiant but an old black Holden, an ex-cop car bought at a government auction, and you and I, we were on our honeymoon, three days' break from the hospital, the sea breeze from the south coast beating my face, flattening my hair through open windows as we roared to our destination past speed limits, past small curved beaches and green headlands.

When we arrived there, we hired a boat (your idea). As the day drew to a close, we got lost up a dark river that became even darker at night. The black jungle of the riverbanks loomed threatening and silent. The mangroves caught us in their tangle of claws, spewing out clouds of angry mosquitoes that attacked my tender honeymoon-bare flesh.

I peered at you in the darkness, at the faint glimmer of a male form standing up the end of the boat. You were wrestling with an outboard motor you clearly knew nothing about. I realised finally that I had just married a complete stranger, and that I might never ever get back to all the things I knew, which I had abandoned so impetuously with scarcely a backward glance.

Was this not supposed to be a honeymoon, with all its scent of diaphanous gowns and luxury? Why, then, were we lost up a darkened river with not so much as a torch? Why couldn't you operate an outboard motor? You were a man, weren't you? I thought longingly of my brothers Johnny and David – they could operate anything. The known male. And then I caught sight of a light in the distance.

'Help! Help!' I screeched. We were going to be found! A search party, nosing its way through the dark towards my screams. And then you were furious at me, for humiliating you by calling for help. You were the hero of the bush, and I didn't trust you to find the way back. I had doubted a hero.

Mishka and Rachel's children had been in my care for five days, going on six. I had managed to get Indie to school just one day, after pre-planning, making her lunch the night before, forcing her school uniform onto her sleeping body, and popping the compulsory sunhat into her waiting school bag.

Well, I felt so proud of myself I had to ring Mum and boast to her. She didn't think that I had performed a remarkable feat. Since Dad had died she still helped look after my younger brother Adrian's little children, and she didn't ring me and say how clever she was! That all their teeth had been cleaned, for instance, and their dresses ironed, hair groomed perfectly. That was normal for her.

So who could I tell of my heroic deeds? Why, Voy, of course. Voy would be full of admiration and adoration and no doubt be relieved that he was not here too. I wished he was. I felt a bit of a lone adult. Like a stranded species among a group of small creatures with very different agendas. *Krasny ludki*, little people!

I needed Voy, to boost my image, set a few standards, make a civilised dinner, open a bottle of wine, compete with the children over me, and generally be the other adult. Or was I imagining a scenario that couldn't happen? Realistically, I had to face facts.

I couldn't get the TV to work, so Voy would have been agitated. Neither could I operate the stereo, nor make myself a cup of coffee to boost my energy levels, because I simply couldn't figure out the grinder. It was big enough to grind a person. No one could have worked this thing, only the mechanically minded Mishka. Voy, were he here, would have just been swearing horribly, frantically pushing all the TV's buttons in vain, and cursing Mishka for not having normal things. And then I would defend my son, saying Mishka's equipment is professional, more sophisticated than ours.

The huge hessian bags of coffee beans sat in a pile, stamped with their country of origin – Papua New Guinea, Columbia, Brazil. They fascinated me, teasing my addiction, as did the tantalising lingering aroma of the ground coffee beans.

I needed my coffee.

Day nine, seven a.m. Standing next to my bed was a small figure in a wet Superman suit. It was Raiden and he had had another bad dream. I had failed. My sleepy arm hooked him in and then he snuggled in with me, a little cuddle module, asleep again, his wet Superman pants soaking into the sheets. I pulled them off and chucked them across the room, ignoring the reek of ammonia. His dreams, hopefully, would be a bit better when he was next to me. I drifted off, deeply content with my familiar role, then came Abraham, and he wriggled in too. Their large bristly heads tucked into my underarms as I closed my eyes against the early-morning sun, safely hemmed in by two dozing, less than fragrant superpowers.

Voy phoned, at night, later, after they had dropped off to sleep. When I told him about Raiden's dreams, he was nearly tempted to come and visit.

'Kot, tell me more of their dreams. I like dreams. I'm interested in *krasny ludki* and dreams.'

'From a distance you mean, like Piaget? Or is it Jung, with the dreams?'

'Yes, it's both of them, of course! But mainly me. I love it, hearing about you and them . . . and yes, from distance of course is good. Please come home with stories. Write them!'

And then at night I dreamed of you. So I dreamed back.

My dearest Olek, I dreamed, I haven't heard from you in a long time now. But sometimes I do dare to imagine you with your little grandsons. You are familiar with them, you know their differences. You try to teach them to play chess, this is your job, you are never the nappy changer! Like Voy, I guess, you would do the special activities. Take the oldest one bushwalking, for instance, camp the night, talk about life and its meaning, about your life in the partisans' forests, handing the obsession down the generations.

Yesterday we drove to Sydney, roaring down the highway in the Valiant, its *Just Married* signs fading with a week of sun and rain. I brought Tally and Rishi back with us here too, so they could all be together, all the cousins. As I expected, they got up to no good. I could tell Indie and Tally were plotting something. But what was it? Giggles and disappearances, a trail of dough and shrieks from passers-by, all of these clues eventually led me to the scene of the crime.

Using my homemade playdough, they had made bombs with eggs concealed inside them and were throwing them over the front gate, where they became little soft pavement mines designed to sabotage unsuspecting pedestrians on their way home.

I cleaned the mess off the pavement patiently, and apologised to the neighbours who had fallen foul of the mines. And secretly I felt proud of the children's ingenuity, and their superior spirit of adventure. It must have come from you I thought, partisan genes perhaps, still clinging on. I thought of the little partisan boy with his *valenki*, performing his serious missions of sabotage on real enemies, not mere neighbours.

That night, instead of me telling 'Goldilocks and the Three Bears', we listened to your voice on the old tape I recorded in the tent on our camping holiday in Spain, exactly one generation ago. It was a bit strange to lie there, feeling your grandchildren staring into my face, listening to your very own voice, still so familiar, your accent so soothing, telling the story of 'The Magic Carpet' and 'Snow White'. I recognised my own voice in the background too, and Nadya's wheezy coughing. And the children's heavy breathing as they huddled closer to you in the tent and snuffled into your neck to feel the warmth of your breath, the salty sunburnt skin on your chest. It bolstered them from their fear of the world outside as they struggled not to sleep, avoiding confronting their own dreams.

44

Nadya's gypsy *orkestra*

I wanted to finish here, Olek, but how could I end before telling you about Nadya's gypsy *orkestra*? Or do you know about it already? This story started with a gypsy's prediction, so perhaps it should end with a gypsy musical celebration. We were sitting at a real concert, and the seats were all full, and it was not just family, but we were all there too. Mum, our matriarch, aunts, uncles, grandparents, children, and grandchildren too. And we were waiting for the gypsy *orkestra* to begin. All the musicians were strung out in a long line and there was Rafal on the keyboards, wearing a pinstriped suit, his dark curly head looking more gypsy than your elegant black-clad daughter, who was showing no trace of gypsy until she started to sing, and then all the warmth, the longing, the soul of the whole of your life, her life, your afterlife, all of our lives, lost lives, your story and a thousand other stories from long before, was pouring into the audience. Warmer, more vibrant, more volatile than molten lava.

Once again I was hiding tears of joy, relief, pride and of everything that wanted to erupt from the pulp of my heart. I got so nervous I lost my wallet – it dribbled from between my fingers. Even taciturn Voy, with his famous reserved judgement, was nervous, but stood up at the end and shouted, 'Bravo! Bravo! Bravo!' And then to me,

266

'Bravo, Kot!' What? Tears in his eyes too? That was the beauty of the moment, the end of one long, hard journey, the beginning of another.

It was five in the morning. I had gone to bed. The afterparty had petered out. Quiet had engulfed the night. Finally. And then I heard it start again. The swelling sound of the piano accordion invading the moist, cool silence of the dawn. The sad songs of a real gypsy man conjuring a strange past that wanted to wake my sleepy heart. A violin started its sobbing, joining the accordion, and I could hear Nadya's voice harmonising. Together they were welcoming the dawn.

Tears oozed from the corners of my eyes. I would like to have just lain in my warm bed letting sadness and happiness weave their spell over me. Perhaps you experienced that, from wherever you watched. This is your time, the dawn, I thought. But then I started to worry again about the neighbours, furious and hating us, deprived of their sleep. You never cared about neighbours, and then suddenly you didn't have to any more. But they're still there, being neighbours. Voy swore gently, 'Kurva! Tell them to shut up, Kot! It is outrageous, it's nearly morning!' His earplugs were simply not coping against this music that had to have its say – it was directly penetrating the soul. I looked at Voy and smiled lovingly upon this wonderful second husband of mine. Was it he who had become the Brit and me the Slav? Had we exchanged our basic natures? Where do we all come from, anyway?

And why does your daughter sing gypsy? Is she a gypsy? People ask me that. Has she got gypsy blood? Well, I think, becoming immediately evasive, on the one hand, perhaps it would be handy for Nadya if I claimed gypsy blood on her behalf. That all goes with being an unscrupulous band mother, doesn't it? On the other hand, I just can't. My family – and hers as well – would deny it strenuously. And the times we live in demand that all scams be revealed. But perhaps when the gypsy held your hand and found the story written into the childish etchings of your brave, young, steady palm, perhaps there was a singing soul in the vision she saw of the wake of your life? And was there just a spot of gypsy blood left there on the little hand, which could have curled for an instant inside the gypsy's weatherworn fist? Whatever the truth, whatever the legend, the power of the gypsy lives.

Acknowledgements

When I first put together some of the jottings and muses collected over my life's journey, I looked through its nicely typed pages and I already thought it was a book. I showed it proudly to a few people who were all brave enough to assure me that it wasn't. It was a dismembered body, a collection of wonderful parts but missing vital organs.

I thank the advice of Lou Sierra, Virginia Wilton, Evan Hanford, Aviva Ziegler and Minnie Nicholas, who are all versed in the art and craft of writing and editing. I thought it would take me a hundred more hours.

It took three years, then, before I could expose my redraft to a few friends and family members whose judgement I knew to be sharp. I thank Niki Zubrycki, Heidi Jackson, Sandra Gross, Sofie Laguna, Kate Kennedy White, Madeleine Meyer, Marion Gluck, Millie Robertson, Judy Law, Helen Hanford, Christina Kennedy, Anastasia Golaj, David Miller and Leah Miller, and of course Jill Kitson for her generous words.

I also wish to thank Robert Hancock, Sakshi Chait, Greg and Lena Rustowski, Mel Shannon, and my daughter-in-law Bem Le Hunte for their valuable tips. And Rafal Dabrowski, my youngest son, whose occasional yawns showed me where to apply the chop, and my sons Jan and Mishka for being the 'mush checkers'.

The historical briefings of my erudite husband, Wojciech (Voy) Dabrowski and also of journalist Eugene Bajkowski who, as a teenager, lived through the war years in the area, were the foundation on which to base an important section of my book. My deepest thanks goes to both of them.

To my adorable grandchildren – Talieson, Rishi, Kashi, Raiden, Abraham and Indigo – I thank for emerging from their usual raucous and messy activities to rescue me when my computer crashed or refused to yield to my commands, and for their inspiration.

I must give special thanks to my sister and brother-in-law Christina and Trevor Kennedy for their generous support and encouragement of my effort through the last few years of writing this book.

Last of all, thanks to my agent Fiona Inglis of Curtis Brown, to my publisher, Julie Gibbs, and to my team at Penguin who have acted as the final midwives of my creation in its struggle towards the light: executive angel Ingrid Ohlsson, my deft and astute editor Rachel Scully, editorial assistant Jessica Crouch and assistant Erin Langlands.

Needless to say, I acknowledge the tolerance and good humour of my family members who have allowed themselves to be my true-to-life characters.